ENTERING
THE
CASTLE

ENTERING THE CASTLE

An Inner Path to God and Your Soul

Caroline Myss

Foreword by Ken Wilber

SIMON &
SCHUSTER

London · New York · Sydney · Toronto

A CBS COMPANY

First published in Great Britain by Simon & Schuster UK Ltd, 2007
A CBS COMPANY

Originally published in the US in 2007 by FREE PRESS,
A Division of Simon & Schuster, Inc.
1230 Avenue of the Americas
New York, NY 10020

Copyright © 2007 by Caroline Myss

Designed by Davina Mock-Maniscalco

1 3 5 7 9 10 8 6 4 2

Simon & Schuster UK Ltd
Africa House
64–78 Kingsway
London WC2B 6AH

www.simonsays.co.uk

Simon & Schuster Australia
Sydney

A CIP catalogue record for this book is available
from the British Library.

ISBN-13: 978-1-8473-7073-0
ISBN-10: 1-8473-7073-X

Printed and Bound in Great Britain by
CPI Bath

For Tom Lavin, the first true companion to my soul, without whom I would never have entered my own Castle.
All my love

CONTENTS

ENTERING
THE
CASTLE

FOREWORD

*E*NTERING THE CASTLE is many things: a guide to the life and times of St. Teresa of Ávila, the extraordinary sixteenth-century saint and contemplative master; a guide to her brilliant meditation text, *The Interior Castle;* and, last but certainly not least, a guide to your soul—a beautiful, tender, radiant, caring, loving, and authentic guide to the territory of your soul.

Mysticism in general and contemplation in particular are such staggeringly vast and often confusing topics that, especially if one is new to either of them, they can prove lethally overwhelming to the soul, right when it is looking for something, if not exactly simplistic, then at least simple enough to ground what might be its confusion, chaos, perhaps fear, perhaps suffering. What I would like to do, then, in just a few pages, is offer the reader some simple experiential reference points that might help to ground some of the central ideas of mystical or contemplative spirituality. I will first give seven of the most central ideas of mysticism and then attempt to give the reader a very quick, direct, experiential grounding in each of them.

The central ideas, if discussed merely theoretically, can sound rather dry and abstract. Here are the seven central ideas: (1) each of us has an outer self and an inner self; (2) the inner self lives in a timeless, eternal now; (3) the inner self is a great mystery, or pure emptiness and unknowingness; (4) the inner self is divine, or perfectly one with infinite spirit in a supreme identity; (5) hell is identification with the outer self; (6) heaven is the discovery and realization of the inner divine self, the supreme identity; (7) the divine self is one with the all, given in grace and sealed in glory.

Now, let's go in search of an experience of each of those items in just a few pages. Tall order? Not really, for you are already aware of, and fully experiencing, each of those items right now, according to the mystics. So let's see.

First, sit back and relax, take a few breaths, then let your awareness come easily to rest in this present moment and simply notice some of the things that you are aware of, right here and right now.

Notice, for example, some of the many things that you can see, things that are already arising effortlessly in your awareness. There are perhaps clouds floating by in the sky, leaves blowing in the wind, raindrops on the roof, the city skyline all brightly lighted against the evening's darkness, or the sun shining brightly on the horizon as it is about to begin its journey across the sky. These things take no effort to be aware of; they are simply arising in your awareness, spontaneously and effortlessly, right now.

Just as there are clouds floating by in the sky, there are thoughts floating by in the space of your mind. Notice that these thoughts arise, stay a bit, and pass. You don't choose most of them; thoughts simply emerge out of what seems to be nothingness or emptiness, parade across the screen of your awareness, and fade back into nothingness. The same with feelings in your body. There might be a sensation of discomfort in my feet; a feeling of warmth in my tummy; a tingling in my fingertips; an intense burst of excitement around my heart; a warm pleasure washing over my body. All these feelings simply arise of their own, stay a bit, and pass.

As I look inward, noticing thoughts and feelings arising in the inner spaces of my own awareness, I can also notice this thing called me or my self. There are many things I might know about myself—some of which I might be pleased with, some of which I might be annoyed with, and some of which I might find positively horrifying or alarming. But whatever I might think about this thing called my self, it certainly seems that there are numerous things I can know about it.

There even seem to be several of these selves, a fact announced by a plethora of pop psychology books. There is my wounded child; my harsh superego; my cynical and even bitter skeptic; my ever-present controller, seeking to control both me and everybody else; my wise old man and wise old woman; my spiritual seeker; my fearful persona, which lets fear make too many of my life's choices for me; the joyous persona, finding a constant current of joy and happiness in this and every moment; to name a prominent few. . . .

But notice something fascinating about all these selves: They are all something that I can see, that I can be aware of, that I can feel and know and describe, in many ways. They can all be seen—but who or what is the seer? All those selves, which I just looked within, saw, and felt, and then described—are objects that can be seen: But what is the subject, the actual self, the actual seer of those seen things, the true knower of those known things?

Get a good sense of yourself right now—just try to be aware of what you call "yourself" right now. Try to see or feel yourself as clearly as you can. Notice that, once you get a sense of seeing or feeling or being aware of yourself right now, what you are seeing is an object, not a true subject. That is, the self that you are see-ing—the self that you call yourself and that you take to be a real self—is actually an object. It's not even a real self or real subject, but simply an object or something that can be seen. Everything that you know about yourself, everything that you are used to calling yourself, is not actually a self or a real subject but just a bunch of objects, a bunch of things that can be seen. But who or what is the seer, the real subject or real self?

To begin with, don't try to see your true self, because any-thing that you can see is just another object, just another thing that can be seen, and not the seer itself. As the mystics are fond of saying, the true self is not this, not that. Rather, as you attempt to get in touch with this real self or subject, just begin by letting go of all the objects that you have previously identified with. Any-thing that you can see or know about yourself is not your true self anyway, but just another object, so let it go, just let it go, and begin instead to disidentify with whatever you thought was your-self. Try this exercise, saying to yourself:

"I have thoughts, but I am not my thoughts. I have feelings, but I am not my feelings. I have desires, but I am not desires. I have wishes, but I am not those wishes. I have intense pleasure and excruciating pain, but I am neither of those. I have a body, but I am not my body. I have a mind, but I am not my mind. All those can be seen, but I am the seer; all those can be known, but I am the knower; all those are merely objects, but I am a real sub-ject or true self, not any passing parts and pieces and objects and things. I am not thoughts, not feelings, not desires, not body, not mind, not this, not that.

So who or what am I?

Before proceeding, let's say that, according to the evidence of our experience right now, we have at least two selves, or two sorts of selves—there is the self that can be seen and known, and the self that cannot be seen or known. There is the unknown seer, and there are all the little selves seen. Philosophers have some fancy words for this: the transcendental self (or pure I AM-ness, which can never be an object, seen or known) and the empirical self (or the empirical ego, which can be seen, known, experienced, and objectified).

Even though the transcendental seer cannot itself be seen—that would be just another object—it nevertheless sees the entire majesty in front of its eyes: Unseen, it sees all; unknown, it knows all; unfelt, it feels all.

For this reason, the true self is often called the witness: It witnesses all that is occurring but cannot itself be turned into an object—as a true subject, it cannot be objectified. It is also called the mirror mind—it effortlessly and spontaneously reflects everything that arises, but does not grasp or keep. The true self is, in some sense, a deep mystery, something that can never be seen, and yet it sees the entire universe in front of it. It is a vast emptiness, and yet out of it the entire world seems to spring.

For the moment, please keep asking yourself, "What is this self of mine?" Keep trying to feel into that question, keep trying to think the thinker, feel the feeler, and see the seer. As you proceed in that fashion, asking yourself, "Who am I?" and gently letting go of all the objects that you thought you were, and as you keep trying to see the seer, you actually won't see anything specific—you won't see any particular things or processes or events or objects (or, if you do, they're just more objects—exactly what you are not trying to find). Rather, as you keep relaxing into the seer, all you will find is a sense of release from objects, release from the small and narrow identities with objects that you used to call you. All you will find, in other words, is not another object but an atmosphere of freedom, liberation, and release—release from the pain and torment of identifying with a bunch of little objects that come, stay a bit, and pass, lacerating you in the process. According to the mystics, the closer you get to your true self, the greater the sense of infinite freedom.

As I rest in the unknown knower, in this pure self or witness, I might notice something else about this self: It doesn't move—it isn't touched by time or motion, date or duration. This transparent witness is aware of time, hence itself is timeless, or existing in the timeless now. The witness is aware of past thoughts, but past thoughts occur now; and the witness is aware of future thoughts, but future thoughts occur now—and when the real past occurred, it was a now moment, and when the real future occurs, it will be a now moment. The only thing the witness is aware of, the only thing that is real, is an endless present, a single now moment through which time passes, but it is not itself touched by time at all, yet rather lives in eternity. And eternity does not mean everlasting time but a moment without time. Wittgenstein saw it clearly: "If we take eternity to mean not infinite temporal duration but timelessness, eternal life belongs to those who live in the present."

So there's another hint: The closer you get to your true self, the more you live in eternity; the more you live in the timeless present, which includes thoughts of the past, the present, and the future, all occurring in the timeless now. So think about the past and future all you want: Just watch them arise in the present.

At this point, the contemplative mystics make one of their most controversial claims, so controversial as to seem almost psychotic, and yet they do so in one thundering voice the world over; they make this identical claim from every known culture, at every known period of recorded history, and in every known human language, and they do this so consistently and so unanimously that this claim is very likely the single most universal spiritual claim that humanity has ever made: The closer you get to your true self, the closer you get to God. And when you totally realize the true self, it is seen to be fully one with, even identical with, God or the Godhead or spirit itself, in what the Sufis call the supreme identity.

Now, this clearly does not mean that your empirical self is God, or that John Doe is God or Jane Smith is the Goddess; it means that your transcendental self—your infinite and eternal self—is God or spirit. Or, put a little more accurately, spirit is not in any fashion separate or separated from the transcendental self of all sentient beings. The transcendental self in every sentient being is spirit in that being, and spirit is the true self of all beings. And that means that 100 percent of spirit is present in your true self, in your deeply inward, radiant sense of I AMness.

Let's pause and look at our list of the mystics' claims, because we have already touched on most of them:

1. We each have an outer self and an inner self. We saw that the outer self (or the empirical ego) is the self that can be seen, while the inner self (or transcendental self) can never be made an object or thing of any sort, but rather is, among other items, a sense of freedom and a great liberation from the known, from the finite, and from the empirical ego.

2. The inner self lives in a timeless, eternal now. Eternity does not mean everlasting time, but a moment without time, which happens to be exactly this moment, when seen correctly as an endless present encompassing all time. The true self is aware of this ever-present, never-ending, eternal moment, through which all time passes—and, while never entering the stream of time itself, remains as its unmoved witness.

3. The inner self is a great mystery, or pure emptiness and unknowingness. Precisely because it can never be known or made an object, the true self is no-thing-ness, pure mysterium, an ongoing unknown knowingness, or cognizing emptiness, or simply, the great mystery of your own being.

4. The inner self is divine, or perfectly one with infinite spirit in a supreme identity. As St. Thomas put it, if the eyeball were colored red, it couldn't see red; but because it is clear or redless or colorless, it can see colors. Just so, because the inner self sees space, it is itself spaceless, or infinite; and because it sees time, it is itself timeless, or eternal. And this infinite and eternal self is the home of spirit in you and in each and every sentient being. The overall number of inner selves is but one. Every person feels exactly the way you do when he feels into his own witness or I

AMness: Since the true self has no objects or qualities, it can't be different in anybody; it is the same radiant divine shining in you and me and all of spirit's creations.

5. Hell is identification with the outer self. Hell is not a place; hell is not somewhere that we go when we are dead; hell is not punishment handed out to us by something or someone else—it is rather our contracting, sinning, separating activity of choosing the wrong self to identify with. We identify with that which we are not, we identify merely and only with the empirical ego, the self that can be seen; and that puny, finite, temporal, limited, and lacerating identity is nothing other than hell. Hell is a horrendous case of mistaken identity. We have forgotten who and what we are, a transcendental self plugged straight into spirit, speaking with the words of God and shining with the radiance of the Goddess. But we identify only with the finite self, the objective self, the self that can be seen, and not the self that is the seer, divine and infinite and eternal.

6. Heaven is the discovery and realization of the inner divine self, the supreme identity. The mystics East and West have long proclaimed that the Kingdom of Heaven is within—because the simple fact is that I AMness is Christ Consciousness, spirit itself, the Godhead in me and as me. The true self in each and every one of us is the true self that Jesus of Nazareth realized—"I and the Father are one"—and that realization, quite simply, transformed him from a temporal Jesus into an eternal Christ, a transformation that he asks us to remember and repeat ourselves.

Of course, this does not mean that my empirical ego is Christ, or that my personal self is Christ. To believe that is, indeed, a schizophrenic delusion. Nobody is saying that my personal self is spirit, but rather that the transcendental witness of that personal self is one with spirit in all beings. Your transcendental self is Christ; your personal self is you.

7. The divine self is one with the all, given in grace and sealed in glory. At some point, as one rests in the inward witness, feeling the atmosphere of freedom, the very sense of an inner

self versus an outer self will often vanish, seen for the illusion it is, leaving only the sense of what the mystics call one taste. My transcendental self gives way to nondual suchness, or what Meister Eckhart called "Is-ness." For spirit is not only the self of all beings, but the such-ness or is-ness or thus-ness of all things. To freedom from any object is thus added the fullness of being one with all objects. I no longer witness the mountains, I am the mountains; I no longer feel the Earth, I am the Earth; I no longer see the ocean, I am the ocean; I no longer pray to spirit, I am spirit. So seamlessly does the world, sacred and profane, arise in one piece that I can find no boundary—not a single fundamentally real boundary—anywhere in the entire universe. There is only the radiant, all-pervading, deeply divine I AMness, within which all the worlds arise and fall, are born and die, explode into being and fade in oblivion, carried along by the one and only thing that is always ever present, even unto the ends of the world: this ultimate mystery in emptiness and release, freedom, and fullness, ground and goal, grace and glory, this self of mine that I can no longer find, as the raindrops in their insistent is-ness beat gently on the roof, a beautiful sound of heartbeat thunder, *thump, thump, thump, thump,* just . . . like . . . that . . .

What we need is a road map, a guidebook, leading from our egos to our transcendental self, one with the divine, grounded in such-ness or is-ness. Around the world, every culture has produced many of these guidebooks, but every culture has a select handful that are venerated above all the others. In the West, it is hard to find a text that is more loved and revered than Teresa of Ávila's *Interior Castle.* Most contemplative traditions have meditation paths that consist of a number of well laid out steps for moving from the hell of our outer selves to the heaven of the divine self (and ultimately their nondual union). Teresa's seven mansions—each of which, in the following pages, is explained by Caroline Myss in beautiful, clear, radiant language—these seven mansions are nothing other than seven steps in this extraordinary path to your own deepest self, or soul, realized in the cloud of unknowing, given by unearned and unexplained grace, and actualized in daily living—an actualization that deepens as this very moment dissolves into the moment of the divine revelation, right here, right now, with this Earth radically transformed from a living hell into a living heaven, the more time is seen as the moving face of eternity, and outward selves, as ornaments of the divine self and radiant such-ness of all the worlds and universes.

Want to find out if those essential points of mysticism that we have so briefly outlined here are, in fact, true? Well, I will tell you the final thing that I personally love about genuine contemplative mysticism: It is scientific—in the sense of experimental, experiential, and evidential. Try Teresa's seven-step interior experiment as taught in *Entering the Castle,* and see for yourself. It's an interior scientific experiment. *Entering the Castle* is fully based on St. Teresa's seven interior mansions, which are explained and elaborated here so beautifully, so clearly, so compassionately, so lightheartedly, so wondrously by my friend Caroline Myss, for whom dearest St. Teresa became not only a spiritual woman who had written a brilliant practice manual, but a saint who saved Caroline's life, showed her her soul, awakened her heart, and set her on the never-ending, always-actualizing, timelessly fulfilled road of practice.

And, dear Caroline, I just know that St. Teresa would say "amen" to this luminous book as the fruit of her calling to you, a calling to all of us to be mystics without monasteries in a world sorely in need of a touch of the divine—divine God, divine Goddess—the true self in each and every one of us, the self looking out at this page and reading every word written on the suchness of its own heart, which you can hear anytime you like, and especially every time it rains, echoing in the beautiful sound of

heartbeat thunder, *thump, thump, thump, thump,* just . . . like . . .
that. . . .

—Ken Wilber

Ken Wilber is the author of more than twenty books, most recently, *Integral Spirituality.* His latest work can be found at www
.kenwilber.com and, along with hundreds of other contemplative spiritual teachers (including dialogues with Caroline Myss),
at www.integralinstitute.org.

A FAR TOO
PERSONAL PREFACE

THE SUMMER BEFORE my fiftieth birthday, standing in the kitchen of my townhouse, I suddenly realized that I did not have a genuine spiritual practice. How ironic, I thought, considering that I lecture so frequently and fluently on spirituality. Although this realization hit me fairly hard, I shrugged it off, telling myself that since I pray regularly and have a Catholic background, a master's in theology, and a well-stocked personal library filled with sacred texts, I'd covered my bases.

Shortly afterward, that autumn, I became interested in the subject of generosity and service and why so many people are compelled to help others. To research the question, I sent out an e-mail via my website asking people to share stories in which they had received an unexpected kindness or had themselves helped someone else in some way. I expected to receive about a hundred letters, but more than fourteen hundred arrived within three weeks. I read every single one. Some were six pages long, others less than three lines, but each one broke my heart wide open. Some days, after reading sixty or seventy letters, I would burst into tears at the tenderness and gratitude—often for the kindnesses of strangers—that they conveyed.

I was stunned by the power that every person has to change, even to save, the life of another human being. The writers were passing on stories of how people and angels had intervened in their lives with words, actions, food, clothing, kindness, holding open a door, offering shelter, and renewing a homeless person's sense of dignity. These stories were living gifts of grace, living proof of God-in-motion on Earth, and I, too, felt the need to pass them on. I wanted other people—you—to know how powerful they really are and how much every single action in life matters.

These stories eventually became the basis of my book *Invisible Acts of Power.* And with that book came the beginning of my spiritual practice.

While writing *Invisible Acts,* I delved into sacred texts from every tradition, searching for the perfect quotations and parables to highlight the book's stories of invisible acts and to illustrate the universal nature of the sacredness of acts of service. I had begun to unplug my phone as soon as I got to my office in order to concentrate on my reading, so the office (and I) felt uncharacteristically calm. One morning, in the peace of my office, I had a flashback to my college days, to a conversation with a nun who had said, "Now remember, Carol, to read a prayer is the same as saying a prayer. Either way, the grace comes through." A chill went through me, not a sentimental chill but a mystical one that gave me a sense of wonder and awe.

Deep in my soul, I realized that during those past weeks in my office, I had actually been on a retreat—a silent, unconscious retreat in which I had immersed myself in sacred teachings. The wondrous human beings who had responded to my interest in service had pierced my heart. Right behind them came the sacred. All this time, while I thought I was doing research, I had in fact crossed into the sweet sanctuary of prayer and contemplation.

In a sudden flash, I saw that I had invited God directly into my life. And in that bright, light-filled instant, as I became absorbed in the connection between love and God, I lost my breath and suffered a grand mal.

Now, we'll just fast forward. Once I had recovered from that nightmare, I knew in my bones that I did not have a seizure disorder, which eventually was confirmed medically. I did realize, however, that, in the words of W. B. Yeats in his brilliant poem "The Song of Wandering Aengus," "a fire was in my head" and in my heart, but most of all, in my soul. I had discovered my soul. In fact, it felt as if a shaft of light were burning within my soul, illuminating it, calling me inward.

It is very risky to speak on behalf of God, especially with a tone of absolute authority. I have often imagined that people who carry on about how God "thinks" human beings should behave must appear to be complete fools to the divine. But it is possible to speak with integrity of our own experiences with the God who has come to us individually. It is from this place that I share my experiences with you. You can draw whatever guidance or insight from these experiences that you want.

I believe that the divine is everywhere and exists within even the most intimate details of our lives. All that we experience today has its purpose in tomorrow's events; sometimes, the purpose is not evident for years of tomorrows. Yet, God prepares you for your spiritual journey, no matter how complicated, painful, or demanding it might become. For this reason, patience, trust, and faith must become constants for you; you cannot, and indeed you must not, even attempt to believe you know what is best for you. The divine will reveal its plan for you; you have to be open to receive it. With this bit of advice, let me now share why and how I came to fall in love with Teresa of Ávila, whose life's work with the soul is the foundation of *Entering the Castle,* as well as my personal spiritual journey and practice.

∽

After the sudden soul awakening in my office, I moved from my townhouse to an old Victorian that I had renovated. I began working with a spiritual director with whom I met at least once a week (and who just happens to be a Jungian and a Catholic theologian whom I believe I was destined to meet). My dreams and interior journey had become more mystical, as if I were being led into new spiritual territory. Even so, everything seemed normal on the surface: I was teaching, writing a new book, and maintaining all my other professional commitments. But nothing was the same behind the scenes. I was moving—or being moved—into another place.

As part of my teaching schedule, I founded an educational institute, CMED (Caroline Myss Education), which at first offered two programs, one on Sacred Contracts and another on Intuition and Mysticism. One winter weekend after my "light" experience, as I was about to begin my first lecture of a three-day workshop, a student asked, "What is your personal spiritual life like?" Normally, I would have given a terse answer, something like, "I pray," followed by, "Next question?" since I have always been ferociously private, sharing only social stories and the like. But this time I decided to answer that question, even though my plans for that morning did not include my spiritual biography, but rather the lives of the Catholic mystics, St. John of the Cross, Ignatius Loyola, and Teresa of Ávila; the afternoon was to be devoted to the Eastern mystics, beginning with my personal favorite, Rumi. But we took a brief detour into my personal beliefs.

The students wanted to know when I had first begun to believe in God, which always strikes me as a funny question. I have always believed in God; I have never had a moment or even a second of doubt. I have always believed in miracles; I grew up in a spiritual dreamland where the presence of the divine was everywhere. I have long had a mystical vision of the world, so teaching the mystics that day seemed natural.

As I moved from my beliefs into discussing the mystics' lives, a student asked, "Aren't seizures known as the mystic's disorder?" Now, at this point, I hadn't said a thing about my seizure. I was a little taken aback. "Yes," I responded, "many mystics had seizures. Teresa of Ávila passed out from them many times." Then, inexplicably, I choked up. I suddenly couldn't teach. I had never before lost my composure while teaching, but I did that morning and, crying, had to leave the stage. A colleague filled in for me for the rest of the morning as I sat on the side with a friend.

I felt odd, vulnerable, frightened. Something was different for me, within me, but I could not identify it. Was I going to have a second seizure? On the stage? I had no idea, but I was nauseated with fear.

That afternoon, though, I began the next session. I always teach standing up and moving around the dais, but this time I sat on a stool. I was holding a copy of *The Interior Castle,* by Teresa of Ávila, even though I had intended to teach *Dark Night of the Soul,* by John of the Cross. I had grabbed the wrong book when I went on stage, but I didn't want to move because I felt so fragile. I thought, Oh, well, it doesn't matter. And I began my talk.

I said, "Teresa of Ávila was a sixteenth-century Carmelite nun who . . ."

Suddenly, I felt a presence, a force near me. Then, I heard, "Daughter, follow me."

It was the voice of Teresa. My immediate response was, "Do not let my students know we have never met, Teresa. Do not let them know."

For the next three days, I taught *The Interior Castle* as if I had studied it all my academic life, when in fact I was only vaguely familiar with it. I followed Teresa into her Castle and, to the best of my ability, articulated the images and information of its interior for my audience of contemporary spiritual sojourners. That weekend, in front of all those students, God gave me a passion and I could do nothing but follow it. That weekend, too, I entered the interior Castle of my soul and began the work that became this book.

Following that workshop, I went home and immediately threw out every single page of seven chapters of a manuscript on which I had been working for months. Monday morning, I phoned my editor to tell her that I needed to start over. We had gone through this sea change once before, during the writing of *Anatomy of the Spirit,* so I told her what had happened and that I was now writing *Entering the Castle.* She reminded me of the deadline and then said, "Go."

Then and only then did I realize what I had done. Like returning from an expensive, long-overdue vacation in which I had wildly treated myself to little and big goodies, I came back down to earth, to the everyday reality and hard work of writing about an essentially ineffable experience. After my weekend of spiritual excess with Teresa of Ávila, after that mystical, gale-force, soul-full workshop, I was alone in my kitchen, about to start writing a new book that I had not even conceived of two days ago. And I was about to rely on the guidance of a sixteenth-century Carmelite nun. In a prayer, I said, "I gotta tell ya, Teresa, I just put my career on the line. This better be real."

Five minutes later, the mail came. In it was a letter from England from someone I did not know. Enclosed with the letter was a bookmark with a handwritten message on the back: "Caroline, I am praying for your health and protection each day. May God guide you with every step. With love and prayers, Colette. Thank you so much for lighting our way."

The front of the bookmark, which I have before me even as I write this, is a picture of a lily pond. The message on the bookmark reads: "Let nothing disturb you. God Alone Suffices. Teresa of Ávila."

I had my proof. And I am never separated from that bookmark.

On another note, I have completely recovered my health. I was prepared not to heal; I was prepared to have to deal with a chronic disorder. I now know what it is to feel as vulnerable as a human being can feel. I was ready to become dependent on others' care, which, for someone as independent as I am, was no comfort. Having to say, "If this is what I must accept, so be it," can feel like chewing glass, but not being able to accept what you cannot change is like having to swallow those shards of glass. I know this to be true from the depths of my soul.

Out of all this, *Entering the Castle* was born. It is truly a work of my soul, as well as of the souls of all the people who gave me *Invisible Acts of Power*. This work, and my soul's journey, could not have begun had it not been for them. I remain ever so grateful to all the people whose stories inspired that precious book.

Entering the Castle is also part of a much greater spiritual awakening—an awakening of the collective soul of humanity. More and more people are being drawn into the work of the great mystics of the Judeo-Christian and Eastern traditions. This yearning for the sacred cannot be satisfied by mainstream religions, which appeal mostly to our heads and hearts. As an evolving spiritual culture, we are now ready to meet our souls.

Yet, it takes great courage to get to know your soul. This is because, once you do come to know it—and engage its power and live according to its authority—the divine itself will come to call. Once you are conscious of your soul, *you* are likely to be "called." Facing that call also requires courage because it can take you to both intensely light and intensely dark places.

When the divine manifested to the mystics of old, they heard, felt, and saw God in all sorts of forms. They followed God into caves and forests, monasteries and ashrams—anywhere they had to go in order to meet again and again. Today, the idea of being called to such a path of spiritual intimacy with God may seem a thing of the past. When you consider the extremes of renunciation, starvation, and mortification for which some notorious mystics were renowned, you might even think it's good that being called seems a thing of the past.

But it is still possible to be called today. And when the call comes, it is virtually certain that it will not ask you to renounce your family and friends and get thee to a nunnery. You *can* get to know your soul and strengthen your soul and prepare yourself for that call. That's what *Entering the Castle* is about: you and your soul and the path to knowing God.

The template for our journey inward, *The Interior Castle,* is a work of Teresa of Ávila, who was herself called to write this spiritual masterpiece after having a vision of the soul as a brilliant, diamondlike, crystal castle with many facets or mansions within it. Specifically, she described seven mansions, each containing many rooms; and in the center mansion lives Jesus—or, for our purposes, God, the sacred, the higher soul, reality, or consciousness—drawing us ever inward. Our route through these mansions and into the center of the soul is through ever-deepening states of prayer and reflection. This vision of the soul's structure became the map of Teresa's interior journey for purification (self-awareness and forgiveness), illumination (higher consciousness and compassion), and union with the sacred.

When I read about the seven mansions of the Interior Castle, I immediately realized that I had found the way to continue the journey I had begun years ago in *Anatomy of the Spirit,* only now I had a path from the mind-body's spirit into the higher soul. *Anatomy of the Spirit* presents the "practical soul," the spirit that works in the everyday world, helping you survive. I'm not saying that you have more than one soul, but you do have different states of consciousness about your soul. In *The Interior Castle*, for instance, Teresa notes that even though we are already in our souls and our souls are in us, we still do need to "enter the Castle [our soul]" in order to gain the deeper state of consciousness we need in order to meet God. *Entering the Castle* is a journey of awakening into our deeper, mystical souls. When you enter the Castle, you move beyond the practical soul and into a capacity to experience God.

Like *Anatomy of the Spirit* and all my other works, *Entering the Castle* is written from a transreligious perspective. It is written not only for Catholics or even just for Christians, but for anyone who yearns to find and follow a calling. It is a search for cosmic, unifying truths.

When you enter your Castle, you will be embarking on a life's journey that will transform you and your relationship with God and the world. You will learn that you need not leave home to meet God and receive grace. You will learn that prayer is a power beyond measure, that it can heal, and that contemplation—essential to maintaining a dialogue with your soul and with God—requires more than just withdrawing into solitude.

It takes great courage to engage with your soul. Even though your soul is your most intimate companion, you may need help in understanding it, identifying its messages, and heeding its call. More than a book, *Entering the Castle* is a guide to your soul, a text of spiritual direction to which you can refer for the rest of your life.

I've written *Entering the Castle* with this image in mind at all times: You, the reader, are in my office, sitting with me, opposite me, and I am speaking with you as if we are alone, in a personal, spiritual discussion. I am visualizing that I am looking into your eyes and praying with you, listening to you, and guiding you into your Castle. I am taking this journey with you on every page.

INTRODUCTION
The Call

SEVERAL YEARS AGO, I gave a workshop at my undergraduate college, Saint Mary-of-the-Woods, in Terre Haute, Indiana. The workshop ran almost a week and took place during an especially hot spell in an area notorious for ninety-plus-degree heat and high humidity. During our first day, at least ten women started crying from the heat, complaining that the college dorm rooms where we stayed were neither air-conditioned nor furnished. The rooms were, in fact, bare and dismally uncomfortable with only beds and ceiling lights, since the students who furnished them during the regular school year had left for the summer.

In spite of all that, or perhaps because of it, I felt that I was home. Back on my old campus, I felt free to teach in a way that I had never before. I felt a freedom of spirit and expression; I discussed the nature of miracles, the lives of saints and mystics, the presence of angels, and why we long for a connection to the divine. The setting and environment were perfect, as the college is also a convent, the Mother House of the Sisters of Providence, and the grounds contain a lovely church and a Blessed Sacrament chapel, as well as a grotto that is a replica of the one at Lourdes, where St. Bernadette had visions of the Blessed Mother.

I mentioned to the participants that, during the week, I would once again attend chapel as I had when I was a student, and that they, too, were free to find their way to any of the sacred places on the convent grounds. One special chapel in the convent has always had at least one person praying in it around the clock since it was built over 150 years ago. I have always loved that extraordinary chapel, and soon many of the participants were meditating in its precious silence, too.

By the end of our first day, no one minded the heat, the dark spartan rooms, the threadbare bath towels, or the dreadful food provided by the college. Together we entered the rarefied atmosphere of the divine. And we closed our retreat as a group joining in a candlelight prayer at the grotto.

That visit woke up something profound in my soul—a desire to find a way to work more directly with that mystical, immediate consciousness of the transcendent—of God—that we all felt there.

This book is that way.

For twenty-five years I have been teaching and writing about human consciousness and spirituality, personal power, and intuition. In *The Creation of Health,* I introduced a profile of the human energy system that showed the emotional/psychological/spiritual stresses underlying seventy-five illnesses. This was also the first book in which I presented my interpretation of the Eastern chakra system, using that spiritual and energetic paradigm as the template for understanding the causes of illness.

My next book, *Anatomy of the Spirit,* presented a "biological theology" and wove together the symbolic meanings of the seven

Christian sacraments, the Eastern chakras, and the mystical Jewish Tree of Life. In *Why People Don't Heal and How They Can,* I took the position that not everyone *wants* to be healthy—they want a "woundology"—and examined what makes many people afraid to heal and consequently sabotage their healing process.

Following those three books on mind-body-spirit health, I turned my attention to archetypes and the collective unconscious in *Sacred Contracts,* starting from the supposition that before we are born we are each assigned a Sacred Contract that we must fulfill in this lifetime. *Invisible Acts of Power* took me down yet another spiritual path, in which I examined the nature of generosity. That book celebrates acts of kindness, but it also explores why people are afraid to be generous, how we struggle with our desire to help others, and our fears that "there is not enough to go around," particularly when we know instinctively that our help empowers other people. In *Invisible Acts,* I also link generosity to the maturation of intuition. The more intuitive you are, the more generous you are, because you cannot help but respond compassionately to others' needs. You want to act invisibly, anonymously; you don't need to be recognized for the good that you do, great or small.

Now, in *Entering the Castle,* I want to help you burst through your ideas and preconceptions about spirituality and intuition and enter into a deeper, more authentic experience of God. It's time to move from intuitive guidance to divine revelation. Many people have sought spiritual power through intuition but have become frustrated. They have confused spiritual longings with their intuitive hits that were pushing them to change, and they have felt they could satisfy these longings with practices such as yoga, meditation, or retreats. Some have attributed spiritual properties to their intuitive skills, thinking of them as spiritual gifts and measures of a highly evolved consciousness—a dangerous misconception.

A spirituality of intuition is a false spirituality. Although intuition can allow you to reshape your ordinary life with a sense of spiritual power—and you may even get some spiritual directives through your intuition—intuition is not a spiritual force. It is a practical skill that you can develop, a matter of the ego, not of the soul. Using intuition as a spiritual practice is like reaching a halfway point between conventional religious traditions and the deeper experience of mysticism and spiritual awakening. Intuition can be a step toward a true spiritual practice, but it is not in itself a spiritual practice. Classic, true spiritual/mystical awakenings cannot be converted into intuitive skills, and intuitive skills should not be considered mystical abilities. Mysticism is a matter of the soul and not the self.

The soul and spirit exist in two different realms. The human spirit represents the self's—the ego's—sense of the divine in the world; it's an expression of one's personality and rational mind, whereas the human soul is the essence of divinity itself.

People crave a grounded, contemporary spirituality that they can practice every day. We don't want to work haphazardly anymore with a hybrid spirituality of intuition and mind-body practices. We want the power of deep mystical prayer and discipline without having to take off to ashrams or adopt extreme practices of deprivation. We don't want to take vows of poverty or chastity. We don't want to renounce family or friends. In short, we want to be mystics without monasteries. *Entering the Castle* provides a way.

Even as we crave spiritual intimacy with the divine, however, we also have deep fears about God and the ways that an encounter with the divine will change our lives. We long for guidance but are terrified of revelation. We pray to know God but fear God's answers. Muhammad, for instance, ran into a cave to hide from the angel Allah sent to enlist him in the service of the divine. Jesus had to face his fears about his calling. There's a popular story told of Graham Greene, the great contemporary British novelist whose characters struggled with their conscience and faith. Greene had waited nearly three years to get a fifteen-minute appointment in Rome with the contemporary mystic-saint Padre Pio. (Padre Pio died in 1968 and was canonized in 2002.) Just before their appointment, Greene attended a Mass that Padre Pio was leading and observed the priest at prayer. Then, without keeping the appointment, he returned to England. When asked why he had left before meeting Padre Pio after having waited so long to see him, Greene allegedly responded that he was not prepared for the way that man could change his life. In other words, Greene knew that his soul would be called, that it would take charge of his life. The only way to try to prevent that, he felt, was to try to keep grace and divinity at a distance.

We, too, instinctively know that answering a call requires that we have some experience of being reduced to ashes—whether that is by releasing old wounds or grudges and allowing them to die and be replaced by forgiveness, or by starting over a career or relationship in a new place or grieving the death of a loved one and rising out of that into a new life.

We are so scared of the divine that we also sometimes reroute our frustration with our spirituality into physical or psychological/emotional disorders. We often hold our fears at bay while we're directing our spirituality into the pursuit of intuitive abilities or other practices, but we most commonly use those practices, such as yoga or meditation, to manage stress and improve our health—which is not why they came into being—rather than to deepen our consciousness and connect to the sacred. As a result, many practitioners end up frozen between worlds, filled with the desire to pursue their spiritual potential but fearing that following it will dismantle their everyday lives, particularly their financial security. Our guide, Teresa of Ávila, was also torn between two worlds, even after she became a nun. She understood that we frequently question the purpose of our lives, that we want to know God and have God in our lives, but that we also want many other things: family, friends, entertainment, food, and music among them.

Yet, we cannot stop our longing for the quest for a deeper spiritual experience, because the attraction to the divine is the most basic force of our lives. Kahlil Gibran called it "life's longing for itself." The pull is more potent than the fear. That's why you're here, now, preparing to enter the Castle.

Entering the Castle gives you a portal into a deeper experience—mysticism. It provides a path to follow in which you can still live in the everyday world of work and family but follow the call to a genuine spiritual practice that gives you a direct connection with the divine. Traditional mystical instruction is far too extreme for us ordinary individuals, yet it is we ordinary individuals who are now seeking a deeper path of divine expression. Teresa sheds light on our spiritual quest, assuring us that life is meaningful and we can find our way out of our doubts and fears.

Mystics are what the word implies—people called to know the divine through its mysteries. Many people today want the mysteries and challenges in their lives solved and resolved quickly, but mystics know that we all have a deeper task: to accept that some challenges come into our lives in defiance of human reason, logic, order, justice, fairness, and even common sense. They know that underlying these challenges is a divine order and sense that may be revealed in time. It doesn't make sense, after all, to sit under a bodhi tree awaiting enlightenment without the promise that enlightenment will eventually come, but wait Gautama did, eventually to become the Buddha, a fully enlightened being. Nor does it make sense to sit for days, or weeks, or even months in positions that silence the body and free the spirit, and yet the first yogis did this over and over, showing the way to others.

You are unlikely to be called in this way, but your call may defy reason, too. In the Castle, you invite the sacred into your life; you learn to pray and to wait, to ready yourself for direction. Mystics know that their instructions will come along with the tasks God sets for them. The command, "Francis, rebuild my church," inspired the man who would come to be known as Francis of Assisi to rebuild a decaying church in a forest. Had he conceived that this command held a second, much greater meaning—to rebuild the Church of Rome—he may have run from the charge (although it would have caught up to him, inevitably, as our calls do).

Some mystics wait just for the pure experience of grace and the divine. Grace is the word we give to the power of God that we recognize in our lives. We long to make this power so real that we can hold it in our hands, or feel it like heat running through our bodies. We want to know that this divine substance *is* real and that it protects us and heals us and flows down from heaven when we request it. Teresa of Ávila's conversations with God, for instance, were even more real to her than her physical life. She felt grace around her and within her. She saw it manifest in visions and heard it in voices. One vision asked her, "Who are you?" and she replied, "I am Teresa of Jesus. Who are you?" "I am Jesus of Teresa," the vision famously replied. The sisters who saw her in her rapt states begged her to teach them the way into the presence of God, which she did in both *The Interior Castle* and *The Way of Perfection*.

As Martin Buber wrote, "living means being addressed." Once you are called, you have no choice but to follow. Perhaps once you are called, heaven has already made the choice for you and you can only surrender to this divine summons, even if that is the last thing you would consciously choose to do. The call awakens you to what is beyond.

The masters also reveal that we do have the strength and

faith deep within our spiritual core to answer the call and embark on the journey into the beyond. "Yea, though I walk through the valley of the shadow of death, I will fear no evil. For thou art with me, Thy rod and thy staff they comfort me." Once you open yourself to God, once God shines a direct light within your soul, your life becomes a journey of faith. Mysteries will seem to fill you to overflowing, but faith and prayer will help you face both the known and the unknown.

Indeed, for the "Holy Anorexics"—Julian of Norwich, Hildegard of Bingen, and Clare of Assisi—their nourishment seemed to come only from their faith. Only the grace they received during spiritual experiences seemed to keep these divinely chosen few functioning where others would have collapsed from weakness, exhaustion, or madness. Their self-imposed suffering became the hallmark of the medieval mystic, an unnecessary extreme now, but, in their time, their example of fortitude in the face of suffering—endurance of bleak conditions and illnesses, poverty, and isolation—inspired thousands of people who also had hardscrabble lives. After all, pain and suffering comes to everyone; that's just life. If a mystic could suffer *that* much in poverty and privation and still have the generosity of spirit and the spiritual energy to heal others, found spiritual communities, write some of the most beautiful spiritual literature and soaring music in the world, and even become a conduit of miracles, then surely God was in his heaven and he would take care of other, ordinary human beings as well.

But what relevance is all this today? How can the experiences of cloistered mystics of four hundred years ago have any practical application to the stresses we encounter in our contemporary society? In fact, we do need their guidance now more than ever. So many people today are experiencing a dark night of the soul (as John of the Cross first defined spiritual alienation) that it qualifies as a spiritual epidemic. The beloved contemporary mystic Mother Teresa said that the real hunger in the West "is the hunger for the soul." No one has provided more precise, thorough routes for self-examination and psychological insight—as well as insight into what the divine expects of us—than the medieval mystics.

The mystics' time has come again. This second great mystical renaissance has been brewing for decades, as we've been asking the questions that bring the divine into direct contact with our souls: "For what purpose have I been born?" and "What is my spiritual path?" and "How can I receive clear guidance?" These are not ordinary questions. They are spiritual invocations, invitations for God to come closer. And when God hears them, God does exactly that.

What does divine intimacy feel like? How do you know if your soul is calling you to live a deeper expression of the divine for the rest of your life? Have you been called? How do you respond? You may find out when you enter the Castle.

COULD YOU BE A MYSTIC WITHOUT A MONASTERY?

I've written this book because I believe thousands upon thousands of us have been anointed to follow our callings. I hope that my interpretation of Teresa's and other mystics' spiritual guidance in a language suited for contemporary times will help you onto your path. As I walk with you into your Castle, I can assure you that you will recognize the ground beneath your feet. Its mansions and rooms will begin to feel very familiar to you. The Castle of your soul is, after all, your rightful home.

PART I
Preparing for the Journey

MYSTICS WITHOUT
MONASTERIES

T HE JOURNEY INTO YOUR SOUL can begin
with a dream. You may not realize it at the time, *Yes.*
but that dream may be telling you that you are
about to come home again, to return to yourself in some essential way. A series of "big dreams" has often prepared me for new
paths.

In March 2003, for instance, I had a dream in which I found
myself walking through the ancient catacombs of Rome, looking
at the crumbling walls where the first Christians prayed and hid
during the centuries they were persecuted, tossed to the lions,
and slain by gladiators. As I explored these great ruins, I came
upon an elevated, flat, rough-hewn stone that I knew had been
used as an altar. Then the dream ended.

Soon, I had a second dream in which I was again in the catacombs, wandering the same path until I came upon the place
where I had found that ancient stone altar, only now, in its place,
was a lovely white marble altar in perfect condition. Then the
dream ended. In my third dream journey into the catacombs, I
returned to the white marble altar to find a candle burning

brightly in the darkness. Had it been lit for me? I wondered. Immediately, I knew it had been. Deep in the middle of that dream, in the place that symbolized the roots of Christian practice—a new transmission of the sacred on Earth—I also knew that this was really not a dream but a call from God. That bright candle called me back to my personal spiritual roots. From there, I began my journey into the light of my own soul.

⌒つ⌒

You never know how God is going to get you. What is God asking of you? What is your soul calling you to do or to be in your life now? What purpose is your life's journey? When you enter the Castle, you will find some answers.

Seeing your soul as a Castle and yourself as a mystic is like having a new lens through which to look at your life. You can see more clearly, notice the shapes of events and patterns more sharply. You don't want to use an old paradigm or an old pair of glasses to find a new path for your soul. And you don't want to use a new pair of glasses in the wrong way.

This morning, for instance, I was having trouble with the clasp on my necklace. I kept fiddling with it at the back of my neck but I just couldn't make it work. So I put on my glasses . . . as if that could let me see behind myself.

You want a new, deeper view of yourself and your life that sees through the visible, ordinary reality and into mystical truth. You don't want to try to look backward. St. Paul wrote that the invisible must be understood by the visible, and that is what a mystic pursues—knowledge of the divine, the absolute. Most people living ordinary lives would not consider themselves mystics, because they don't understand what a mystic is or they think mystics reside only in monasteries pursuing absurd compulsions to starve themselves. This is an outdated view.

These days, many people—no doubt you, too—are being

called into a deeper experience of God in many ways. That is what a mystic is—someone who wants to engage in direct dialogue with God. That desire ignites an interior flame that burns for the rest of your life, lighting your way. "Great fire can follow a small spark," wrote Dante. Perhaps you feel a mysterious stirring deep within you, a restlessness or anticipation that you don't understand. Perhaps you have a sense that you need to get in harmony with an unseen order—it could be the beginnings of your mystical birth. For some people, a soul calling reveals itself in an instant. But most of us have to contemplate the guidance we receive in order to understand and respond to it. To help us read God's symbols and mysteries, we turn to the spiritual masters—the mystics.

The fairly recent availability of sacred literature and spiritual teachings from all world traditions has brought the experience of the mystic out of the monastery and into our contemporary culture. Sacred literature stirs the soul. Vessels of divine guidance, many mystical texts were long guarded from the general public. Even some ordained brothers and sisters did not work with them because they were not prepared, and one does not toy with the sacred. The anonymous author of *The Cloud of Unknowing* warns readers not to talk lightly of its contents or to give the book to anyone who is not prepared to spend some time in sincerely trying to understand it because of the unexpected effects its contents could have. Before opening *Loyola's Personal Writings,* or *The Dark Night of the Soul,* or *The Interior Castle,* a monk would pray to enter a field of grace because he knew his soul would be aroused by the spiritual truths within them and compelled to explore the mysteries they contain. Teresa of Ávila, for instance, had her first mystical experience after reading St. Augustine's *Confessions.*

Today, however, we read these texts in coffee shops and our homes, often oblivious to the fact that we may be awakening something deeper as we read. Arousing the soul has profound consequences, for once it announces itself it requires attention, prayer, spiritual direction; it wants to express itself through acts of compassion and service. Your soul is your connection with eternity, your intermediary between Earth and heaven, between your everyday physical life and a higher reality. It is your calm eye in the hurricane of a chaotic world—yet, it burns to realize its purpose: to communicate with God. It waits impatiently for the opportunity and avenue to unveil itself to you—your own divinity, the God within you.

What does "unveiling your own divinity" really mean? Are you filled with awe at the thought of God within you? That's impossible, because you cannot imagine awe, you can only experience it. In the Castle you will connect to your divinity—and give your soul an opportunity to stretch out a bit instead of being bound in, as most are, by the routines of daily life, the race to get and to spend. There you will comprehend a fragment of the awe and power by which the early mystics were willingly held captive throughout their lives. As *The Cloud of Unknowing* states, "Those who feel the mysterious action of the Spirit in their inmost being . . . [who] taste something of contemplative love in the very core of their being . . . should such folk read this book, I believe they will be greatly encouraged and reassured." Feed your soul just once with words and experiences that bypass the mind's reflex to edit out "dangerously stimulating spiritual content" and the awakening begins.

Consider these words of Teresa of Ávila from *The Interior Castle* (Starr): "I began to think of the soul as if it were a castle made of a single diamond or of very clear crystal, in which there are many rooms, just as in heaven there are many mansions . . . some above, others below, others at each side; and in the center and midst of them all is the chiefest mansion where the most secret things pass between God and the soul."

Who would not be seduced by those words? What secrets does God hold for you? If you could find a way into those beautiful mansions in your soul where a dialogue between you and God is possible, would you not pursue that?

But you have a major obstacle to overcome in order to communicate with God: your reliance on your mind in matters of the spirit. Usually, for instance, you pray for help or guidance about everyday matters, such as your health, your career and finances, or your romantic, familial, or other relationships. You expect the answer to the prayer to come in a conventional form, perhaps as a new job or relationship. And you generally look, listen, feel, and think your way through the guidance: You tend to intellectualize it.

The mind, however, is useless in finding a way into mystical waters. As I said to one person who was describing his yearnings to experience God, and his frustrations, "Your mind is exhausted in its search. You need to finally let your soul have at it. Get your mind out of your soul's way." The mind, as Teresa would say, is simply not strong enough to make the journey. Coming to God is the soul's task. And the awakened soul will agitate and pull at you until you wade in and begin to reach out to the divine. To help you anticipate some of the challenges you will encounter in the unknown depths through which you will be swimming, *Entering the Castle* provides a mystical map and practices that guide and orient you, your mind, and your soul.

All mystics, medieval and contemporary, East and West, Christian and Jewish, Hindu and Buddhist, were familiar with the consequences of exposure to mystical truths. They are, symbolically speaking, blinding. They can stun you, "knock you off your horse and blind you for three days," as they did to Saul on the road to Damascus. They short-circuit you until you get your bearings. You never know what you will uncover when diving into the unknown—your subconscious and soul. The journey absolutely changes you. You need the guidance and counsel of mystics who have gone before you.

As a medical intuitive, I did a reading on a man who, as I learned in my reading, dealt in stolen goods. I told him that I saw that he was a criminal. He said that he felt as if he had been "caught by heaven red-handed," which was a bit of an exaggeration, as I told him, but he vowed to change right then and there. Several weeks later he phoned to give me an update on his newly reformed, crime-free life, and said, "I gotta tell ya, turning honest is limiting my choices here."

Exposure to truth changes your life, period—whether that truth is a revelation about personal honesty and integrity or a divine revelation that reorganizes your place in the universe. This is why most people run from truth rather than toward it.

But mystics sought refuge in monasteries because they wanted to be knocked off their horses by truth, right? They wanted their apparitions and stigmata and miracles. They wanted their mystical road maps. The outside world was no place for people with this type of phenomenal—if not outrageous—relationship to God. Maybe so, but given the personal, spiritual, social, financial, business, and political problems and challenges facing us today, we do need this kind of power out in the world. We need the insight that comes from intimacy with God. We even seek such spiritual guidance by going on weekend retreats or vacations at ashrams and monasteries, spiritually seductive places that recharge body and soul. But more than relaxation and de-stressing, we are seeking a genuine encounter with the power of grace. We want the faith of the mystic. We want a sense of the divine to seep into our cell tissue. We want to believe that we are being watched over by God.

By welcoming seekers of all faiths, ashrams and monasteries are sharing, both symbolically and physically, the mystical space, practices, prayers, and power of the contemplative life. They are helping to create mystics who can go out into the world. The contemporary mystic more often than not does not reside in a monastery. This new mystic's community is that of humanity itself, not a walled city or cloister. Like the first Buddhists, Taoists,

Who would like my prayers? point.

and Christians, the contemporary mystic is called to represent an invisible power in the world through a personal spiritual practice, through the power of prayer, through living consciously and practicing compassion, and through becoming a channel for grace. Like the mystics who changed the world even though they remained behind monastic doors, a mystic without a monastery serves visibly in his or her personal life, among friends, family, co-workers, strangers, and adversaries, and invisibly, through prayer and channeling grace into the greater world.

As a contemporary mystic, you are measured by the quality of attitude you bring to all your tasks, by your capacity to be a model of generosity, and by challenging the fear that there is not enough to go around in this world—whether that is money, love, food, fame, power, attention, success, or social position. Mystical service means modeling calm in chaos, kindness amid anger, forgiveness at all times, personal integrity—to live, in other words, mindful that every second offers a choice either to channel grace or to withhold it.

No one, by the way, is expected to master these ideals. Your goal in your practice is not perfection. Your goal is to live consciously and in accordance with the highest degree of truth that your soul can maintain. You practice living with truth so that it becomes part of your soul. For example, consider the commandment "Thou shalt not steal"; for some people, honoring that truth unconditionally is second nature. They are well past the point where they can be tempted to steal. But another spiritual directive, "Forgive those who trespass against you," or "Forgive your brother seven times seventy"—as often as you have to, for forgiveness is a higher path than vengeance, and a conscious soul must forgive—may not yet be one that these same impeccably honest people can honor all the time. They are not yet able to be unconditionally forgiving. But life is a journey of practicing consciousness, not perfecting it.

Some of my workshops can be more life-changing for me than for my students in bringing home a spiritual insight. During the course of one extraordinary workshop, for instance, we examined the nature of consciousness, specifically:

- What exactly does it mean to be conscious and to act consciously?
- How conscious do you want to be?
- How do you act unconscious—in other words, how often do you pretend to be unaware of the consequences of your actions and their incongruity with your beliefs—when you are really quite aware of what you're doing?
- What makes it so difficult for you to act according to your beliefs?
- If given a chance to become more conscious or to have more money, which "more" would you take? (Ninety-nine percent of the people in the room took the money.)

Most people did not want to answer me at all, but one brave man raised his hand and shared that he was not prepared to live as conscious a life as he knew he should or could because he didn't think it was fair. Being "more conscious" than the people he lived with made him resent them. I asked him to describe what he meant by "more conscious" and he said, "Well, since I'm the one studying all this consciousness material and learning about the power of positive attitudes and how we need to forgive in order to heal, it seems I'm always the one who has to do the forgiving. Everyone else in the house gets to stay resentful because they are not as conscious of the toxic health consequences of being unforgiving or angry. So I'm always the one who has to be the more giving and the more understanding. I'm always the one who has to see things as illusions and symbolically, while everyone else gets to take them literally and stay bitter or greedy or lustful or angry or whatever.

"To be honest, it seems that the more unconscious you are in this world, the more fun you have. And to be honest again, I am not ready to be as forgiving as one is supposed to be on the spiritual path. I am not ready to be compassionate toward everyone. I just don't feel that way and I can't fake it. I still need to feel superior to others in order for me to keep my world in order. I do feel better than people who do not have an education and people who refuse to go to work, and that's all there is to it. I do feel superior to rapists and murderers and no one can convince me otherwise. I am not prepared to see the goodness in those people. They are not good people; they are evil and cruel and some are unredeemable, at least so far as I am concerned. It's a waste of time for me to think good thoughts about them and serves no purpose whatsoever. That's someone else's calling in this lifetime.

"And so long as I am being really honest, I still need to exaggerate, which is a public way of admitting I still need to lie on occasion. I don't steal, I never commit petty crimes or any street stuff. But at the interpersonal level, I still need to 'break the law,' the laws of God and conscience. So the fact is I am more conscious of deliberately choosing to not be conscious than my commitment to maintain a conscious life. It's just too hard sometimes and, as I said, it doesn't seem fair to have to work harder than other people who are just so unconscious."

After this surprisingly honest confession, many other people admitted that they felt the same way. Living a conscious life was just too painful or too hard, or too unfair, and they didn't feel that they had reaped any of the benefits of being conscious. They feel that they have to lie in order to get by in life. They can't give up judging other people. Just the thought of having to live that conscious a life is overwhelming. They could discuss a philosophical, metaphysical truth such as, "We are all interconnected," but they could not yet make it real in their personal lives.

But that's what practice will do. That's what it's for—to become more conscious, to embody consciousness, to live in congruence with your beliefs and act on them in the world. That's what a mystic does.

To understand this challenge more fully, let's look at the nature of divine paradox.

Spiritual Paradox

Paradox is the language through which God communicates with us. Of course, we do the same in return. We delight, for example, in imagining God in nature or seeing the divine expressed in the birth of a child. In these settings and events—cameos of the divine—the "alchemy for awe" is perfect. When we have these divine moments, we are usually feeling spiritually or physically safe. Our hearts are open and our spiritual defenses are down. We do not expect to hear the voice of God in the mouth of a newborn or flaring out from a setting sun, so we feel safe looking at the world around us and can afford to see God everywhere.

We are rarely open, however, to seeing the presence of God within ourselves and we fear intimacy with the divine unless it is on our terms. When we need help, we want that help to come exactly as we need it, exactly when we need it, causing as little discomfort as possible. We want constant proof that God hears our prayers and monitors our physical survival, but we do not really want to make eye contact with the divine because of the consequences: After encountering God, we would have to live a relentlessly conscious, compassionate life, and we would have to overlook the behavior of people in our world who continue to live as we once did, consciously unconscious, and treat them with understanding and compassion.

Investing time and energy in learning about higher-consciousness teachings and practices, and then deciding that you would prefer not to be quite that conscious, will lead you into spiritual chaos. Your fear of God will feed itself with superstitions about a divinity who punishes, who takes away your wealth and makes you ill. Yet, paradoxically, you have no option but to pray to that God to help you maintain your wealth and your health—and your faith. You will attempt to look for God every-where in your life but not really want to see him anywhere; at least you will not want to see him in a way that makes the divine undeniably real.

Deep in our cell tissue, we know that a mystical experience of the divine melts away doubts. We want it, we fear it, we know that it will empower our souls to reorganize our lives and priori-ties. We know instinctively that the more mystically we see the world, the more we will be inspired to take action. So, to keep this mystical consciousness at bay, to keep the status quo, we de-liberately nurture doubts in ourselves and in God.

In the first mansions of the Castle, you address this conflict between the pull of earthly emotions and higher laws. You aim to work on them, level by level, and to see deeper into them until you can consciously animate the power of higher truths in your system. To animate a truth is to feel it, sense it, recognize it mov-ing within your soul. And with this consciousness comes the responsibility to pray for the strength to think and act in accor-dance with it, to live it—and also to pray for the "poor in con-sciousness." When you see, experience, breathe, feel, and know in your soul that God is in all people (even though they do not see the same in you), *you* have to be the peacemaker, the for-giver, the nonviolent one, the caregiver, the one who does not judge because you now *must* see clearly. You have to act at one with your faith. As the great mythologist Edith Hamilton wrote, "Faith is not belief. Belief is passive. Faith is active."

CONTEMPORARY MYSTICS

Mystics without monasteries come from every walk of life, from every spiritual tradition, and from no spiritual tradition. In fact, having a religious background thick with awe and icons was never essential. Contemporary mystics cannot be typecast and can look like anyone, from anywhere—from an organic farmer, to a politician, to a soldier, to a couple, to new parents, to a retired postal worker. Some people who ended up the most fervent mystics started out as near agnostics and even street people, such as St. Augustine, once a notorious womanizer. The English mystic Richard Rolle of Hampole, author of *The Fire of Love*, wrote that he had wasted his youth on worldly, dissolute pursuits. A dramatic conversion experience, like that of St. Francis, who heard a voice out of nowhere command him to rebuild "My" church, often happens to the last person you would expect to be called. That call out of the blue is what makes the conversion so dramatic. After all, there's no point in converting someone who is already a devout believer. Better to go after someone worth the chase. A fighter against a cause, once converted to the cause, becomes the best fighter for it.

Mystics like Francis of Assisi or Teresa of Ávila are living proof that God does exist. Heaven called each by name. In some way, everyone on a spiritual path wants to be called by name into an intimate connection to the divine. No one wants to wander lost in this world. Perhaps everyone is not as passionate about climbing the highest mountains, so to speak, but I have not met anyone whose goal was to remain lost in a fog of meaninglessness until he or she disincarnates. We want personal, direct guidance.

Even though many people are called out of the blue to be mystics, it is possible to invite the experience of mysticism into your life and actively pursue a deeper experience of God. Contemporary mystics seek a new kind of relationship with God— one of partnership in discovering their purpose. In fact, one way to seek a sense of the sacred and personal revelation is to ask, "For what reason was I born? What is the greater purpose and meaning of my life? How am I meant to be of service?"

With these three questions you are calling out to God, inviting God into your life to change you at some level—to unlock your soul's purpose. These questions indicate that you are ready for a more mature relationship with God. You admit to yourself and to the divine, "I'm ready now to work with you and be directed to know my soul and my destiny."

After making such an invocation, you begin to see a significant difference between your ego-centered life in the world and your soul's outlook. For example, the ego is consumed with physical survival; it charts courses to control its environment and everyone in its environment. We all begin life directed by our egos; our survival demands that. We live for a long time dominated by questions such as, "What's mine?" and "How much can I have?" and "How can I feel more safe?" But eventually we say, "There has to be more than this." Then, an inner earthquake begins to split the landscape of your life. You find yourself at a crossroads where the voice of the soul pushes you to choose a new road that will take you to your real, authentic purpose. And, in case you've forgotten, your highest purpose is never a matter of title, power, wealth, and goods—as hard as that is for the ego to accept. Your highest purpose is what your soul can accomplish in union with your ego and God, not in opposition to them.

Asking any one of those three questions about your life's meaning and purpose is like tampering with mystical power tools. They cut through the thickest denial, bulldoze the most densely constructed life, and dismantle the most intricate house of lies. They lead you to discard what you no longer need so that you can change your course and move into the next stage of your life. These questions can guide you into the Castle.

I frequently ask people in my audience, "How many of you have ever asked God or the divine, or however you refer to heaven, these questions?" I already know that every one of them has, but I am always eager to see how many will admit to it. Usually, only half the room will. Those who won't are holding back for only one reason: They fear that God will see them admit to it and would take it as an invitation to immediately change their lives.

How clearly, how intimately, do you want God to see *you*?

When you pray to have your calling revealed to you, you are actually asking for a life that benefits at least one person other than yourself. That is the mystic's life purpose—to know his or her soul and put it to use in a spiritually radical form of service to others. And mysticism is spiritually radical. For one thing, you enter into a realm of consciousness that is truly "extra" ordinary. Second, your interior life becomes more valid, more real than your exterior life. Yet, you are still very much of the world, as you can see in the following lives of two very different contemporary mystics.

Edgar Mitchell was an astronaut on *Apollo 14,* a historic flight to the moon. When he was traveling back to Earth, he had an experience for which, he has said, nothing in his life prepared him. Viewing Earth from space, he was filled with an absolute inner conviction that our planet is part of a living system in a conscious universe. Within two years of his flight, Mitchell founded the Institute of Noetic Sciences to explore the frontiers of human consciousness and possibilities for global peace.

Another man I know had a near-death experience in which he encountered a being of light that guided him through a review of his life. He saw examples of "what could have been" in his life had he had the courage to make different choices—choices motivated by faith instead of fear. He was given another chance at life and returned to his body. He now lives what he describes as a far more "open and loving life" in which he is no longer afraid to be a devoted husband, a supportive friend, and an honest individual. That is his highest calling. He did not feel compelled to build a healing center or jump into a huge, global project to make a difference in the world, but he lives a life congruent with his faith and his soul's directions. He, too, is a mystic.

To be a mystic without a monastery means that you make a conscious decision to stop being motivated by fear—fear that you don't have enough, that you have to have more to meet your basic needs. And you replace that fear with faith and compassion. In effect, you become a powerful instrument of God's grace. Infused with a force greater than our own—a divine intention, assistance, or insight that is spiritually rejuvenating—grace is energy that can fill you with a luminous awareness different from everyday consciousness. It motivates your spirit and lights your path from within.

A spiritual awakening generally conforms to a so-called mystical blueprint. Some find their path through having everything taken from them, through a loved one's death, or through some other tragedy. An experience of loss or divorce in which you basically die to an old life and are reborn into a new one is archetypal to the mystic. "Old things are passed away; behold all things are become new." (Cor. 5:17) Others awaken to a talent or gift or are called to a project that they simply have to pursue—one that may make no logical or financial sense but to which they must commit nonetheless. The experiences that unfold after an awakening, however, can be as various as the people who are called. You may feel as though you are flying by the seat of your pants, taking each day as it comes. You learn to rely on a kind of mystical common sense, which is essentially a combination of patience, courage, and faith in the outrageous spiritual guidance you're receiving as you follow divine instructions. "And be not conformed to this world: but be ye transformed by the renewing of your mind, that ye may prove what is that good, and acceptable, and perfect, will of God." (Rom. 12:1–2) You also learn to rely on the power of prayer, of which we will explore several types.

Like you, the medieval mystics wanted a connection to the sacred, but they knew how to manage an intense relationship with the divine. Teresa of Ávila in particular knew her way into the soul and to God, and her map and prayers help us find our way into the same Castle that she discovered four hundred years ago. To pursue this mystical path, you will have to adopt some of the practices of our medieval elders to support your soul. Daily prayer and a regular observation of silence, for example, were a part of their lives. Silence is the soul's oxygen, "the true friend who never betrays," wrote Confucius; "the one and only voice of God," according to Melville. In silence, you can hear your soul's guidance. Of course, an observation of complete silence is simply not realistic in the world today, but a practice of silence in your spiritual life is both realistic and essential.

I've watched people chat away their grace, so to speak. They discuss their spiritual lives as casually as family matters or sports. In fact, today there seems to be more of a social taboo about discussing politics than about one's personal spiritual life. I've seen people toss out into general conversation the spiritual guidance they had received during moments of prayer, as if it were ordinary information. People seem to get impatient about their experiences and guidance and want quick answers and clear interpretations from heaven and from others. Don't be like them. Hold the grace within you. Let it penetrate deeply into your soul, your cell tissue, your thoughts, your memories, your fears. Allow grace to expand your soul as only it can.

Some people think they need attention and feedback from others to validate their spiritual experience as special. I've been in conversations in which people became competitive about their mystical experiences. In one exchange, for example, one woman said to another, "When I do a healing, my hands get hot and I feel sensations running through my entire body." Immediately, the other woman responded, "Oh, I started out with those sensations but I've since progressed to seeing light around my clients. I no longer have to heat up like that. That type of thing is for beginners." Rather than learn from each other, their need for ego-reinforcement reduced what could have been a rich sharing into a common competition, revealing that neither was yet a truly gifted healer.

Contain your experience with the divine so that it does not escape you but rather reshapes you. Be silent. Silence will help you avoid engaging in the games of competition and illusion that regularly seduce us in the outside world. Silence also helps you avoid distraction. It helps focus the busy mind—the mind that always has to be doing something, thinking something, the mind that always has to be otherwise engaged lest it become introspective and allow the soul's voice to override its own. The silence I am describing is a silence that you use to contain the grace you receive when you enter the Castle of your soul. This quality of silence allows you to engage in discernment. You carry this silence within you, even when you are with others. It allows you to hold your center amid the chaos in your life; it keeps you clear so that you do not do or say things you will regret or make decisions out of fear. Silence is a learned practice that requires far more than just not talking. Not talking is not silence; it's just not talking.

Daily silence, prayer, and contemplation are traditional practices that you must adopt as a contemporary mystic outside the monastery, but none requires that you leave your family, start a new business, move to another state, quit a job, become celibate, or take a vow of poverty. You do these practices in the life you have now. They will enhance your life and the life of every person around you.

These contemplative practices are similar to those of the medieval mystics, but modern mystics are also necessarily quite different in mind-set and attitude. Many medieval mystics—Francis of Assisi, Catherine of Siena, Meister Eckhart—were bold and fearless. Others were reckless in the extreme and loved to express their devotion to God dramatically. Fasting to the point of starvation and self-inflicted floggings as penance were just a few of the extreme measures to which they went as a way of living or illustrating their faith.

As foolish as their behavior might seem today, these people identified in a physical way with the suffering, crucified Jesus. They wanted to relate to that figure as literally as possible; they wanted to touch that figure; they thought they could ascend to heaven through the same passage of suffering that this figure of the divine represented. This medieval viewpoint can seem particularly remote, since, from the 1960s, many contemporary theologians have envisioned Jesus as a cosmic Christ, a universal divine being who represents love for all humanity, and today we tend to focus on Jesus' teachings and practice of compassion rather than on his physical death.

But medieval mystics saw their suffering as a sign from God that they were loved. Suffering was their way of being mindful of God every second of their lives. They did not want to take their thoughts away from God for a moment; constant pain served them as a divine companion, a reminder not to be distracted. They endured severe illnesses and disabilities, persevering through them in their spiritual quests. Those mystics had their version of suffering and today we have ours, but even today, suffering, reward, and punishment are the three most popular faces of God. And all are attributed to divine will, now as then, and we still seek the strength to endure them.

Today many people commonly cause their own suffering, often for far lesser reasons than spiritual enlightenment, using their emotional and other wounds to manipulate others, to make them feel guilty or dependent. Many use the language of suffering to communicate the content of their hearts and minds because they lack a solid sense of self and cannot say that they are angry, hurt, or afraid. Yet, today we fear suffering more than we seek it. And we confuse our fear of suffering with our fear of the consequences of surrendering to divine will. We fear that becoming close to God will result not in blessings and beauty but in pain and loss. I believe that a part of the calling of the contemporary mystic is to de-animate this suffering relationship with the divine, transform it to one of fearless intimacy.

Nonetheless, for the medieval mystics, enduring extreme illnesses and relentless pain brought a strength and stamina to their souls. They became able to endure direct contact with the divine. And direct contact does require endurance. Muhammad wrote that every revelation seemed to tear his soul from his body; Isaiah was so overwhelmed by his vision of God in the Temple that he cried out in anguish. It was said that even angels couldn't withstand the sight of the divine and would shield themselves from God with their wings. Moses could not look into the burning bush. Even the ancient Greek gods assumed forms of animals or human beings that people could look at without fear and without being burned up at the sight of their awe-full glory. There will be consequences of contact in your spiritual and physical world, whether the contact is a message or other guidance, an apparition, or the "blessing" of a gift, say a gift for healing or precognition. And the mystics' insights and practices—not their suffering—will help you develop the strength to endure.

Using the mystical practices of prayer, contemplation, and self-inquiry, *Entering the Castle* prepares you for authentic mystical experiences and helps you overcome your fears of them. Your experiences may include ecstatic moments of oneness, light, transformation, or healing, but you also may have some darker feelings of isolation and depression. Several renowned mystics went through periods of depression. For instance, Teresa of Lisieux, "the Little Flower," who lived in the nineteenth century, prayed to know God more deeply and then fell into an abyss of doubt. Rather than give Teresa a preview of heaven, God instead seemed to abandon her even while she was living a life of complete devotion. Living with this sense of disconnection caused great suffering for her, but because she felt the despair so familiar to other people who live in doubt, she was able to identify with them and help them find a way out through a devotion to God made of small ways and daily tasks—a path of love and trust in God that she called The Little Way.

In Teresa of Lisieux's words, the "Lord needs from us neither great deeds nor profound thoughts. Neither intelligence nor talents. He cherishes simplicity. Our Lord does not look so much at the greatness of our actions, nor even at their difficulty, but at the love with which we do them." She likely did not know of the Tao Te Ching, the great Eastern mystical text, which also advises, "Do the great while it is still small," but their similar insights proves the universality of mystical insight. In a similar vein, Teresa of

Ávila also observed, "God lives also among the pots and pans,"* in other words in our daily actions. Generations of monastic cooks in both the East and the West have also noted the importance of mindfulness. Thirteenth-century head cook and Zen Master Dogen's "Instructions to the Cook" recommends we practice in our whole life, for our whole life. Teresa of Ávila said, "When eating partridge, eat partridge. When praying, pray," meaning that there is a time for every activity and for putting our full attention on each moment. She could have been echoing the Buddha, who said, when you walk, just walk; when you eat, just eat.

Bear in mind that some of the medieval mystics' lives represent extremes. Their dramatic inner transformations led them to change the world around them. Many of their religious communities are active, and their faith inspires us and wisdom guides us still, continuing to change us and our world. You will likely not be subjected to the trials of St. John the Divine or Job or the depression or ecstasy of the Teresas on your path, but you may face other spiritual paradoxes. Why would God plunge a devoted person like Teresa of Lisieux into a great sea of uncertainty? What possible good could come from making a believer become a doubter? Therein lies the mystery that has always characterized the relationship between us humans and God. No one escapes this life without some crises of faith or questions about where his life is going, no matter how many times his prayers are answered.

TERESA OF ÁVILA'S SIGNIFICANCE

As an abbess and a nun, Teresa was known for her beauty, charm, and administrative skills, and her take-no-prisoners form of spiritual direction. The physical facts of her life are these: Famous in

* These quotes from Teresa and their anecdotes are from Mirabai Starr's inspired, gorgeous commentary and translation of *The Interior Castle.*

her lifetime for her wisdom and visions, she was born in Ávila, Spain, on March 28, 1515, and died on October 4, 1582. Her family were *conversos*, Jews who had publicly converted to Catholicism during the Inquisition. Teresa became the Patroness of Spain, was canonized a saint in 1622, and in 1970 was made a Doctor of the Catholic Church, the most respected title given to a scholar, theologian, or mystic for his or her contribution to Christian enlightenment.

Teresa's spiritual biography is far more intriguing. Her intimate spiritual relationship with Jesus inspired many nuns to adopt the practice of wearing wedding bands upon taking final vows as a symbol that they were brides of Christ. Yet, like many mystics, Teresa did not begin her life with a burning desire to have a mystical relationship with God, or even to be a nun. As a young girl of twelve, she was sent to a convent by her father for education and discipline after the death of her mother, which had devastated her. During her eighteen months with those nuns, whom Teresa found particularly loving and spiritually devoted, she felt called to the monastic life. At the age of eighteen, most scholars agree, she entered the Carmelite Order of the Incarnation, against her father's wishes. But later in his life, inspired by his daughter's example, her father also became devout.

In her autobiography, Teresa dismisses most of the first two decades of her life as a nun, writing that she neglected God and was attracted to the social life in the convent. Spanish through and through, full of music, Teresa loved to play the tambourine and drums, sing, and dance. She also loved food—loved cooking it and loved eating it.

Although her prayer life was painfully frustrating, boring, and empty over those years, that changed just as she was entering midlife. At thirty-nine, Teresa had a classic mystical breakthrough, one that we could even call a conversion. Teresa was already a believer, of course, but her faith had not become experiential; it was mental, habitual, and governed by ritual. But on this particular day, Teresa experienced her first intense mystical encounter with Jesus while walking down the hallway of her convent. Pausing at a statue of Christ known as the *Ecce Homo,* Teresa fell prostrate on the floor, sobbing, as the pain of Jesus being flogged became real to her for the first time. In that moment, Jesus "incarnated" within her and she felt him in every fiber of her body and soul. When she finally composed herself, after weeping for hours, Teresa the mystic had been born.

From that moment on, Teresa had numerous mystical experiences, which she called "divine favors," because one can never tell when God will visit. One can only be a willing recipient of a mystical experience, which is solely and completely determined by the divine. Her mystical experiences progressed to become increasingly cosmic, transcending any she had ever heard or read about—she was seen to levitate by other nuns, and also had indescribable out-of-body states and illuminations in which she was fully conscious of separating from her senses and transcending physical realities.

Teresa explodes the myth about mystics that, once God has called you, your life becomes one of suffering and poverty. In her case, and in other cases like that of the great Sufi mystic Rumi, God consumed Teresa and Teresa consumed God, yet they prepared the way for the rest of us to discover a rich feast for the soul.

WHY NOW?

Why is this the right time for the transition of divine resources from inside monasteries to the outside world?

First, the "new age" isn't new any longer. It's middle-aged and needs a makeover. The human consciousness movement opened society to many spiritual traditions and alternative healing methods. Yoga and meditation studios and health food stores have sprung up everywhere. I call the last half century the age of the psyche, since we developed the language and vocabulary that allowed us to explore the vast domain of the psyche, discovering, among so many other dimensions, the power of intuition, archetypes, and the collective unconscious and spirit. People have always been intuitive, of course, but never before have multiple cultures experienced the rise of a subculture of psychics, intuitives, and healers as during the past fifty years. Interest in psychic abilities caught on like fire and hasn't subsided.

Ultimately, this liberation of the psyche provided the essential birth canal for the self, or individualization, the greater expression of the personal ego. Personal empowerment and self-esteem—the emergence of the self—are the core accomplishments of the past fifty years. Concepts such as speaking one's truth, getting in touch with one's inner child, and developing personal boundaries are all products of the age of the psyche and individualization. They represent the evolution of conscious choice. That management of one's personal power of choice defines a conscious human being.

Another radical social change to which the human consciousness movement gave rise is the freedom to pursue a spiritual path separate and apart from the religious tradition of one's birth. This has catalyzed the emergence of the contemporary mystic. These changes in society—the breaking down of conventional boundaries between religions and cultures and the birth of selfhood—were essential to laying the proper groundwork for a new soul practice of mysticism. So part of the answer to "Why now?" is that all the preparation has been done.

Yet, psychic and spiritual chaos now saturate and fog our collective airwaves. In the early days of the human consciousness movement, the psychospiritual chaos was different: We were breaking cultural, religious, and social traditions, most of which needed to be broken. Yet, with that dismantling of many ancient spiritual rules and rituals, we created a new wall between us and the experience of the sacred—blocking not our access to the sacred but our experience of the sacred. I am not suggesting that an Iron Curtain arose between us and God, or that this wall was in any way a punitive response from heaven. I am saying that traditions such as the Latin Mass in Roman Catholicism and the Gregorian chants created an atmosphere of reverence that has not been replaced by equally awe-inspiring rituals. Guitar Masses just don't have the same effect as a choir filling a candle-lit church with the sacred words and music of the Gregorians or Hildegard. Again, I am not by any means suggesting that the Mass should have remained in Latin or that people should not haul their guitars into church (well, maybe I am suggesting that); but I am saying that the rituals that generated awe and spine-tingling inspiration that opened mind and body to the feeling that miracles happen were lost. In the efforts to make the Mass and other forms of worship more approachable, the element of the mystical and the miraculous, the invocation of the sacred, was lost.

People are starving for this awe and for the sacred. This is why people make pilgrimages to sacred sites and participate in sacred rituals from various native traditions. They want to touch, see, and feel the sacred. They want to be bound to the sacred by a ceremony, by a vow. They want some type of link to God that cannot be acquired by meditation alone, at least not by those who cannot study that discipline with a genuine spiritual master.

This is why the mystics and I suggest, no, *insist* that you have a spiritual practice, a discipline in which every day something is expected of you as an individual. You are not left to your own devices, your own schedule. You maintain rituals that invoke grace and generate a connection with the sacred in your daily life. I know that this is necessary.

The absence of the sacred and the rituals that invoke it are part of the reason why people are turning to fundamentalist, reactionary religions. In their own way, these are rigorous theologies that include social, individual, and mass rituals. In some religions, attendance at these ritual prayers or church, synagogue, or mosque services are even mandated by the state. These religions bring order to their believers' lives in a chaotic world. They provide a doctrine of beliefs and a code of honor, which are essential supplements for the soul.

What fundamentalism is to a culture in chaos, mysticism is to a soul in chaos. The mystic's life is disciplined but, oddly enough, not complicated. The contemporary mystic responds to his soul's call to become an effective force in the world. His theology maintains divine intimacy through prayer and contemplation, through living a spiritually congruent life, and through being a living channel for grace in whatever earthly capacity he is called to serve. The contemporary mystic is called upon to live as an invisible power, a healer in disguise, a person who truly knows that every word, thought, deed, and act of human touch has the potential to help, comfort, and make a difference. A mystic recognizes that his good works are connections to the goodness and love of God, extensions of God. In Rumi's words, "Do a favor. The soul's work shines like gold."

You do not need a particular religion or secret prayer, mantra, or icon to be a mystic. You are ready to live a deeper theology, not just to read about it. You are ready finally to heal from your painful past, to stop seeing your spirituality as a means of personal healing and entitlement. You are ready to see spirituality as a power for the healing of others. You are ready to build a soul with stamina. Divine timing and human need make the time right for this new soul-calling.

It takes patience and inner work to excavate the many rooms in the mansions of your soul. Yet, in each one you will discover another domain of your being—your spiritual gifts, your divine jewels, as Teresa of Ávila describes them. It takes courage to discover these jewels within you because then you have to use them and wear them out in the world in this lifetime—because your soul will not allow you to forget them or hide them. You are more infinitely beautiful than you can imagine, and more infinitely gifted and blessed than words can describe.

2

APPROACHING THE CASTLE: READYING THE SOUL

THE SOUL HAS BEEN DESCRIBED in beautiful metaphors throughout world literature. Dame Julian of Norwich, an English mystic, wrote that God opened her inner eye and showed her her soul in the middle of her heart: "as large as an infinite world and like a blessed kingdom . . . a glorious city." Like Teresa of Ávila, Dame Julian saw God within the center of her soul, which for us and for God is a place of peace and rest. Rumi saw the soul as having many aspects, in one poem calling it a strange tree that sometimes grows an apple and sometimes a pumpkin, sometimes causing trouble and sometimes remedying it. He wrote that the soul can be like a honey balm that restores our health or it can be restless like a tiger; sometimes the soul can help the heart grow a greater understanding, and sometimes it overturns everything we think we understand.

The origins of the word *soul* may lie in the Middle English *soule,* from the Old English *sawol,* or the Old High German *seula,* which all hold that the soul is our nonphysical essence. Its sacredness and connection to God are widely accepted by theologians as well as psychologists. Jung, for instance, wrote that the soul is "an entity endowed with the consciousness of its relationship to deity."

Yet, even with the help of poets and saints, it can be difficult to make your own soul "real" and to locate this inner source of divinity. All mystics agree that the mind and body are different from the soul. But the soul is often obscured by the clamor of our inner chaos, our doubts and fears. It would be wonderful if getting to your soul were as simple as closing your eyes and focusing. It is not, but focusing on the Castle and entering it prayerfully, step by step, is the most effective way to meet your soul.

Please begin with the understanding that there is a very clear distinction between your soul and your "soul as Castle." Your soul is your divine essence, your eternal self. Imagine dying and completely ceasing to exist. You can't. You have a need to be eternal, and your soul is designed for it. That part of you that cannot imagine an end point is the beginning point of the soul.

Your soul as Castle is a powerful metaphor that induces mystical intimacy. The Castle represents a deeper, interior state of consciousness, beyond the five sensory domains of the mind and beyond your mental understanding of soul. Here is a way to work with that image:

Imagine a Castle—not a palace, but a Castle built with heavy, thick, protective stone walls. Imagine a moat surrounding that Castle and a drawbridge over it. The Castle is isolated, exposed atop a hill overlooking miles and miles of land. Visualize yourself as your soul, as an infinite energy, a great wind flowing into and out of the sun. See yourself not as your body, but yourself in your spirit or soul or energy form approaching this Castle. Visualize crossing the drawbridge, going under the archway and into the courtyard. Imagine that you have withdrawn from the world. All becomes silent.

Stand in the center of the courtyard and command the drawbridge to close behind you. Once you close this drawbridge, you are safe from everything. Stand in silence as you sense the thickness of the walls surrounding you, protecting you. Now, using your breath to keep you focused and grounded, visualize your soul melting into the stone walls of your Castle, penetrating the cold stone and animating the walls with the energy and heat from your breath. You are becoming one with your Castle.

Make this Castle your home, your safety net, your place of silence, your retreat. Your soul as Castle is a mystical sanctuary into which you can retreat whenever you need to gather your strength, clear your mind of debris, or regain your footing. It is an inner sanctum in which you gain access to grace and sublime guidance.

Now that you have experienced your soul as Castle through that exercise, I want you to have the greater intention that your soul becomes a Castle. Make this state of soul consciousness an active part of your ordinary life. Practice seeing your life as a calling. Act in line with that calling to be of mystical service in the world. This is not something that you can organize into hours and days like an ordinary forty-hour-a-week job. A calling isn't a job; it's a passion. You become your calling; you embody the power that is your Castle. Your soul as Castle represents you fully in the world. It is as active in your life as your mind and heart. When you imagine yourself in your Castle, when you pray there or meditate, do as the Buddha recommended: "Sit with the dignity of a king or a queen; when you move through your day, remain centered in this dignity."

Your Castle, or soul, is in a state of near-perfection, even though your self is not. But perfection is not your goal—spiritual practice is your goal. A spiritual practice is the backbone you need to start any type of calling or transformation—spiritual, personal, or physical. You cannot change anything in your life with intention alone, which can become a watered-down, occasional hope that you'll get to tomorrow: I intend to start exercising; I intend to get my desk in order; I intend to change my eating habits. Intention without discipline is useless.

Personal transformations require the inner work of self-examination, contemplation, and prayer. You must learn to love the discipline of the interior life and all that it requires of you. The practices in *Entering the Castle* draw on many such spiritual traditions. The Western mystical path, for instance, requires the study of scripture, meditation, and prayer. As theologian and former nun Karen Armstrong writes in *Visions of God,* the reading of scripture led to prayer, which "enabled a monk to enter into himself and discover what he needed to change in the light of divine truth. . . . In the scriptures . . . the monk had an encounter with the divine and felt he was in some mysterious sense studying God himself. Muslims evolved a very similar attitude toward the Koran. As the monk studied God's Word he would frequently find his heart lifting itself up to God for a few brief intense moments"— an experience of mystical insight and union, in other words.

Meditation today means something quite different from the medieval practice, when it meant "study" more than "contemplation"—something similar to Jewish or Muslim tradition in which the reader chants and memorizes scripture. With chanting meditation, Armstrong points out, the words awaken the soul with a kind of sacred music and allow it to enter a deeper truth. Similarly, in the East, Buddhists used mantras (chants or prayers), visualizations, and mudras (symbolic gestures that awaken the spirit) to invoke forms of the Buddha's speech, mind, and body. By communing with these aspects of the Buddha, they aimed to transform themselves and the world around them just as Western mystics did. They attained Buddha nature—the fully awakened state.

Today, self-examination, prayer, and contemplation—the disciplines of conscious effort—are still the best ways to transfer your center of power from the external world to your interior world. Even with these practices and your determination, however, you will face one obstacle after another, one trial and test after another. That is a simple fact for all mystics. One recurrent challenge will be the resurgence of your fears that entering your soul will change your life. You don't need to head off to a convent or monastery to submit totally to your soul and God as in the old days. That was then and this is now—and now is different. Now your role is to empower the life you have and the person you are—and the person you could be—with the energy of grace that listening to your soul gives you.

The journey into your soul builds your inner strength; your soul as Castle is a mystical fortress of personal power. Entering the Castle is about your relationship to God and about your becoming strong enough to receive God and engage in an unobstructed, unmediated spiritual dialogue with the divine. You are searching out this "soul within your soul," this hidden Castle, so that you gradually, slowly, become conscious, congruent. For how long have you been a mass of contradictions? How long have you claimed to have faith while living full of doubt? How long have you told yourself you were devoted to living a conscious life, but have really done very little to pursue this business of truly becoming conscious? There comes a moment when you must come to terms with your contradictions. If you truly believe that this life has spiritual purpose and that you were born to find your purpose—then how can that belief not take charge of your entire life? Everything else in your life should become a servant or a means to finding and living that one truth.

Approaching your Castle requires that:

1. You continually work to make your soul "real."
2. You shed expectations and false assumptions. This, too, is a continual task because you always have (and always have had)

expectations of God. As you enter your Castle and find your soul within your soul, you will wonder, again and again, Am I doing this the right way? Buddha taught, "Don't keep searching for the truth, just let go of your opinions."

∽

To make your soul real, you begin by identifying how it speaks to you.

RECOGNIZING YOUR SOUL'S VOICE

"How do I know if it's my soul talking to me or my imagination?" many people ask. Poetry can touch your soul. A sunset and a warm breeze can suffuse you with profound sensations of love and serenity that make you feel as if you are hovering above the smallness of your life, at one with a greater being. From this spiritual altitude, you have a greater perspective on your problems and stresses. At least for that moment, your faith in God is absolute. But within minutes, your mind once again asserts itself and you are unable to sustain that state of consciousness, no matter how much you want to. But the indelible imprint of that single moment's encounter with the divine remains. No other precious memory can compare, and it is so powerful that you long to return to it.

Remember a moment like that right now. Animate every sensation that you associate with it. (By "animate," I mean focus your senses on that memory so that it comes to life again. See, feel, smell, hear, and taste it.) Enter into the experience of that moment—that memory—completely. Even if you can animate that sense of tranquility for only five seconds, that five seconds is enough to give you a sense of separation from your ordinary world and a connection with the divine. What did you animate?

A transcendent perception of merging with nature? A heightened psychic state when you felt bliss, or had a vision, or heard vocal guidance, or had an out-of-body experience? Or did you remember a shadow experience, such as a desperate state of internal chaos, depression, or isolation and detachment from the physical world? These negative states can also connect you to a soul consciousness. John of the Cross, for example, named his experience the "dark night of the soul," and described the soul going "from itself and from all things," and "dying to them all and to itself." And yet this isolation animated profound insights on the soul's relationship to God that he recorded in his luminous work, *Dark Night of the Soul.*

A heightened sense of your soul is an indicator that the divine has entered your Castle with very clear intent. When your soul has become animated by the divine, you feel a dramatic increase in the sensation that something is different or about to happen, but you just don't know what. You may lose your ability to focus your attention on your professional or personal life, but in a way that is different from normal distraction.

That clear intent of the divine, paradoxically, is to engage you in a mystery. For instance, the divine may manifest in your life in a series of challenges meant to wake you up from thinking that you control your world and everyone in it. Or perhaps God sends you something to endure that seems to have no purpose, no meaning, and is, at least from your perspective, completely undeserved. You will ask yourself, "Why me? What have I done to deserve this? Why do I have to endure this? What is the reason?" This mystery may make you struggle to explain what you perceive as an injustice until you accept what God has chosen for you. This is the archetypal challenge of Job come to call. Such mysteries have no logic, no order or reason behind them, and that is precisely the point: We are meant to learn that our understanding of God's ways, of divine logic or order, will always have human limitations. When Moses got to the top of Mount Sinai, his experience of God was a cloud of unknowing. The human mind can't comprehend the enormity of God's reality. Like other mystics, if we really want to know God, we have to get rid of our preconceptions about God.

The story of Job represents our quintessential argument with the divine, that there should be justice and order within the very fabric of creation itself. Job was a man of great piety who trusted in God completely. Yet, God sent him one affliction after another to dismantle his perfect world and test his faith: He lost his health, his family, his wealth. His friends told him to stop serving this God of his, who would repay faith with such undeserved punishments. Job remained steadfast through many tragedies, but ultimately he reached his limit and lost his faith in cosmic fair play. Then Job wanted to put Yahweh on trial for his unrighteous acts against a righteous man. When Yahweh finally speaks to Job, he asks him—among other wondrous questions that are meant to show the insurmountable difference between divine and human wisdom—"Where were you when I founded the earth? Speak, if you have any wisdom." (Job 38:1) Job drops to his knees, physically and symbolically, quickly realizing the unquestionable greatness of God.

God's message in the story of Job is that heaven has a design and plan far greater than what can be shown to any human being. All that is within the vast scope of creation has a purpose known to God, including each human life. Job's falling to his knees symbolizes the mystical act of surrender we all must make in order to trust God's plan for us within the vast scheme of creation. We all have to surrender our need for our world to be ordered according to our conceptions of justice, logic, and rational motives. Just as you must have realized by now that your world does not, in fact, revolve around you—that you have very little authority over your life and that even making it alive until sundown is not in your hands—you must reach the stage of spiritual maturity where you surrender to God.

Job's life represents our desire to have God reward our goodness with goodness and punish only those who deserve it. Thousands of years later, we still rail against a God who does not observe the rules of earthly justice—even though we have been shown again and again that *deserve* is not a word that we should ever ask God to apply to us. Job teaches us the power of humility. He also teaches us about the power of endurance, but not just our ability to endure suffering or loss. Job's is really an endurance test of the soul's mystical capacity: Can it endure an encounter with God? Enduring a revelation of the divine plan and accepting it builds strength of soul.

A mystical experience fills your soul with undeniable proof that you are intimately known by an omniscient God, but it can be shattering in its revelation of the inconceivably vast distance between God and Earth. A man I know had a spontaneous mystical experience. (Most people are unprepared for mystical experiences, which is why they can be so unsettling.) In his case, he "heard" instructions on what to do with his life and knew instantly that this voice came from God. He had been praying for guidance for a very long time, having lost his job more than a year earlier, but instead of following the instructions, which were that he move to Portland, Oregon, and study yoga, he shared his experience with his friends, all of whom advised him against following these orders. Their negative reactions were not what he had expected and soon he became withdrawn, isolated and depressed, guilty and shamed. He knew that he had had a divine intervention but was not strong enough to act on the guidance. In his own way, he had "seen" God, which should have been proof enough that all would be well, no matter how difficult the days ahead might be, but he was not able to endure it.

No doubt you are wondering why that mystical experience happened to him. Simple. He was ready for it. Mystical experiences happen when you are ready. But while his soul was ready—he heard the direction and recognized that he should follow it—he needed to strengthen his faith in order to follow it. He needed to get his mind and ego out of his soul's way. Whenever you turn over your faith to your mind to manage, you always end up in a crisis of faith.

SOUL QUALITIES

The soul is a fact, but it is not physical. This can make it difficult to understand what it is and where it is within you. Survivors of near-death experiences attest that some part of them apparently detaches from their physical bodies following the death of the body, but while that's proof of the soul for them, it doesn't prove it to us.

The soul is like divine music that only God can hear; it is the force of endless resurrection; the soul is like a fire that never goes out. These metaphors create brief, seductive glimpses of the soul, but in a crisis, when you need to maintain your strength of character or when you feel that you are standing alone in the world, you want to feel one with your soul. You want to become so comfortable in the skin of your soul that you do not feel separate from this eternal part of you. That's what I hope working in the Castle will do for you.

Sacred literature and maps describing the structure of the soul all suggest that it is a vessel of power about which you can learn in gradual stages. In Teresa of Ávila's seven mansions, and in the Castle, you experience your soul through seven stages of consciousness and ever-deepening prayer. You uncover the different qualities of power that each soul contains, all of which the individual needs to explore and refine, including humility, dignity, integrity, honor, wisdom, justice, harmony, and endurance. These qualities, which are also described in the Tree of Life from the kabbalistic tradition of Judaism, enable a soul to discover its own divinity and, consequently, to embody the qualities of light essential to an experience of God. A soul with these characteristics is strong enough to be in direct contact with God—it is a soul with stamina.

Interestingly, the Hindus and Buddhists also mapped seven chakras, or levels of spiritual consciousness, in the body. The Jewish spiritual text known as The Zohar, in which the Tree of Life appears, was written after a mystic had a vision of seven palaces or levels of heaven and seven of hell. All these templates show that each level of consciousness is unique, each purposeful, each a center of creative soul power that must be brought into full consciousness of its own divinity. That gradual empowerment is the nature of the journey to enlightenment or, in the language of Teresa, of mystical union with the divine.

Spiritual teachers and mystics universally instruct us to develop these qualities, which can shatter fear, break the bondage of an illusion, and supply us with the courage we need to follow seemingly illogical inner guidance. Two stories, one quite famous, are perfect examples of a soul with the strength to trust in God and follow his guidance. A young girl named Bernadette had six visions of Mary. By the time of her sixth vision, thousands of people had gathered at the grotto to witness her kneeling before a bush. In front of the bush was the Madonna, whom only Bernadette had seen, but who had assured Bernadette that on this Sunday, she would give the people proof of her visitations. As the people watched Bernadette, hoping to see the type of proof that would dazzle them, Bernadette began to put mud on her face and to dig a hole in the earth with her hands. Then she stuffed her mouth with grass. The crowd suspected that she had gone mad and began laughing at her, but Bernadette took no notice of them at all. Eventually the crowd left, without noticing that a spring had begun to trickle up from where Bernadette had dug her small hole. That spring became the healing waters of Lourdes. Bernadette embodied humility, conviction in her faith, and endurance, among so many other soul qualities, all of which were repeatedly tested in the years that followed as intimidating Church investigators rigorously questioned her about her experiences. With no witness who could come forward to verify the visions, Bernadette had to stand alone, with her soul.

The next story is neither dramatic nor the least bit famous, but it also shows a soul with stamina. A remarkable woman I met years ago received spontaneous guidance to start a food program for the homeless in her neighborhood. This might not sound like a big deal, except that this woman herself was homeless at the time. What seemed to precipitate the guidance was that, one day, in the depths of her suffering and hunger, she saw another homeless person and prayed, "Dear God, isn't there a way that I can help him?" The tragedy of this other homeless person's condition made her forget about her situation for a moment as she prayed for him and not for herself. Immediately, she heard the instructions, "Go to the church and tell them to help you start a program to feed the homeless." She was scared to death, afraid of being rejected and humiliated by the priest, but, as she told me, "I knew what I knew and I knew what God told me to do and that was all there was to it." She marched over to her neighborhood Catholic church the next morning and told the priest that she had been ordered by God to begin a program to feed the homeless and that he *was* going to help her. And he did. Shortly after that, she was hired as the church secretary and given a place to live and begin a new life.

Without stamina, the soul cannot change directions or engage in healing or grab hold of opportunities. For instance, when first confronted with a diagnosis of a serious illness, most people truly want to heal. But those who have the best chance of making it have engaged their souls in the healing process. The moment, the very second your emotions, mind, or body is weakened, your soul communicates instructions to get you back into harmony. You must be willing to listen and act on those instructions immediately.

For instance, we all want healthy cardiovascular systems. Emotional stress, obviously, is highly toxic for the heart. A woman I met at a workshop had suffered a heart attack three years prior to our meeting. She said that she was determined to live a spiritually conscious, physically healthy life, but that she was in a very stressful marriage. Every time she prayed for guidance, she got the feeling that she should leave her marriage. "But," she asked me, "was that guidance really right?"

Was the guidance right? Is *right* even the appropriate word to apply to a discussion of guidance? I told her that she had prayed for her highest choice—that is, the choice that would maximize her health and her spiritual life—and that choice was to pursue a life path that would bring her back to health. Whether she was strong enough to follow her highest option was up to her. I could tell that she was not going to make that choice, because she feared being alone more than she wanted to be healthy. In effect, she had already made her choice, but she was not ready to admit to it. Her soul did not yet have the stamina to listen to its own instructions, to follow the path to her highest potential.

You need to develop a soul with stamina as you maintain your spiritual practices. In fact, the practices will help you grow stronger; for you are not just trying to have a regular spiritual practice, you are pursuing your own empowerment. A spiritual life is not about finding ways to feel good. It's not about how to get guidance on how to stay safe in this world. A spiritual life means that you excavate your false gods, fears, and illusions that hold you prisoner in this world. You face these false powers and free yourself from them in order to know the true power of God. You face the fact that you cling to your husband, your friends, your children, in order to have them meet your needs. You face that you are an addict and you push beyond your lies about yourself. Having faced these false gods and delusions, you release them. Then, you will no longer wonder about God, because you will have found your route to knowing God. Facing personal truths and purging yourself of addictions or manipulative habits require strength, courage, humility, faith, and the other qualities of a soul with stamina, because you are not just changing yourself; you are changing your universe. Your soul is a compass. Change one coordinate in your spiritual compass and you change your entire life's direction.

The journey into your Castle gives you an expanded understanding of the meaning and purpose of life. It reveals greater truths to you, but you must develop the stamina to live in accordance with them. Your mind alone is inadequate to the task and your heart is too emotional. Your soul tells you, "Everything is in the hands of a force greater than what you perceive in the present moment. Let go. Do not let the illusion of the moment seduce you into a misperception. Let it go. Other guidance is at work that you cannot see or hear. You are not alone. Let go. Surrender." Only a soul with stamina *can truly believe* those instructions and have the faith to follow them. The mind can repeat them like a mantra but cannot truly force itself to believe.

Build the stamina of your soul: It's a necessity. You begin building this stamina by doing the work in each of the seven mansions and its many rooms.

Another way to make your soul real, to separate its particular energy from that of your imagination and emotions, is to recall some sensations or experiences that stand out, that were particularly distinct or out of character yet had a profound effect on you. I'll share an example with you that reflects exactly the type of experience I want you to search for in your mental archives.

My niece, Rachel, who was thirteen years old at the time, asked me what was the difference between a promise and a vow. I paused before I answered, looked at her face, noticed that we were in an unremarkable setting, and realized that her question had all the earmarks of a moment of spiritual awakening. She was beginning to sense the subtle but dramatically different power fields that distinguish the ego from the soul. Her out-of-the-blue question told me that her soul had begun to speak to her. This question needed more than an ordinary answer; it needed an offering of wisdom that Rachel could store in her soul.

I told Rachel that promises are agreements that she as a person makes between herself and her friends and her family. They are agreements of honor. When you break a promise, the part of you that lets you know you've broken your word is called your conscience. I asked her if she could remember what the biggest promise was that she had ever made in her life so far, and she answered, "I don't know. I can't remember all the promises I've made." I asked her, "Have any of the promises you made changed your whole life in any way?" She couldn't think of any. I asked, "Have you broken any promises that you've made?" That question made her uncomfortable, but she replied, "Yeah, I guess, but everyone does. I try not to, though."

Unlike a promise, I told her, a vow is an agreement that your soul makes with God. You make a vow when you are ready to make a commitment to live your life a certain way. Even in cases where you make a vow to another person, you are also making an agreement with God, so a vow is sacred and therefore has cosmic consequences that promises do not. Vows are so powerful, I explained, that most people can live up to the demands of only one or two vows at the most over the course of their entire lives. When and if the time came for her to make a vow, she would have to make certain that her soul was in complete agreement with all that the vow would require of her. I added that the time for vow making would not happen until she was an adult, so she had a few years to go before she would have to consider such matters as a part of her daily life.

Rachel seemed to accept my explanations and then our moment was over; she moved on to ask me if we could go to a bookstore. She showed no indication that she understood the cosmic significance of our mystical dialogue, yet I knew our conversation had locked into her memory. She would think about our conversation several times and would never again make a promise without giving it serious, conscious thought. Rachel's life compass had shifted.

This type of experience reflects how the soul gradually awakens us to its relationship to the divine. The soul is destined to encounter God on a schedule, no matter how distracted we might be at these moments in our lives. Just as we go through puberty to become physically mature, we go through life experiences to become spiritually mature and awaken to our soul's presence. A single question that comes from the soul—like Rachel's—can reorganize your entire cosmology.

Another example of a soul becoming real concerns a man who was trying to control his abusive temper. According to him, he didn't want to yell at the people he loved and worked with and create chaos in their lives, but, as he said, "I just couldn't help myself before. I would see things that annoyed me and I would explode." In addition to going to counseling about his temper, he started to meditate, believing that the practice would calm his nerves. "I really didn't think I could do the meditation thing because I have ADD and meditation is not for people like me who are on Ritalin, you know what I mean? But then one day, as I was trying to do my breathing exercise, I was wondering, Why am I so violent? Is there something wrong deep inside of me? Dear God, what is wrong with me? I suddenly felt this calmness come over me that was not me, I can tell you that. And then I felt something deep from within tell me that my life would not fall apart at all if I stopped screaming. . . . 'Just stop screaming. It hurts me.' I was shocked because that was not me talking, but it was me—talking to me. Who was this 'me' inside of me? I believe that was my soul talking to me. I was hurting my soul. I suddenly realized how violent I was, violent inwardly toward myself as well as toward others. Everything in my life has been different since that experience." This man's soul made itself real in a way that he could hear and understand.

These stories show the ways that the divine penetrates the

pulse of your soul—one question at a time and right on schedule. Divine timing is involved in every facet of your life. It triggers the right time for you to wonder about why things happen
as they do, or the difference between a vow and a promise, or
even why bad things happen to good people. These questions
are themselves preludes to mystical awakenings, telling heaven
that you are ready to grapple with bigger, weightier truths.

A Moment of Contemplation: Soul Consciousness

When have you paused for a moment, in the middle of your ordinary life, to wonder about the existence of something greater
than yourself—a world purpose or truth? Perhaps a thought,
question, or insight seemed just to drop out of the sky to register
brightly on your mental radar, completely distinct and separate
from anything you were doing or thinking at the time. Perhaps
you suddenly thought, Does God really hear my prayers? or,
What purpose does suffering on this Earth serve? or, Is there a
way to serve peace in times of war? or, Lord, how should I understand the essence of your nature? Have you ever wondered
where in the huge cosmic plane your endeavors have a place?

These questions contain a particular type of psychic energy
that can draw you into a sense of timelessness. They momentarily lift you out of your body, and, in that rarefied air, your mind
transcends your ordinary consciousness, opening to thoughts
and perceptions about life, God, and truth. The very weightless-
ness of these thoughts alerts you to the fact that you are in a
higher atmosphere of consciousness that is separate and apart
from the personal. Suddenly a sound or someone calling your
name breaks the spell and you fall back to earth, aware that you
were "somewhere else" for a moment. You might call this experience daydreaming, but imagine being able to enter into that
same transpersonal, transcendent state on purpose. Engaging
that clear level of consciousness by choice is what it means to
enter your Castle, or enter fully into your soul. Like any interior

work, achieving that quality of consciousness within your Castle takes practice, focus, and contemplation. As paradoxical as this sounds, you have to be attached to your commitment to learn how to detach from earthly consciousness.

As a first step, keep in mind what daydreaming feels like as a focus. You daydream all the time and it is effortless. Remember that. Daydreaming is a very real form of detaching from your ordinary consciousness and transcending the here and now of your life. Daydreaming is consciously shifting from your conditioned five-sensory survival mode to internal perception. One of the most effective ways is to repeat a prayer or a line of poetry that lifts your thoughts through inspiration. Let me suggest the following prayer as an exercise in withdrawing your consciousness from the physical world of time and space. Teresa of Ávila wrote this prayer, and I am especially fond of it, as it could easily speak for the people who are mystics without monasteries of our world, today. You can substitute more ecumenical wording for Christ (God, the divine) if it helps you hear the cosmic soul of her words.

YOU ARE CHRIST'S HANDS

God has no body now on earth but yours,
    No hands but yours,
    No feet but yours,
Yours are the eyes through which he is to look out
    God's compassion to the world;
Yours are the feet with which he is to go about
    Doing good;
Yours are the hands with which he is to bless men now.

Teresa of Ávila

THE DEEPER PATH:
SELF-EXAMINATION AND CONTEMPLATION

Another way of coming to know your soul is through self-examination and contemplation. Self-examination and contemplation go hand in hand as a spiritual practice; the first part of your practice reviews your personality or ego, and your conscience, and the second part feeds your soul.

Self-examination is the practice of accountability to your soul. You review how well you live in congruence with the truths that you know and believe most deeply. Living in truth is more crucial than speaking your truth. Teresa of Lisieux wrote that "it was far more valuable to speak to God than to speak about God for there is so much self-love in spiritual conversations." In a similar vein, it is far better to "become" your truth than to speak your truth. Self-examination is the practice of becoming your truth. This is an essential practice for every person who consciously enters the Castle of the soul.

It is spiritually seductive to imagine your interior as a Castle that only you can enter, a secret space that is filled with grace, a place of healing, a source of guidance. This interior place—your Castle—is real, just as your soul is real, just as your thoughts and emotions are real. These aren't just words or an exercise in active imagination. They are sacred forms and images that get you to the essence of spiritual nature—a unity of soul and God, psyche and body, spirit and body. Entering your Castle enables you to begin a dialogue with your soul and with God. I cannot emphasize that enough, nor can I tell you how exquisite that dialogue eventually becomes. But it's work. It's work to get to know yourself, and why you are the way you are, and why you love what you do and have the passions that you do. You require work. You are not a simple act of creation; you are complex and creative and conscious and unconscious.

Among the many voices that you will inevitably hear within

your Castle—and there will be many, as each fear has a voice of its own—one voice is a permanent resident: your conscience. In entering your Castle, you also enter directly into the nervous system of your conscience. Teresa locates the activities of the conscience in the First and Second Mansions.

People fear their conscience, which makes the practice of self-examination and contemplation all the more essential. Your conscience is the voice you run away from the most, the "I don't want to talk about this now" voice. In your conscience is a Pandora's box of guilt, shame, and all the fragments of your shadow that you—and everyone—would just as soon not confront. Yet, confrontation of the shadow, acknowledgment of your conscience, is core to any spiritual path. You feel guilty not just about words you spoke in anger that you cannot take back but about acts of betrayal that you cannot undo. You also feel guilty about opportunities that you let slip by for all the many reasons people do this: fear of taking on something alone, fear of failing, fear of hurting someone who does not want to see you change your life or move forward or away. You may feel guilty about simply wanting to work hard enough to make something happen for yourself. Let's face it: There is always something to feel guilty about.

The Castle is not a "health spa for the soul," however. Self-examination and self-reflection are not primarily healing practices, although they most certainly have healing effects. You maintain these practices whether or not you have a personal, spiritual agenda, such as working through guilt. Below is an example of how you might use a classic technique of self-examination to work through guilt. Your purpose is not to make you feel bad about yourself but to understand what motivates you, what your underlying forces are deep within your psyche and soul.

1. As with all inner work, you must be alone and undisturbed.
2. Separate the issue from the individuals involved.

3. Reflect upon your own actions, not the actions of others.
4. Look for the motives and reasons, fears and weaknesses in your actions.

When you discover a motivation or fear, bring it into the light to heal it, which will require a different process entirely that includes contemplation and prayer. You may also require the support of a spiritual director or a soul companion, as Teresa describes individuals who understand the awakening process and needs of the soul.

Self-examination is exactly what the word implies—it is the discipline of continually looking within and examining the self. God is not the only great mystery in this universe. You are a stranger to yourself in many ways, especially if you do not yet know your own highest potential or the power of your soul or the depths of your own shadow, for that matter.

Contemplation, the complement to self-examination, nourishes your soul. It stimulates your relationship with the divine. "Silence is the friend who never betrays," wrote Confucius. "Silence is the one and only voice of God," wrote Melville. All religious traditions have a history of seeking silence as a path to God, the Light, and the Way.

Silence is an invitation to the divine to come forward, to reveal itself to you—as a presence more than as active guidance. You wait to experience the presence of God without an agenda, without a prayer list filled with requests that cover myriad fears and insecurities. This is a new experience for many people who seem to lack the patience to wait for God. They want to "pray and run," speak their list of requests in their mind as if they're presenting a shopping list to Santa at Christmas, and then tell themselves that they are officially protected by God because they've just prayed for protection.

Contemplation is the discipline of piercing through the ego's self-centeredness and impatience. It may include enduring the boredom—sometimes for years—of waiting for God to show up. Contemplation is like falling into your soul and away from the world. Buddha speaks about the world being "illusion," which you can understand mentally, but detaching from your illusions is where the work comes in. You have to realize how thickly intertwined you are with an illusion, such as the need for a certain person's approval. Then you have to set about the long and arduous task of examining how that attachment to wanting that person's approval shapes your character, your integrity, and maybe even your honesty with yourself. Then you have to consider how much your life will change if—or when—you finally muster the courage to detach from the perception that you desperately need that person's approval. When you free yourself from that perception, you have freed yourself from the illusion that someone outside of you rules you inwardly. But first, in order to do all that, you have to persuade yourself, bribe yourself, find the strength within yourself to face the fact that your world will change once you shatter an illusion. And you find this strength through contemplation and prayer.

To enter into contemplative silence, emptiness, and nonaction, you can use prayers and meditation, writing or journaling about spiritual questions. For instance, give yourself this assignment for journaling: "Joy, grief, hope, and fear are the four passions of the soul. Of these four, on which do I dwell the most? How do I understand joy and the soul? Do I create joy in my life or do I expect joy to be created for me?"

A Moment of Contemplation

This brief contemplative exercise will prepare you to enter your Castle. Ask yourself, "Where do I encounter God?"

Is your first response to look up, as if God is a resident of a sky-heaven or in the domed ceiling of your church? Do you envision a favorite landscape or forest or garden? Be honest about your very first gut response, not your intellectual response. Do you first have to pull the image of God down into your heart and belly in order to reply, "God is within me"? Do you relate to an inner God or is God primarily an external force for you? Contemplate this truth: "The divine is present within me." Can you accept that and feel the truth of that presence?

This exercise in contemplation takes you to your "location" of God, a location that is already fixed, like a street address, and comes from a mixture of your childhood and your religious and superstitious traditions. One of the tasks in your First and Second Mansions is to dismantle the God of your ideals and your childhood so that you can receive God as God in your life. Just as your soul has no single physical location in your body, but you envision it in your Castle in order to work with it, to work with God you have to envision his whereabouts.

UNVEILING GOD: THE FOUR VEILS OF GOD

Mystics see the presence of God everywhere and in everything. Francis of Assisi had numerous accomplishments, but he is remembered most for the day he stopped by the roadside to speak with a bird. At that moment, Francis was in a mystical experience in which he felt, saw, and heard the divine in everything around him, including all of God's creatures. He saw that God had created all that is, and that all that is, is a manifestation of divinity, birds and human beings included.

You are fully divine. Those words may sound spiritually elegant but, like so many other lovely mystical teachings, remain hollow until a light goes on inside you and you feel this truth in your body, heart, and mind, as Francis felt it on that day when he became one with the whole of God's creation.

One day, I realized that truth is light, as the mystics say, and few of us can live at the speed of divine light. Few of us can handle seeing God in everyone and in everything every minute of every day. We can visit that truth every now and again—perhaps in poetry or in a retreat in the seclusion of a monastery where we are safely contained within a small space and not exposed to a sea of God's people—but few of our souls are strong enough to generate continuous compassion, understanding, love, nonviolence, and generosity of mind and heart, words and deeds. But that is what a person living in spiritual congruence is expected to do—to shine light where there is none, but not to expect light to be shone in return. Light is always returned, of course, but one type of suffering ends when we no longer expect light to be returned by all those we help along the way.

I realized on that day that—simply put—we can't take that much God. We just can't handle too much truth coming at us too fast. We like truth, but in small, controllable doses. We like to apply truth when and how we choose and to whom we please. By analogy, imagine that you lived in the age before electricity and one day you were awakened into a future in which cars, airplanes, electric lights, computers, televisions, telephones, CDs, DVDs, and CNN existed. In your old world, you had to wait up to six months to get a letter from someone; that was the speed at which your consciousness could handle an exchange of information. Then suddenly you were in a world in which information, details, and facts came at you at the speed of light, changing your world faster than you could process the data. You would collapse from an inability to cope with too much speed and too much information.

The same principle applies to our exposure to divine energy. From the second you incarnate, your soul is in dialogue with divinity, and it is expressing and experiencing its own divinity instinctively. Your mind may choose whether to believe in a spiritual path or in a God, but your soul has no such choice. Your soul develops from your first breath, if not before.

When you enter your Castle, you embark on a journey that alters the speed at which you are capable of experiencing God. You separate from ego, which connects you to the five-sensory world and ordinary time and space, in which your relationship to the divine is manifested through physical form and physical life. For instance, we call a sudden healing a miracle because it occurs beyond the speed of our five-sensory world. In the Castle, you experience God outside of time and space—at the speed of light. Timelessness is the speed of God. It is we who cannot cope with that speed within our time-regulated world. Timelessness is mystical time.

How can you attain such an altitude of consciousness? The more congruent your self and soul become, the more you open to experience God within the mystical realm. You will work on this in the First Mansion of the Castle.

The Four Veils of God

God exists in many forms and disguises, as Teresa would say, in the details of the world you live in and inside you, within your soul. As you approach the Castle, you recognize more of God's presence and locate him in his visible and invisible manifestations. Seeing through the Four Veils of God also helps you see four aspects of your soul.

Organic Divinity: The First Veil

Many people now grow up in households that have no religious affiliation. Their parents did not attend any church and they felt absolutely no connection to any religion. They were never baptized or welcomed to Earth with a ritual that welcomes the soul into its new body. Regardless of how present or absent they imagine God to be, the result for some is often that God becomes a concept or theory: God as morals, God as ethics, God as poetry and metaphor, God as presented in theologies. Most people with religious training tend to see God as punisher/redeemer, savior/ protector, God as parent, and as man incarnate. These expressions of God make aspects of the divine attainable, accessible, at least to some part of our sensory system. Although we cannot see God, we can at least grasp, understand, discuss, theorize, and theologize.

A mental God is perhaps God's most common disguise. Because their minds think of God as an abstract theory, they believe that their hearts, unconscious, physical bodies, and souls are also separate from divinity and unaffected by it. With a mental God, the goal is to control God as opposed to be controlled by God. Thus, a separation of interior power, such as the mental God from the mystical experience of God, must be maintained. Yet, their emotional beings and souls are connected to God regardless of what their minds think. Long before we reach the active intellectual stage of our lives, the divine has already broken ground with the soul. We have a theology in our biology. It is instinctual, just as birds know their paths, beavers build dams, and whales communicate with one another. We are born with knowledge of natural laws, through which the divine reveals or animates its presence in our bones, blood, tissues—our cellular beings. This is God as "organic divinity," in the cycles of nature, an organic intelligence that is inherent in the order of life and operative at the cellular level, a constant life force.

Organic divinity incarnates into each soul as a primal sense of right and wrong, good and bad behavior that is life-affirming. Instincts are our first expression of intuitive and individual power; asserting them helps us survive. And because physical survival is an obvious priority, for many people their first relationship to God is one of "food and faith." That is, God is known through the superstitions that develop around finding a means to survive in the physical world. The survival or organic God is a God of "stuff" and a resource for getting that stuff.

When you attempt to control and establish order in your external world, you are connecting through your instincts to organic divinity. Order and control equal survival. But order will ultimately deteriorate and you will lose control because no human being can control the external world, although everyone will try and fail. Instincts help us survive on the physical plane but are not enough for us to understand our souls or to know God. At the limits of your instincts, however, is another part of your soul and aspect of divinity—one that underlies disorder and change.

I once had a conversation with a man whose young son had recently died. He was deep in mourning, and as I looked at him I knew he would live the rest of his life in mourning. In shock because, in his interior theology and map of life, a parent dies before his child, not the other way around, he kept repeating, "How could this happen? Why did this happen? Why did God do this?" No one could have given him an answer that could take away his pain or justify the death of his son. In his theology, he believed he would die first. That was a given; indeed, for him, it was a covenant with God. What map was he supposed to grab on to, now? He had not only lost his son, he had lost his cosmic map, which included his relationship with God, his spiritual rituals and their power. He was left to wonder if there really was a God. For this man to heal, he would have to consider that God operates outside the organic structure of nature. God may have ordered his earthly world to have summer follow spring each year, but God did not *have* to make that happen. This random factor in the nature of God would require a leap of faith in this man's consciousness, for he could not envision or trust in a random God. Waking up to the random nature—or divine paradox—of God is often the crisis that makes people move beyond an organic relationship to God.

A Moment of Contemplation

Let me now put you in touch with this organic divinity. It has always pulsated in your cell tissue. Organic divinity contains the first level of mystery—the impetus for your pursuit of the mystical. Here is where you first encounter God, in the primal relationship between you and the God of survival, the God who governs the rebirth of life out of chaos and disorder. This is the God who rules the seasons, who turns the clock of everything, who animates all basic life forces. This is the God in whom you need to begin to trust before you venture further into the deeper waters of your interior life, the interior domain of your Castle.

You can tell yourself that you do indeed trust in this God, but do you really believe that your basic needs will be met in life? Do you require order in your physical world to feel safe? What do you pray for? How many prayers do you offer for safety? For protection? How many prayers do you make that stem from your desire to survive? How many prayers do you offer in surrender? How much do you fear that if you surrender, God will reduce you to poverty? Do you still need a reason for even one experience or trauma that happened to you? Do you still question why chaos swept through your life and reordered the plans you had?

The organic God is the one we fear the most, the one for whom we wear icons of protection and conduct cleansings of ourselves and our homes to release the bad spirits. This is the God of superstitions and fears that our rational minds should be able to exorcise, but can't because these superstitions are primal. This God was in your bones long before any other God was in your conscious mind.

Conscience and Personal Choice: The Second Veil

The Second Veil of God is in your conscience. Unlike your natural instincts, your conscience is an internal system connected both to God and to your soul. It weighs your choices and matures with you even if you don't have a formal religion or theology. The divinity in your conscience inspires you to choose to be good, generous, kind, honest, moral, and ethical—to express characteristics of the soul. Your ego can blame as many people as you want for the choices that you make, but at the end of the day, your conscience—your soul—does not assign blame. Your conscience pierces through this Second Veil of God to show you that the soul is different from the ego and that you will always have to distinguish between the two.

Unlike your instincts, which equip you to deal with the external world and its challenges and threats, all of which you perceive as coming toward you, your conscience engages the conflicts, strengths, and weaknesses coming from within you. With your conscience, you govern and express your appetite for power choice by choice. Your conscience walks with you in the trenches of your everyday life as you try to discern between the positive and the negative. Your conscience is your soul's compass on Earth, maneuvering the flow and direction of your innate ability to create or destroy, including physical life. You turn to your conscience to battle your personal shadow—which is fed by feelings of guilt, anger, selfishness, and feelings of personal injustice and of entitlement.

Your personal divinity, also called charism or your special grace, begins to show itself through this Second Veil as yearnings for true selfhood and connection with God. Inevitably, on the rough waters of the seas of choice, circumstances will arise that you cannot resolve or work through by your conscience alone. You will be prompted to cross into the next level of the mystical journey when you ask what there is beyond what you perceive: "For what purpose was I born? What is the meaning of my life?"

These questions pierce the Third Veil.

Inner Guidance: The Third Veil

Unlike the question, "Why did my son die before me?" which implores the divine to explain an earthly event and end our personal suffering, the question, "For what reason was I born?" asks for personal revelation. You ask to have the meaning and purpose of your life revealed to you because you can no longer bring order to the chaos of your physical world, or because the order you have brought has failed to satisfy something inside you. Questioning your life purpose invites the divine to come closer, to pull you inward so that you can hear direction and revelation. It alters your relationship to yourself as well as to God, placing the journey of your soul at the forefront of your life path and making the ego its servant. This invocation asks to see the face of God, to encounter the force of the divine one-on-one through direct guidance. This is the eye of the needle through which your personal transformation will be dragged from inner chaos to a still point.

Paradoxically, your soul thrives on chaos because it recognizes the hand of the divine at work in upheavals that push you toward transformation. The mystery of organic divinity lies in order, but the mystery of the God that speaks through your inner guidance comes out of disorder and vibrates through gut instincts and debates of conscience. You begin to expand your conscience into a more transcendent consciousness. The power and consequences of personal choices become more evident to you; you realize that you are responsible for the consequences of your attitudes and beliefs, and you strive to become ever more conscious through a devoted spiritual practice through which you receive guidance. You participate with God in uncovering your purpose.

The soul is a relentless companion. It never rests in seeking its freedom and voice. It will do what it has to do to release your physical body, your mind, and your emotions from the debris of untruths and self-deceptions that keep you chained and unable to see your purpose. People often wonder why their spiritual lives began with an illness or a life trauma; illnesses and life crises are often the ways the soul finally gets through to you to take charge of your life. In your Castle are many mansions. Among them is one that holds your potential to heal yourself. That alone is worth the journey.

The final veil, the fourth, is the Mystic's Veil.

The Mystic's Veil: Pierced by the Light

A mystic is called to come into an intimate relationship with divinity. A calling is not a job, a career, or an occupation, but a pursuit that transcends ordinary life. Your soul becomes a channel for grace. This changes everything, and it changes nothing. You don't float away, divorce your mate, take off for the hills, or fast, but you have a passion to be congruent, to have your instincts, conscience, intuitive guidance, and mystical relationship to God exist in harmony. You may live a perfectly ordinary life in the world, but your interior life is anything but ordinary. You continue your external life, but on the inside you are awakened, fearless, conscious, a resource for others.

A Moment of Contemplation

You know you are being called. Your soul is unsatisfied, starving for purpose. Some part of you knows—feels a pull beyond reason deep within the core of your being—that God is calling you by name. And you realize that you must have an intimate relationship with God above all else. A life of mental prayer and an occasional weekend workshop and massage will no longer suffice as your spiritual life. You finally recognize that you need to experience God—and you need to experience your divinity, your route to God. You enter through the Castle, but the Castle is a metaphor for your divinity. The divine typically selects those who would prefer not to be selected, but only you know if you have the devotion to become a channel for grace. That choice, however, is not entirely yours. What is entirely in your hands is the quality of your inner dedication to becoming conscious.

Your soul will move you always deeper within yourself. You cannot stop that process any more than you can stop aging. You will enter your Castle eventually—inevitably—because the mystic in you longs to go home; it longs to stop running from a fear of chaos. You crave an end to being possessed by your fears of not surviving, of not having enough food, money, or security. You want to trust life itself and the God that gave you life. You want to surrender yourself into that same cosmic trust that the mystics had—and have—that your needs will be met. You want to find your highest potential—and enough strength of soul to free yourself from the need to have others recognize, approve of, and applaud who you are and what you do. You want to heal from the burdens of resentment. You want to be liberated from the people you have yet to forgive and the guilt you carry because you need to be forgiven. You want to be free to live without fear, but most of all, you want to cease fearing yourself, your soul, and your God.

That's what's in it for you. No matter how much you fear entering your Castle, the fact is that you are your Castle. Ultimately, this is a journey about personal courage and faith; your soul knew long before now that you would inevitably enter your Castle.

3

CROSSING THE DRAWBRIDGE: THE KEY TO THE CASTLE

IN MEDIEVAL ENGLAND, a mystic who wanted to become a hermit had to get a license or special blessing from his bishop. Today, you don't need a special permit to search to know God, but, even though you already possess your soul and are even possessed by it, you must nonetheless consciously seek an entry into it. Crossing the drawbridge represents your transition from ordinary life to a commitment to explore a mystical relationship.

Prayer is the bridge into your castle. Through prayer, you quiet your mind. You cannot engage your soul through relaxation or the power of imagination alone. Those are just mind-body techniques for mind-body work. Your mind is not your Castle. To enter the sacred interior of your Castle you have to pray and give conscious attention and dedication to your journey. You are embarking on an internalized liturgy, as the great chronicler of mysticism and rituals, Mircea Eliade, might have put it; you are entering a Gnostic system of ancient wisdom and practice. This is a journey of discovery, of the liberation of the self. You are scaffolding your soul with stamina for the remainder of your life. Most of all, by entering your Castle you develop a relationship between you and God.

The most effective way to make the transition from the idea of your soul as Castle to actually entering the Castle is to become familiar with its blueprint before you step inside. Visualize yourself at the foot of the drawbridge to your Castle. Within your Castle are seven mansions. They are not necessarily vertical, one on top of another. Rather, according to Teresa of Ávila, these mansions are arranged "some above, others below, others at each side; and in the center and midst of them all is the chiefest mansion—where God lives."

Each of the seven mansions represents an elevated place in the soul for self-examination and encounters with God. At each mansion you increase your understanding of your soul and gain a deeper capacity to experience and know God. Each mansion represents a stage of development and self-discovery in which you peel off layer upon layer as you go into room after room. In each room, you face an issue or a strength, talent, challenge, memory, history, or wound that exerts control over you. In many instances, you will confront shadow aspects of the self that you need to reconcile, release, or heal. You will also uncover various aspects of your soul, some familiar, many unfamiliar. Some of these rooms you have opened, some you have sealed, and some you have yet to discover. Your task is to enter these rooms, clear out the debris, and discover hidden treasures and untapped inner gifts that you are meant to recognize and develop as part of your soul. This is the essential work of the soul-journer.

I have noticed again and again that the rooms in the lower three mansions that contain gifts and blessings are the ones most tightly sealed and hardest to open. People fear these treasure vaults because they know that the divine power they contain, once freed, will change their lives. In fact, the work you do in every mansion, room by room, allows your life to change. And by doing this work your soul builds stamina and its insights grow richer, more intimate and revealing. Each mansion has as many rooms as your soul needs—and then some.

For Teresa, the seven mansions are a map of mystical ascension that displays the full spectrum of what you may experience on your journey to know God through coming to know yourself. Without a map, you can become overwhelmed by the soul's complexity and the divine's magnitude, so the Castle contains numerous exercises of deep self-examination, contemplation, and prayer. I will explain the different ways you may experience God, grace, and divine love as your soul and psyche awaken.

As a new pilgrim on the path of the soul, you progress in stages, so we start by carefully and methodically examining how thoroughly entrenched you are within the physical world and its various power structures. Your attachments are sources of pain and distraction, a position shared by spiritual teachers from Buddha to Teresa. You work within one mansion at a time and then move to the next. But you will find that you need to return to certain rooms in a mansion several times before moving on.

In the lower three mansions, you do the serious work for clearing the soul. There, you discover your "reptiles"—as Teresa called them—those interior sufferings of mind, heart, and spirit that you need to face and expel from your soul. Reptiles see better at night. Symbolically, they haunt the mind and gnaw at the heart. The reptilian part of the brain is one of the most primitive—it reacts without conscience; it is the unconscious part of the brain stem and our higher consciousness strives to control it.

As you uncover your reptiles, you must learn to wait for God, which is not easy. Chances are you are impatient and anticipate great and wondrous results immediately on entering the Castle. Expectations are reptiles of the worst kind, whether they are expectations of your sojourn into your Castle or any expectations you have of life. Some of Teresa's nuns had expectations of quickly meeting God as well, but, as she told them, you must first confront this sense of entitlement about God so that you can actually encounter God. You have to put aside your expectations of the Castle as well, and what it holds and how it may change you or your life.

The work that occurs in the mansions and the manner in which you experience God are distinctly different between the lower three mansions and the upper four. When you enter the Fourth Mansion, the experiences of transcendence and divine contact with God begin. At the Fourth Mansion, it is as if the divine meets you halfway through your journey into your soul. And the divine accompanies you the rest of the way to full union, awakening, or enlightenment.

God comes to greet you and sweeps you spontaneously into altered states of consciousness. Teresa gives the impression in her writings that these experiences of ascension occur naturally by the time you are in the Fourth Mansion, because God is waiting for you there. "Love is free" in the Fourth Mansion, according to Teresa. Here the individual heart becomes a cosmic resource for love, a vessel for what Teresa called the "sacred heart," the mystical heart of the cosmic Christ or cosmic consciousness—a universal force of grace. At this level of soul development, you can channel love beyond your personal needs and reasons—prayer becomes the means through which you let love flow through your soul and into the world.

From the Fourth Mansion on, you are absorbed into ever-deepening states of grace and spiritual consciousness, direct manifestations of the divine. Your soul is stretched to cosmic proportions. As the soul increases its strength, it can withstand increasing expressions of grace and God. Always the goal remains the same: to stretch the soul in preparation for becoming a container of divine love in the world. In the Fifth Mansion, holiness and its many expressions become the state of consciousness. Holiness is not a characteristic that we relate to very easily today.

When we think of being holy, we think of saints or gurus, not usually of ordinary people. But holiness is actually an exquisite power of the soul that emerges once a soul has matured into wholeness. The soul becomes a subtle but powerful container of light that heals, transforms, and inspires those whom it shines upon.

In the Sixth Mansion, Teresa acknowledges the difficulties that confront the individual in pursuit of God, including unreasonable "orders from above," which may include some seemingly impossible trial. But the "unreasonable God" is not one you can avoid, even if you avoid the Sixth Mansion. The fact is that we are all given something—or many somethings—to endure in this lifetime that test our faith, love, and resilience. These challenges are unavoidable and often seem unfair, but that is exactly the point—to push you into accepting without question that which God deems necessary.

Finally, the soul ascends to the Seventh Mansion, to a fearless bliss in which it is consciously united with the divine. All tests between the individual and God cease in this mansion. Teresa could barely find words to describe this mansion, which is her bodhi tree of enlightenment.

At this point, standing on your drawbridge, you may well think: I live an ordinary life in the real world, not in a cloistered community. What possible value could come from my meeting my soul? Why would I want to risk changing my life? What is the point, practically speaking, of tampering with mystical transformation for someone like me in the day-to-day world of relationships, work, mortgages, friendships, family, politics? Maybe I should continue to maintain a spiritual practice in which my experience with God is largely in my head.

You should take the time to consider these questions, but it may help you to know more of what the Castle is and what entering it can bring you. For Teresa, entering the Castle represented releasing her soul into the full presence of God. As the pathfinder into this uncharted territory of the soul, Teresa prepared the way for others, and her entire life showed the power of her discoveries in the Castle.

Would Teresa be in a cloister today? I doubt it. She would be where you are—out in the world.

Let me give you a preview of what the First Mansion holds. I'd like you to see how each room of each mansion is a facet of the cosmic hologram that is your life. Your soul is infinitely more than the fleeting glimpse you may have experienced during meditation or in a ritual. Your soul is a masterpiece of divinity in miniature. Its power is connected to the whole of creation. But it is not enough for you to read that and acknowledge it, and think, Oh, I know that. It's just incredible but I can see that. But really you *can't* "hear" that truth and "get it." You have to walk deliberately into the Castle and look into this truth, one facet at a time. You have to connect to this truth in body, mind, and spirit, consciously and viscerally and fully. You have to earn the experience of making that truth *real* for you, beyond the domain of your five senses, through deep inner work and prayer. Your purpose lies within the Castle, where you will understand that the reason you have descended into physical life is to unleash the power of your soul upon Earth. To enter into your Castle is not a journey that takes you *away* from the world; rather, it brings you directly *into* the world. It brings you fully into your soul, and into your power in the world.

Ironically, people who are not in touch with their souls live in fear and spend their lives running away from the world, even though it looks as if they are working and living right in the middle of everything. Yet, the mystic, who might look as if he or she has run away from the world, is in fact living right in the world, far more present and empowered. Mystics change the world around them more dynamically and more positively than can ever be measured. The mystic works on the invisible plane, relying on God, prayer, and grace. It has always been this way and it always will be.

But, let's face it, the world is as seductive as it is frightening, and that is the paradox you will confront in the First Mansion. Teresa knew well that the journey into the Castle is arduous for many reasons, not the least of which is that, while in the First Mansion, you will try to figure out a way to serve two masters and get away with it. That is, you will want to remain attached to the power dynamics of your physical life while attempting to jump-start wondrous mystical experiences. You'll soon discover that this won't work, but it does lead you to realize that you have a relationship to the archetypal pattern of chaos. When a situation becomes unreasonable or uncontrollable, chaos erupts. You, too, can be unreasonable and uncontrollable, so, not only does chaos happen in your life, you also create chaos, sometimes inadvertently, sometimes deliberately. Ultimately you create chaos as a means of avoiding a confrontation with truth or divine guidance. These are some of the matters and spiritual directives that you will examine in the rooms of your First Mansion.

To begin to understand the relationship of your soul to chaos in the First Mansion, for example, you start by examining your personal or ego relationship to chaos, including the personal and spiritual discontent you feel, the disorganization and drama you foster in your life, or the anxiety you have that chaos will occur if you do not adhere to a ferociously organized schedule. You do this in your First Mansion because this is the mansion most closely connected to your external world. It is the ground floor, the domain of physical power and chaos. In the appropriate room, you focus on how you create chaos in this world, how you call it into your life to distract yourself and others, to cloud your and others' reason and confuse emotions. In this room, you would ask yourself:

"Do I enjoy my ability to create chaos?"

"How often do I create chaos instead of tranquility?"

"Does chaos control me more than my inner guidance? If I

were directed to trust and have faith that all would be well, would the chaos around me have more power over me than the message coming from my soul?"

These are just a few sample questions from the rooms of the First Mansion, but they are life-changing. This type of close-to-the-bone introspection is an act of soul progression, as Teresa would describe it. Even if you do not have an ultimate goal of mystical union, even if you are not seeking to go through all seven mansions to know God, you will benefit from confronting the gripping hold that chaos has over you. You will dramatically improve your life, at the very least. Even if you want simply to reduce stress, the results of going through the First Mansion will be profoundly liberating. This self-examination will open a cosmic portal and give you a vastly expanded awareness of the consequences of your actions and reactions, personal motivations, and choices. You will become more self-aware and conscious of how your choices reflect your personal power agendas. In fact, you will have a new, more conscious, intimate relationship to power.

But, if your goal is to involve God in your life and know your higher purpose, examining chaos will make your prayers and contemplation and all your inner work more dynamic. This work is more than self-observation. You are awakening your soul. Through your inner struggles, you open yourself to guidance. Your journey will become sacred and mystical rather than psychological-spiritual. From the First Mansion you can proceed, step by step, to the center of the soul's Castle, where God is calling to you, where he lives inside you. "The kingdom of heaven is within," as Jesus taught, and one way to enter it is through the soul's Castle. Once in the center, you share your truths and secrets with God directly.

Teresa became able to reach this place of mystical union and dialogue after long practice of prayer, self-examination, and contemplation. She did not seek mystical experiences or force moments of rapture when she engaged in these spiritual practices—they came upon her spontaneously as gifts from God, sometimes when she was working in the kitchen, sometimes when she was alone in prayer. Pursuing the mystical path is both a calling and a choice. The divine comes to call in any number of ways; you must choose your response.

∂

Visualize taking a step from your everyday world onto the beginning of the drawbridge to your Castle. Stop there for a moment as you read this, anticipating your next steps toward the Castle.

A Moment of Contemplation

The first call of creation came through God's voice when he said, "And let there be light." Silence contains light, although not the type of light you can see. Silence is thick with the light of the divine. This light seduced and continues to seduce mystics. A direct encounter with this light is a direct encounter with God. Through encounters with this light comes illumination—the experience of being absorbed into divine consciousness and then returned to earth. You seek silence, solitude, tranquility, and resolution to difficulties not just because that seems a more natural and healthy way to be; you are drawn to the silence because inner silence and calm are seductive. You may tell yourself that you have to get away from all your stress or that you need your own space in order to think through the problems of the day, but the truth is that you want to stop thinking—period. That craving for silence, that desire to be alone and quiet for even a few minutes, is a soul need. Your mind may need quiet, but your soul craves silence. Quiet does not satisfy the soul—only silence does. You can begin to find this silence in the Castle, where God fills the soul with a sense of silence beyond quiet, beyond peace.

There, God stills your mind, your body, and your emotions in a state of silent prayer that Teresa called the Prayer of Quiet.

SPIRITUAL DETACHMENT

Examining your attachments to the material world might seem, at first, a throwback monastic discipline that has no role in your present life. But it is a valuable practice for changing your life as well as for healing illness. Any serious redirection or healing requires that you define what holds power over you and what you attempt to control or have power over. You locate the fragments of your spirit that you have left in your past with power objects— which can be anything from expensive property to social status to money or any material goods that symbolize authority for you—or powerful people and disentangle, detach, and collect them. This is, in fact, what you also do in therapy—examine where you are entrenched in relationships or memories. Even if you are not ill or in therapy, if you want to become a conscious human being whose spirit, mind, and body are integrated and whose actions are congruent with your values, you must examine all your relationships to power.

Teresa instructed her nuns, too, to develop a heightened awareness to any and all sources of emotional stress, attachments, and power struggles that manifested themselves in their world. No monastic wall, no matter how high and thick, can prevent competition or jealousy. But as the sisters gained awareness of the causes of their struggles, they worked with prayer and contemplation to detach from them—just as you will do.

Profoundly insightful and therapeutic as her methods are, Teresa would not have called this inner work healing; but we would and we do, which is a difference worth noting. Healing is a major theme in contemporary spiritual culture. We have woven spiritual practices into the health industry, and the result is that our spiritual path and our healing path often become one and the same. The map of the seven mansions is rooted in prayer, not in healing. Teresa assumed that each person entering the journey into the Castle was not yet aware or not yet awakened, but considered his or her soul full of grace. To Teresa, the only soul without grace was the soul of a person who did not pray or who consciously committed sin. It baffled Teresa that a person could forgo the pleasure of prayer, of being with God. Of all the many mysteries in the universe, that, for her, was the unsolvable one.

Teresa believed, as do many spiritual masters, that attachments are distractions from the soul's ultimate calling to become an intimate companion of God. Your attachments buffer you from the presence of God in your life; they substitute for contact with the divine. An object or situation that captures the power of your soul dilutes your capacity to pray with full attention. Buddhist teachings parallel this position perfectly: Distractions lead a soul away from the present moment, from the here and now, which is the only reality that should concern you. All the rest is illusion. As the Buddha taught, the cause of suffering is attachment; the end of attachment will mean the end of suffering.

Spiritual detachment is the means by which you withdraw from distractions of power so that you can experience the authentic power of God that is pure love. You may not know what it means to be loved *by God*. If the only experience of love you have had is that of loving another person, then how could you possibly comprehend what it means to be fully embraced by God? You discover that you are loved fully by God through experiences of complete dependency upon this invisible force of Divinity, this truly unknowable source of grace and benevolence that enters most profoundly into your life during your most vulnerable moments. For Teresa, attachments to earthly power of any kind (which manifest as jealousy, haunting memories, or sexual passions) indicate that your soul has not yet grasped certain truths about its nature and purpose. These attachments often stem from fears of abandonment, isolation, loneliness, starvation, and poverty. Such attachments cause suffering, regardless of whether you live in the world or in a monastery.

Detachment is a spiritual necessity because you cannot serve two realities simultaneously. You cannot be honest and dishonest at the same time; you cannot be married and single at the same time; you cannot forgive and remain bitter; you cannot truly let go yet continue to hold on; and you cannot acknowledge the higher reality of a spiritual life and divine guidance yet do things or hold beliefs that defy your spiritual principles. Herein lies the cosmic battleground for the soul on matters of attachment: At the end of the day, what power is more seductive to you—Earth's or God's?

No one answers that question just once. You are confronted with it many times. Every time you close your eyes and ask for guidance, you know deep in your soul that the answer will always necessitate that you make a choice between faith in the unseen domain of God and the material world.

Because of this reluctance to trust, people spend their entire lives standing on the drawbridge to their souls—knowing that they are being divinely called, feeling a yearning to know God. Yet, they cannot bring themselves to cross the bridge to the soul because they fear what might become of their attachments. They ask themselves, "What if God wants my money? What if God takes my house? What if this business of soul exploration results in my ending up alone like a nun in a monastery?" Your attachments are the moats around your Castle that prevent you from entering your Castle. You cannot imagine yourself free of them in concept. You think they keep you on the Earth. Who, you ask, would you be without them? Attachments to your worldly goods and to the traumas and pains of your past are, without a doubt, the greatest impediments to a spiritual life. This is what Jesus meant when he said that it is easier for a rich man to pass through the eye of a needle than to enter the kingdom of heaven. Your need to protect your physical life and power base in the material world continually competes with your trust in God. Do you really think that if God wanted your money or house you could prevent him from declaring eminent domain?

Remember detachment does not mean giving up your earthly belongings, as the mystics did when they entered their monasteries. Detachment means that you withdraw the authority that social status or money or an emotional wound has over you. The object or status becomes unessential as you come to know the true authority of your soul and God. It is then that you realize that these are mere substitutes for power and ways of protecting yourself from in the world. Detachment releases you from the need to protect yourself by clinging to objects that substitute for faith in God. You do *not* need to give them up, but you *do* need to see clearly why you cling to each of them with such passion.

A Moment of Contemplation: Guidance for Detaching

You leave fragments of your spirit here and there over the years. These pieces are glued—like barnacles on a ship—to various places, objects, people, memories, and unfinished business. Although detaching from them can be extremely difficult, detachment is a far more natural practice for your soul as well as emotions and mental health than holding on to the dead zone of your past. With practice it gets easier but the practice is rigorous. The following exercise in detachment is brief but powerful.

Think about something that qualifies as an attachment for you, something that you really struggle with. You know that you should have detached from this situation, person, or memory long ago, but it hangs on and on. Enter into silence and pray for guidance for how to resolve this situation. See the person, situation, or thing; feel how your spirit is stuck there. Ask, "How can I get free?"

What did you hear as guidance? What sign came to you to

tell you your prayer was answered? Perhaps, you think, you didn't pray long enough or hard enough to receive an answer to your prayer. But perhaps the answer came so swiftly, immediately, that you dismissed it because you have been clinging for so long.

Enter into prayer again and go past your hurt, your pride, your ego, your fear, and face the attachment and the reasons you hold on to it. All these reasons are about power. Nothing else. No one holds on to any attachment unless there's some energy connection, some currency of power involved. Even your worst, most painful memories hold the power of pain, a pain that gives you the "right" to ask for certain things, treatment, sympathy, or other entitlements. What is the root of your attachment, the power you're trying to hold on to?

Now imagine detaching completely from that object that is weighing down your soul and draining your energy. What part of you struggles with detaching the most? Pride? Fear? How much is due to an unwillingness to let your physical world change? Scrape off the barnacles, cut the cord, sever your power connection. Now what will happen? What will change?

This exercise helps you see the power both of your soul and of your attachments. With that insight into this basic soul struggle, ask yourself, "Do I really want to receive clear, direct guidance?" If you receive guidance that compromises your physical comfort, would you be willing to follow it? Few can answer yes unconditionally. Even ancient mystics who received the clearest directives in the most profound visions found it difficult at times to carry out the guidance they received. That conflict is part of our relationship with heaven: We are drawn to God, we are terrified of God, we rely on this God we cannot see, we do not trust this God completely, and yet, in spite of all our confusion, we cannot stop ourselves from continuing to walk toward our Castle.

AND THEN THERE ARE THE REPTILES

Once inside your Castle, you will encounter your reptiles. Even though the human soul is indeed made in the image and likeness of God, it has to face the "venomous creatures and reptiles of the world" as a part of its journey to God.

Our psyches and souls harbor these same symbolic reptiles that Teresa and her nuns identified four hundred years ago, such as hatred, jealousy, envy, vengeance, arrogance, dishonesty, and vanity. Some we call by different names: memories of emotional and physical abuse, guilt, inability to forgive and the need to be forgiven, addictions, codependence. Yet, "reptiles" is a perfect name for all these sufferings of the soul, because, just like reptiles, they stalk us under the cover of darkness, discovering our weaknesses and slithering past defenses. Once they get into the Castle, Teresa writes, they are very difficult to get out. Who has not been kept up at night by the stress of dark emotions? We would all like to clear our minds and souls of these reptiles.

As difficult as they are to get out of the Castle once they're in, "reptiles and venomous creatures" rarely get into any of the mansions beyond the third. Teresa writes that the Fourth Mansion and above are far too pure for them. A reptile cannot survive in the presence of the light of the divine. In any case, by the time you are ready to enter the Fourth Mansion, you will have already evicted most of the obvious reptiles from your soul just by virtue of the rigors of the journey itself.

Yet even in the middle of this often dark but essential work is an ever-presence of God that, according to Teresa, continually reinforces your inner light, courage, fortitude, and passion for a deep inner life. No matter how much the inner life demands of you, the rewards are always far greater than what you can imagine. But first you have to make it through boot camp, with its reptiles and need for discipline, dedication, and a rigorous training program. You cannot expect to see results immediately. You have to hang in there and go the distance.

I have often thought that if a way could be found to communicate the tranquility that comes from finally *knowing* God, a tranquility that melts away everyday fears and replaces low self-esteem with empowered humbleness, then those would be the most powerful words ever written. But words alone will never be able to contain the experience of God—we must each earn our way to that precious, inner state of tranquility.

TRANSITIONING BETWEEN WORLDS

Teresa wrote *The Interior Castle* to guide others into a conscious relationship with God. Today, many people are prone to say that they are committed to living a conscious life (not "devoted," but "committed," which has no direct spiritual implications, and does not commit the individual to a particular God or spiritual practice). This leaves those individuals free of any serious spiritual responsibilities, such as a rigorous daily spiritual practice. Often, this goal of living a conscious life includes the determination to become healthy and empowered, always seeking to keep one step ahead of discontentment and discomfort and always looking for personal fulfillment.

The commitment to a spiritual path requires more discipline and rigor than the choice to live a conscious life. Yet even the choice to become conscious needs to follow rules and stages. A devotion to becoming conscious is every bit as arduous as attaining mystical union with God, even if on the surface it appears to be less God directed. Those who are serious about becoming conscious will discover that it's the same goal that Teresa and her nuns had of becoming conscious souls. Changing the vocabulary doesn't change the journey.

One difference in the pursuit of these goals, however, is that the nuns were under a vow to pursue their spiritual lives. We do not take any vows to practice our spirituality. We are free to stop and start our spiritual lives, catch as catch can. We can put together bits and pieces of whatever traditions we like, frequently adding holistic health or intuitive practices, melding all of them into a custom-designed spiritual path. Some days we meditate, some days we don't, depending on whether we have the time or need to de-stress in a noon yoga class. Some people, of course, are very disciplined about their practice, but they are in the minority, and generally their aim is not to know God intimately. Their aim is often to build self-esteem or maintain a healthy, fit body—self-focus, again.

A vow elevates a spiritual practice to one of spiritual devotion. It is incomprehensible for most people today to take a vow before God that says, "I shall be devoted to my spiritual practice without distraction because I recognize that I have this life for a brief time in order to be of divine service and gain personal illumination with God." Taking such a vow is out of step with our spiritual culture. We are very relaxed about matters of the sacred. We do not emphasize devotion to the sacred out of the same sense of awe and reverence that is so common in monasteries, but that has nothing to do with whether a person is actually in a monastery. Reverence and devotion open the soul to intimacy with God and go far deeper than exploring personal matters of healing. You cannot stop and start a true soul practice. Once you consciously enter your Castle, you set in motion a journey that has no end point. Mystical experiences begin when you finally leave personal agendas with God behind.

Make no mistake about this fact: The world is our monastery now. Our spiritual challenges unfold within our personal lives and the external world. When you pursue a relationship with your soul and God through the Castle, you are answering a call. You are being called to build your spiritual stamina so that you can channel grace in this world and for this world. Our new monastery, the world, is in desperate need of the strength of your soul.

SHALL YOU CROSS THE DRAWBRIDGE?

I have so often looked into people's eyes and seen pure fear as they asked me about their lives. I could see so easily what "could be" for them, if only they were not so afraid. I could see that truly their lives would work out for them and all would be well. Yes, it would be rough for a bit after Diane left her job and Jack closed his company, for example, but they had no idea—*none*—how extraordinary their lives would become. I did. I didn't know how or what or when, but I did know that they were being invited to cross their drawbridge. That would make all the difference in the world for them. Why would the journey make so much difference? Up until now, they had known only fear. Finally, they were going to discover the power of their souls.

In preparation for entry into the Castle, I've selected a poem from my favorite poet and mystic, Emily Dickinson. I've taken some liberties with this poem to support the journey into the Castle.

UNTO ME? I DO NOT KNOW YOU—

by Emily Dickinson

"Unto me?" I do not know you—
Where may be your House *and Castle?*

"I am Jesus—Late of Judea—
Now—of Paradise"—

Wagons—have you—to convey me?
This is far from Thence—

"Arms of Mine—sufficient Phaeton—
Trust Omnipotence"—

I am spotted—"I am Pardon"—
I am small—"The Least

Is esteemed in Heaven the Chiefest—
Occupy my House and *my Castle*"—

—from *Poetry as Prayer*
by Reverend John Delli Carpini

ᕋ

Now, begin to walk over the drawbridge and through the gate to your Castle. As you go, say this prayer:

"I open myself to divine guidance. I surrender myself to become as a channel for grace, healing, and service as God directs my life."

You are now in the courtyard of your Castle, deep within your soul. The ground beneath your feet sparkles like heavy, crushed crystal. Feel yourself standing firmly on this crystal, within the safe, quiet, thick walls of your Castle. Breathe in the silence of your soul for a few moments. You have begun.

PART II
The Soul's Journey

THE FIRST MANSION

The Power of Prayer, Humility, Chaos, and Divine Seduction

In humility is the greatest freedom. As long as you have to defend the imaginary self that you think is important, you lose your piece of heart. As soon as you compare that shadow with the shadows of other people, you lose all joy, because you have begun to trade in unrealities and there is no joy in things that do not exist.

—*Thomas Merton*

FOR ME, entering my Castle was like coming home. This is because prayer—the key to the Castle—has always been a constant in my life. As soon as I could comprehend instructions as a toddler, I was taught that my day should begin and end with a prayer to God and my guardian angel, who stood over my right shoulder all day to look after me. Prayer has been like an inner chapel that I enter when I want or need to gain a higher perspective on life. Prayer lets me look through the lens of the sacred.

I want to make a point of distinguishing between wanting and needing to enter into prayer in order to shift perspectives. You don't always have to be motivated by need to pray. More often than I *need to,* I *want to* see from a different perspective. This is the motivation that calls me into prayer. Through prayer, we all can distinguish truth from illusion, and I love the liberating feeling of truth. Nonetheless, as I began working with Teresa's gentle presence in my life, I realized that I did not pray at the level she was describing, so I began a more disciplined practice of prayer and contemplation.

That decision required that I change a few routines around my home, beginning with initiating silence. Normally I would have a couple of cups of coffee in the morning while watching the news and scanning my e-mail. I would get infuriated over events, yell and walk around the kitchen, calm down a little, drink more coffee, watch more news, and then carry on about the shape of the world to whoever walked into my kitchen—and someone is always walking into my kitchen. One morning, in a fury over some political incident, I slammed a box onto the kitchen counter and a coffee cake popped out as if it had been fired from a rocket pad. It flew across the room, hit my cousin in the head, then smashed all over the floor. That incident said to me that I was becoming as out of control as the world around me and that I needed to withdraw in order to write this book. I needed to get inside the Castle, to detach and pray.

"Let my soul go where I cannot go and let my soul go only with God." I repeated these words again and again. I also repeated, "I detach as I pray. I put my soul in God's hands to serve only good in this situation that I feel powerless to change."

With these prayers, I felt a tiny flame of hope ignite. Hope is the face of grace, and it reminds us that ultimately the world is not in the hands of greedy politicians or terrorists or corporate moguls or fundamentalists praying for Armageddon. The world is in the hands of God. This prayer brought me back to my senses, to my center, to where I function best, "in the world but not of the world."

And for the first time in my life, I understood the true power of prayer. It is the invocation of grace. Prayer has the capacity to lift you off the Earth at the speed of light. Because I wanted to experience what Teresa writes about, because I passionately wanted to get *into* my Castle, I followed her instructions on prayer.

Soon I was in the First Mansion of my Castle.

PRAYERS FOR THE CASTLE

There is no shortcut into the Castle. The only way to enter is through prayer and meditation, but Teresa differentiates between what she considers authentic prayer and "word habits of the mind." In the latter, we are not conscious of what we are saying. When someone prays automatically, without a focused awareness of whom she is talking to and what she is asking, she is not praying, no matter how much her lips are moving, Teresa writes. "If she gets into the habit of addressing the Magnificent One as if he were her servant, never questioning the manner in which she is expressing herself, merely letting whatever pops into her head fall out of her mouth, spilling words she has learned by simple repetition, she is not praying." *(The Interior Castle*, Starr) In authentic prayer, on the other hand, we're conscious of the purpose of our prayer, which is to communicate with God. Even if you cannot sustain this awareness through an entire prayer, however, as long as you are truly reflective some of the time, your prayer will be authentic.

Prayer draws you into the energy field of the sacred and protects your soul. Because the soul resides within you, you can never be separated from it, but, Teresa notes, "Remember, there are many different ways to 'be' in a place." Prayer is the key to the Castle gate, and it unlocks the meaning of *be.* Your soul within your soul—your Castle—is another way to be; it is a level of reality you hold within you and to which you go through prayer. The Castle is a place of being, not of thinking or pondering or emoting. It is your center, where you transcend the five-sensory self and issues of your physical life. This is your place of faith in something greater. It is a given that God lives here.

Once inside your Castle, you imagine the soul as a companion with whom you also communicate through prayer and contemplation. You go beyond a basic intellectual image of the soul as your essence or connection to eternity and animate its image—you make your soul real as a "sacred other," a part of your self. And with this beloved inner companion, you find that your soul becomes your bridge to God.

Inside the Castle, you cultivate a perspective that sees beyond the worries, ambitions, and ordinary issues of your life. This is not easy to do, but give up complaining. Give up being a pessimist. Give up thinking life owes you anything. Give up being lazy and wishing things were easier all the time. In short, give up wishing your life were other than the way it is and *do* something with the life you have. Reaching for your sacred other requires that you love or appreciate at least part of your life, that you are striving to make the most of your life, and that you recognize that life is a gift. The sacred other is not difficult to find. But your own worthiness and appreciation of your life may be difficult for you to find—and that's the raw truth.

As you pursue your sacred other, remind yourself that this journey does not require you to toss out your belongings and walk away from the world you know and all the people you love. Rather, your goal is to transcend the controlling influence that the false gods of the outside world—like stress, money, and peer pressure—have on you and your relationship to God. Mystics like Teresa, Francis, and John of the Cross lived in a kind of fearless bliss; they functioned fully in the physical world, but their bodies were servants to their souls. Eventually their worlds also became servants to their souls as their teachings attracted followers and they implemented the instructions they had received from God. A contemporary example of a mystic of the world was the saint Mother Teresa. Without a cent to her name, she died one of the most powerful citizens of India, if not of the planet.

These individuals did not constantly ask, "What if there isn't enough? What about my 401(k) and retirement account? What if my plans don't work out the way I want? They relied on prayer and grace and saw the world first through the eyes of their souls and trusted that a greater force protected them, a force so great that no human being could challenge it. Paradoxically, so many others, with everything material at their disposal, hesitate to do anything to change the world. The mystics' lives were extreme—in their miracles, escapades, and accomplishments—so that others could witness the power of the soul in action with the divine as partner.

You will not be called into monastic service as a result of entering your Castle—I promise you. You can, however, know in your own way the fearless bliss that the monastics did. It is not a grace that the mind or heart can generate. It comes through your soul. It begins to flow into your being as you nurture a relationship through prayer with the sacred other within your Castle.

THE STAGES OF PRAYER

Prayer is the way to self-knowledge and to knowledge of God. For Teresa, the lifelong search for and refinement of self-knowledge was a creed. She could not comprehend how a person could stop exploring her soul or exhaust her curiosity about what God wants of her.

Though prayers can be simple, their power and mystery are not. Prayer unites your conscious self and your soul with God. It alters your consciousness, which allows you to enter the Castle's seven different levels of consciousness. In prayer, you open your soul to become available to God—available to listen, to receive, to be. Prayer removes you from anger, from the chaos of ordinary concerns or aggressive thoughts, and allows you to dwell on spiritual phrases and transcendent truths that lift your consciousness.

Logically, you would ask, "But what sort of prayers should I say? What are the right prayers to get into my Castle? Are some prayers more effective than others?" Teresa addresses these questions as she describes three categories of prayers and how we progress through each. For Teresa, repetitive prayer, such as saying the rosary or a mantra, is the most basic form of prayer, but it reflects a soul afraid to approach God. When repeating words, you have no chance to *listen and receive*. "The quieter we become, the more we hear," wrote Ram Dass, the modern mystic who wrote *Be Here Now*. The intention of repetitive prayer is to comfort you, which it does, but that comfort is self-generated, not a product of divine grace. Although repetitive prayers do not invoke divine guidance in the same way as a practice of contemplation and creative, spontaneous prayer, they are certainly useful and blessed. As you begin your daily prayer practice, you can use them to help you make prayer time a habit.

The **prayer of** *recollection,* as Teresa calls the first stage of prayer, is a higher form of prayer to which you gradually progress from repetitive prayer. In a recollection prayer you re-collect yourself and pray yourself into wholeness. You gather together parts of your spirit that you have neglected, forgotten, or attached to others. In recalling your spirit to yourself, you detach from all outside influences. This type of prayer will be a part of your practice in Mansions One through Three, where your task is to come to "know thyself," to go beyond your ego and your personality and discover the content and character of your soul.

To help you in this discovery, you engage in conversations with your soul in each room. This conversational prayer marks the development of the courage to be open to an exchange with God. In dialogue you open your soul to God's voice. To begin the conversation, Teresa suggests saying a prayer—even a repetitive prayer—and then quieting yourself and listening for a period of time, as if you are establishing a practice of dialogue. Pray and listen. Pray and listen. What do you hear?

At the same level, the companion to the prayer of recollection is the **prayer of *contemplation*,** in which you enter into silence for the purpose of self-reflection. In this state, you can read sacred texts or inspirational teachings and consider how to apply them to your life; but mainly, you reflect on your actions, thoughts, and deeds. Your dialogues with your soul in each room will reveal many things, including pain, shame, and other raw emotions and insights about yourself, but you're not doing this to feel bad or to invite self-pity or guilt. You're mining these chunks of raw emotions so that you can find the value hidden within them. Sit with each discovery until you can see through the raw ore to the gold or jewel it holds. At every opportunity, choose fearlessness: Do not run from whatever you discover, whether you find pain or untapped talent. Be fearless. Fearlessness is bliss.

Don't measure your progress through the mansions by how fast you get through the exercises. Your mind can play tricks on you and will tell you many times that you have completed the work in one room. You may even think that you have completed the work in an evening or an hour. But, as you soon discover, opening up one room opens up more rooms that reflect the content of your personal life.

From the moment you begin this work, you will start to see the world from a different perspective, from the vantage point of your Castle, from whatever room in which you are standing. If, for example, you are working in a room that examines how you deal with change, you will call upon that state of mind the next time you stand amid chaos. You will turn automatically to prayer, if only to say, "Help me act with wisdom in the middle of this upheaval. Do not let me contaminate my soul or the souls of any individuals with whom I am in contact." With that prayer, you bring grace into that moment's unfolding and shift to the perspective of a room within your Castle that will guide you in how to respond. This is true awareness. This is the soul in action in the world.

Ultimately, the only authentic progress you make is through prayer. There is no way to determine how long you will remain at any stage of prayer or in any mansion: Teresa spent years progressing from one stage to the next, although the more you come to peace with the mystical practice of detachment, the further and deeper you will go.

Beyond the prayer of recollection is **the prayer of** *quiet,* in which you engage in the Fourth and Fifth Mansions. At this stage, you have matured past the need to use prayer for petitioning favors or for a personal safety net. You have detached from the quest for psychological or emotional tranquility into a state of soul tranquility. Doubts and fears about your ability to survive in the physical world are gone. You have moved into an unconditional trust that yields a mystical "quietude," as Teresa describes it, a divine bliss that is given to you spontaneously, a taste of heaven.

In the third level of prayer, the **prayer of** *union,* you experience a mystical state of union with God. This generally corresponds with the Sixth and Seventh Mansions. In such a state, your senses and mind are numbed, in a state of suspension. In one of her experiences of mystical union, Teresa noted, her senses wanted to go with her when God called, but they and her mind were simply too fragile. Only her soul could withstand the presence of God.

Prayer is your way through darkness, prayer is your way into the light, prayer is your way to maintain your field of grace. Prayer is your way into the Castle and through the Castle and it is the way to maintain your connection to your Castle. Let me recommend that you draw upon the prayers of all the major traditions to help you, dedicating one day each week to a different tradition. Open your soul to the wisdom and truth in all traditions. Prayer is your way to God.

I recommend this prayer for entering the Castle:

The Prayer of Entry

I cross the bridge into the silent bliss of my interior Castle. I close the drawbridge and forbid all outside influences from entry into this holy place that is my soul. Here in my Castle, I am alone with God. Under God's light and companionship I discover the depth and beauty of my soul. I embrace the power of prayer. I open myself to divine guidance. I surrender myself to become as a channel for grace, healing, and service as God directs my life.

Here I embrace my devotion to the divine. And here I pause in this silence to animate my soul's dignity. I feel my interior self calling me. I resonate deeply to my own divinity. I am prepared now to encounter, to become, to dialogue with my own divinity, that which is God within me.

Here in my Castle, my faith becomes a fire, cleansing my soul of every fear. Each time I enter my Castle, I trust even more deeply in the presence and wisdom of God in my life. I surrender my mind, my heart, my need for safety, and my need for rational explanations and orderly instructions to God's will for me. I trust that all that is in my life is as it should be. I release the need to know why events happen as they do, whether painful or glorious. I release the need to let others know they have harmed me. I release my fear of being abandoned on this Earth and left to face my life alone. I release my fear of becoming infirm. I surrender in trust that I am on this Earth with purpose. I am guided, I am cared for, every prayer is heard, and every prayer is answered. I am a channel for grace and delight in the silent bliss that surrounds me in the sa-

cred center of my Castle, in the intimate presence of
God. In this silence, the only voice I hear is God's.

ᴄ᷁ᴐ᷁

You are now in the energy field of the First Mansion. Here, your
soul begins its journey toward self-knowledge, illumination, and
God. You will come to know, feel, and recognize your soul by
working on the spiritual and earthly challenges contained within
each room. Each challenge or spiritual exercise has a significance and purpose essential to the evolution of your soul. One
room at a time, you increase your self-knowledge and refine it
slowly, gradually.

The first three challenges you face in this mansion are
power, control, and the ego. Teresa led her nuns into the First
Mansion through the door of humility, a subject she continually
emphasized in her teachings—and a concern of many other
great spiritual teachers, from Jesus to Gandhi. There is no more
appropriate place to begin.

THE POWER OF HUMILITY

Humility is a quality of character that you must have on the spiritual path. It is also the quality that is most misunderstood and
misinterpreted. Most people confuse humility and humbleness
with being humiliated, about which they have an ingrained, par-
alyzing fear that controls their psyches, emotions, and actions.
Humiliation is an experience of powerlessness or of assault on
your self-esteem, but humility, understood within a spiritual context, is the portal to complete liberation.

Small wonder that people confuse humbleness with humiliation, since some of the *Oxford English Dictionary* definitions of
humble include "low in rank [and] respect." The word *humility*—

referring to the quality of being humble—is from the Latin *humilis* and *humus,* "earth," and is related to the Greek *chtōn,* "earthy," and *chamai,* "on the ground." Humility does not mean that you hold yourself in low esteem or deny yourself respect, recognition, power, status, or accomplishments. Humility in the Castle is a virtue and you begin your quest for it on the ground floor of the First Mansion.

The truly humble person has little fear of what God will ask of her or him because no task is too small or insignificant, demeaning or worthless. Many of the great mystics were given wild and bizarre instructions during meditation. These orders were not meant to humiliate them, but to show that the extraordinary could be attained through unconditional faith. They were living, breathing examples of unconditional faith. Many contemporary mystics who will never be famous have received equally challenging, even outlandish guidance that struck other people as foolish or risky. But their fearlessness and humility allowed them to follow through regardless of the social, financial, political, or personal consequences.

One man I know was deep in prayer when he heard an inner voice instruct him to "bring healing to the hospital." At first, he had no idea what that meant. He wasn't a physician and had no professional association with any hospital, but he was a practitioner of holistic healing. He let the idea "cook" a bit, then approached his local hospital to see if the administrators would allow him to teach a seminar to the nurses on the basic principles of the human energy system, which could help them provide holistic care for their patients. They said no, so he went on to contact another hospital and then another. Finally, one hospital said yes. His seminar was so popular that he was invited back to give more, and soon he was giving them monthly, instructing nurses, physicians, and other staff on holistic healing practices, which the hospital gradually adopted.

Was this man frightened when he heard this guidance? Yes and no. He was frightened at first *because* he knew it was authentic and he did not want to fail. And he did not know where to begin or what to anticipate. What scared him most was his realization that he had to rely on his own cleverness more than he had ever had to in his ordinary life, while knowing he had the backup power of divine intervention going for him. You don't follow divine instructions because the task is guaranteed to be successful; rather, you perform the task unconditionally because that is what you are instructed to do. It's a no-questions-asked order, just as a miracle is a no-questions-asked favor from God.

The challenge, of course, is in exploring your vulnerabilities and strengths and allowing yourself to be humble about them. What do you perceive as your earthly power? Is it a relationship—romantic, financial or business, political, or friendship—that gives you a (false) sense of safety? Is it a status job or house, social club, or neighborhood? Would you feel humiliated if you lost it or were stripped of it? Discerning the authentic power of your soul is the basis of your work in the First Mansion. Every other act of self-discovery depends on how well you lay this foundation of humility.

The Grace of Humility

Grace has many qualities and many expressions, among them: compassion, wisdom, patience, vision, endurance, humor, joy, intuition, holy foolishness, resilience, forgiveness, hope, gratitude, ecstasy, generosity, creativity, fearless bliss, and humility. Each quality of grace in turn has its own capacity to influence, heal, and affect change in your psyche and body. Humility, for example, allows you to recognize and acknowledge all the positive qualities of body, mind, and spirit in another person. Humility disarms the competitive voice that whispers to you, "There is not enough. What about you? You must be first. You need more. You deserve the reward, the attention, the status, and the money far more than that other person does."

Feeling humiliated by someone can frequently activate your

shadow, and, for example, foster feelings of vengeance or resent-ment—but maintaining an attitude of humbleness provides you with a shield of detachment. Humility enables you to under-stand another person's motivations and to transcend any nega-tivity. It can help you to realize that the actions of a frightened or negative person are rarely directed at you personally. Anyone qualifies as a target for an angry person.

It's more challenging now than ever before to be humble in our culture, since we place so much value on the individual and self-empowerment. In our contemporary attitudes, self-empowerment and humility make strange bedfellows; yet, para-doxically, no two qualities are better matched. Humility means that you do not need to deny others respect, attention, acclaim, or power because you need more than they do. Humility gives you the strength to be detached from the need for praise and (false) power, and to avoid the pitfall of craving approval. Pride is the worst of all toxins and the opposite force of humility. It takes hold of you in an instant and makes you a prisoner of the ego and the world around you. You might have millions of dol-lars, own five homes, employ two hundred people and think you are free because you are the boss, but you are probably a puppet of your pride, which requires you to have all that in order to feel that you have power and identity.

When I bring up humiliation versus the power of being hum-ble in my workshops, the entire audience seems to have a collec-tive flashback to some childhood humiliation. The memory is written all over their faces in an instant, their body language changes, and an atmosphere of vulnerability comes over every-one. Humiliation is disempowerment, but humbleness, as Teresa taught, is a powerful shield for the soul. Without humility, you are not in balance; the smallest motion can rock your boat and upset you. A person doesn't greet you properly; you aren't the first in line; you're not seated in the first row; you're not waited on in a restaurant fast enough; you aren't invited to a cer-tain party—how dare they! You can't go outside looking like *that* because what would "they" say? Someone makes a critical remark and you are destroyed for weeks, months, perhaps years; maybe you even need therapy to cope. A relationship disintegrates because pride prevents reconciliation. A humble person would move through all these incidents without leaving a wake.

True humility is releasing the need to have to win, to have to have the last word, to have to always have your insecurities reinforced with endless support. Humility is the ability to help someone who has injured you, to say you're sorry, not to wait years for the other person to apologize before you speak to him. Humility is the ability to appreciate the many people who devote their lives to helping you make your dreams come true, whether in a corporate setting in which you earn millions of dollars or in a small business or in your family.

Choosing to walk the humble path—and to stay on it—requires that you reflect frequently: "What is my true power?" and "Whose approval really matters—those who live outside my Castle or the company I keep inside my Castle?" And when God speaks to you, humility is the capacity to say, "Yes," instead of, "But what will others think if I do that?"

You cannot master humbleness just once or all at once. It is a daily life practice because, without a doubt, the fear of being humiliated is the most controlling voice in our psyches. Teresa and other spiritual directors from other traditions understood this basic truth of human nature. Many people who are looking for their purpose, their highest potential, are frustrated and exhausted by their quest because they think they can't see the next step they're meant to take. But even when that next step is right in front of them—which it always is—most would find a reason not to move forward. Some would say, "Well, the time is just not right," and others, "I'm just not sure." Their excuses are always the same but in the end, all excuses boil down to the fear of humiliation.

These individuals are waiting for something that will never come: They want guidance in a package, like a severance package or portfolio. And they want their guidance package to contain: (1) specifics of what they should do and with whom, usually with a guarantee that other people involved will do all the "high risk" work; (2) a guarantee that they will not have to invest one cent of their own money but will make a great deal in return doing the minimum; (3) a guarantee that they will not have to move, reorganize their lives, or become uncomfortable in any way, shape, or form; and, most important of all, (4) a guarantee that they will not, they *must not,* fail. Oh, and being admired by others in this "highest potential project" would also be nice.

In short, they want guarantees that they will win the race before they even run it. Rather than face the fearful demons or reptiles within them, most people make up stories, telling themselves that they are just too confused, or they just "can't quite hear their guidance," or that the time to move forward is simply not *now.* But their time will never come as long as they fear humiliation.

Humility becomes your protective shield because few see the humble as threatening. That is why humble, poor, shoeless mystics and many other magnificent humble individuals so often become the healers and peacemakers. They walk where others fear to tread because others fear being humiliated and the humble do not. Therefore, the humble are sent the tasks that are truly powerful, though they themselves appear powerless to people who see through the eyes of pride. To people wearing "hubris shades," the tasks appear to be simple, naïve, unworldly, out-of-touch; and those "born in a manger" or those who "sit under a bodhi tree" seem far too humble to cause any stir in the world. And in such humbleness is hidden the protection of God. Humility protected all the great spiritual masters—Jesus, most certainly; with humility, Gandhi defeated the British Empire.

This is a mystical truth: God does assign outrageous, relentless tasks to those he calls. And here is the second mystical truth: In order to endure your tasks, you *must* be humble. Humility is your greatest shield in this world. Humility is also the foundation to a mystical union with God. Take this truth with you as you explore your First Mansion.

Rooms for Refining Humility

Before you enter the rooms, make sure you have a journal and pen or pencil with you or a laptop in which you can write. You must never leave a room empty-handed. Find and write about something in every room to take with you into the world. If you write in your journal that you are having trouble reaching your soul in a certain room, add an explanation for why you think you are having that difficulty. You won't be able to empty any one room entirely in one visit, and some you'll never empty—but you'll *know* the contents. As the days/weeks/months of your life continue, each room fills up again and again—some far more than others, of course. And, although I have constructed seven rooms in this next section for you to enter and explore, you can always add other rooms that you feel you need. Each mansion can go on forever!

Note that while the instructions are to continue from one room to the next, *you* decide the pace at which you work. You may want to work on only one room per week, for example. These are rigorous exercises. They build your soul's strength to move spiritual boulders and make way for light. Do not try to move rapidly through the Castle; in any case, it's impossible (as Teresa herself noted). If you need to leave the Castle after only one room or two, please first say a prayer of closure or recite the Exit Prayer at the end of this mansion (p. 162).

Keep this thought in your awareness: You want to connect with your soul. You want to know yourself and how you relate to every part of your life, even parts you have yet to discover. Your

Castle is your place of truth. You are about to meet reptiles you do not even realize live within you and to discover that you have a dungeon in your soul in which you keep prisoners, people you refuse to forgive and desire to punish. This is the journey of discovering your mysteries. By walking into these rooms one by one, again and again, you call forth your soul.

As you penetrate deep into your interior self, beyond the chatter of your mind, you free your soul—*yourself*—from the illusions that have held you captive all your life. Many of those illusions are painful, but recognizing them for what they are is liberating. In meeting your soul, you are getting out of a type of earthbound madness. You are allowing yourself to live the rest of your life without fear of what will become of you on this Earth. That alone is a worthy goal—to live fearlessly. You come to realize that you can take care of yourself because you are in touch with your interior self, detached from everyday fears and insecurities. Within you is an unquenchable desire to live a wildly free life in which you are liberated from the self-imposed restrictions that come from the fear of humiliation and the fear of others' opinions, including your own self-critical nature. *That* is fearless bliss.

So, with that goal in mind, take a moment now to pray. You are beginning your journey into your soul. You and your soul are alone with God. Bless this journey that you are on. And bless you.

You are in your Castle courtyard. You enter the First Mansion. Imagine a long hall that has countless rooms. Yet, in spite of its infinite length, the hall is charming and comfortable, not daunting or intimidating. You are now going to find your way into one of the rooms along this hallway. You will do this not just once but many times. Each room represents a particular quest, a place where you can talk with your soul. Each room is furnished in a different way: Some are elegant, clear, almost Zen-like in their spareness; others will be dusty, cluttered, piled high with mementos.

THE FIRST ROOM:
How the Fear of Being Humiliated Controls You

Visualize yourself in front of the first room in this first hallway. See the plain wooden door. It is familiar, ordinary-looking. See yourself opening it and entering this first room, which is comfortable, warm, and cozy. Be fully present in this room. Take your time and, step by step, cross the floor to a gorgeous stone fireplace where a welcoming fire is crackling in the grate. Take a seat in one of the two big comfortable chairs facing each other in front of the hearth. But do not relax. Relaxation puts you to sleep.

Imagine that your soul comes to sit in that chair across from you. You can actually give form to your soul, give it your face, hair, and clothing. You recognize this soul. You know it. You just haven't given yourself time or opportunity to see it, acknowledge it, or be with it. Keep yourself focused and present. If you drift, and you will—this is just your first journey—return yourself to the image that you are conversing with your soul. After any distraction, simply return.

Soul Work: Your task in this room is to examine your fears about humiliations and how they have influenced your choices throughout your life. Have they influenced what you studied in school, the career you chose, the mate you have, the place you live, the religion you practice, the friends you maintain, the charities to which you give? Tell your soul what you would really like if you did not fear to admit it, if you did not fear you'd hurt someone else, if you did not fear change. Talk to your soul as if it were a beloved companion, a wiser aspect of yourself, which it is. Allow it to respond, and write down what it says in your journal. Ask for at least five examples of how the fear of being humiliated has affected you. Ask your soul to remember: How did it try to communicate to you during these years? How did it let you know that you were repressing guidance or changing a life course as a result of this fear? Go beyond simply identifying hurts. You are looking for the consequences of disconnecting from your soul.

Now, consider and write down how the fear of being humiliated is controlling your life *right now*. Ask and answer this through your soul. How are you repressing your *soul's purpose* from emerging in your life because you fear humiliation? What do you and your soul long to express? Do you want to break out of some constraining situation? Or perhaps you long for just the freedom to establish your inner life without feeling self-conscious? Go into your soul—always go into your soul. The temptation is to let your mind do the talking, but the mind does not belong in the Castle. Tell yourself again and again, "I do not want to think. I want to listen and receive."

After you've written all you can at this point, prepare yourself to leave this room. You will no doubt need to revisit it at several points on your journey in order to work through the control that this fear has over you. This is true for everyone.

Thank your soul for the insights it has given you in this room and make your way back into the infinite hallway, shutting the door behind you, knowing that this safe room and comforting fire—and your soul in its familiar guise—are available to you whenever you need to return.

THE SECOND ROOM:
Ways You Have Been Humiliated

Return now to the Castle hallway lighted by torches attached to the thick stone walls, which hold the outside world at bay. You stop in front of a room whose door is similarly plain and ordinary. When you open it, you find that this room is fairly simple, too, but also has a comfortable set of chairs in front of a cozy fireplace. There are shelves and nooks and niches with little doors ajar surrounding this hearth, but they are empty, suggesting that you are to fill them with the insights that you discover in this room.

Take your seat and imagine your soul in the chair across from you. Your task is to recall the ways in which you have been humiliated. Everyone has been humiliated and most people recall those incidents no matter how long ago they happened. Humiliations shape your life as much as your DNA does. In this room, though, you can safely talk with your soul about them and how those experiences shaped your behavior, your personality, your fears, and your habits.

Soul Work: Open yourself to the insights your soul has for you. Record them in your journal. Remember: You are in this room to dialogue, which means to listen as well as to speak. Lean back in your chair by the fireplace and let your soul communicate with you. Just be open. Receive. How deep is the scar tissue from your experience? How have these experiences influenced you? As you recognize each incident, place it on a shelf in one of the niches or cubbyholes. Now that you know these memories are there and you have written in your journal how they have affected you, you can close the cabinet doors on them. You've faced them, dealt with them. Now release them.

Rest quietly for a minute and experience the sensation of feeling empty, having released so much hidden weight—your inner reptiles. As before, after you have faced and written all you can for now, thank your soul for its memories and messages.

Take your leave, knowing that if you have to do more work in this room, you can return.

For now, though, you want to go back into the hallway, where you see another door that resembles the first two plain wooden doors, only this door shines with a high varnish in which you can almost see your reflection. This is the room you have to enter.

THE THIRD ROOM:
How You Have Humiliated Others

Just as you have been humiliated, you have also humiliated others. In this room, you and your soul will find memories of the acts by which you have harmed others overtly or secretly. You enter this safe room and go over to a window, before which are two chairs. Sit in one chair; your soul sits in the other. The light coming in through the window is soft and reflective, perfect for introspection and self-examination.

Soul Work: Ask your soul to help you recall instances when you humiliated other people. As you list them in your journal, also write down why you chose to act that way. You may *not* use the excuse "because I was afraid"; that is a catchall excuse that lets you off the hook. The bar is set much higher for you in the Castle. You need to own up to your reasons for your behavior and be accountable in each of the rooms of the Castle. And you need to maintain complete honesty in these dialogues between you and your soul. This is the practice of self-reflection.

After you've recalled five old scenes and recorded them in your journal, look for a pattern in your reasons for humiliating others. Then, shut the journal, thank your soul for its truthfulness, and leave this room for now.

Back in the hall, you can see more rooms to enter and explore. If you need to leave the Castle for now, say your prayer of closure or the Exit Prayer (see p. 162). If you're going on, approach the door of your fourth room, where you will examine your associations with the concepts of humility and humbleness.

THE FOURTH ROOM:
Ten Associations with Humility

This door is different; it's two sliding doors with a Zen-like design of light wood and rice paper. Slide the doors apart and let yourself into the quiet, spare room. Here you will examine what you think and feel about humility. As you enter the fourth room, notice how beautiful its bare wooden floors are. They are smooth, clean, and have a kind of glow that highlights the beautiful pattern of the wood and its simple elegance. In front of a simple stone fireplace are two round cushions for you to sit on so that you are close to the ground. Call on your soul to come and take a seat with you.

Once again, your thoughts turn to the subject of humility. Humility is grace, a power of the soul, but you have to believe and feel that. If at the personality/ego level you think that humbleness is disempowering or humiliating, you are headed for a spiritual crash. To embrace the grace of humility, you must begin by confronting your personal discomfort with seeing yourself as a humble person on this Earth and what that means to you.

*S*oul Work: Ask your soul what it associates with being humble. You're seeking ten positive and ten negative associations with humility. If you associate humility with certain people, write their names in your journal, and elaborate on whether you see them as humble or humiliated. Did they see themselves as humble or humiliated? Did you admire or avoid and pity them? Is poverty necessarily a part of being humble? Do you associate being humble with taking orders from others rather than having personal authority? When you're finished, take your leave, knowing that you can return to this peaceful room should you need to reconnect with models of humility.

Gently slide open the doors and close them behind you as you return to the hallway, preparing yourself to enter the next room and the next question.

THE FIFTH ROOM:
What Would Humiliate Me Today?

The fifth room's door might stick a little and you may need to push to get inside, just as you may need to push yourself to ask and answer the next questions. This door is made of a heavy metal, but you need to get through it to meet your soul. This exercise, again, requires you to be very honest with yourself. Imagine your soul sitting opposite, if this is useful, and begin your dialogue. Make sure to note your insights in your journal.

*S*oul Work, Part 1: *On private matters and public situations that could be potentially humiliating:* Do you have a secret that you would not ever want others to know—not your spouse or part-ner, not your parents, not your children or siblings? Don't think just of your actions—do you have thoughts that would be humil-iating to admit? Attitudes you hold but don't want others to sus-pect? Are you harboring an opinion about someone else that would be embarrassing to you if he or she knew? Have you done something at work or home to which you don't want to admit, which could embarrass you? Would being asked to do certain tasks at work humiliate you? Would not being part of a certain so-cial group become a source of humiliation for you? Would not being able to wear designer clothing or fly first class or have cer-tain job privileges humiliate you? Would having to take orders from certain people be humiliating for you? Why? With these many examples in mind, continue to examine your life and vul-nerabilities around this question.

Soul Work, Part 2: On matters of God and humiliation: Do you fear that God will humiliate you if you surrendered your life in trust to him? Have you ever felt "spiritually humiliated"? Reflect on the prayers that you have made in the course of your life in which you asked for guidance. When did you make these requests—in crises or grief? Note them in your journal. Now, think deeply about this: Did you place conditions on your prayers? Did you say you would change or do something in return for an answer to your prayer? Did you hesitate when you phrased your request? Did you immediately think about what you would not want to be guided to do? Or what you could *not* do if asked? Ask your soul to go into its memory bank and to open yours. Be absolutely truthful. Write at least five an-swers in your journal. When you really can't push yourself to admit any more, close your journal, and thank your soul for its help.

As you lift your eyes from your journal, you'll notice that this room leads directly into the sixth room. It is almost as if this room with its heavy metal door is an anteroom to the next, one of the biggest rooms in the First Mansion. The sixth room is like a vast, cluttered warehouse, piled high with things, events, and memories you would rather forget but that you have to face and clear out.

THE SIXTH ROOM:
Lost Opportunities and Acts of Self-Betrayal

Although we cannot avoid pain in life, much of the pain we experience is self-inflicted. Specifically, when we do not act honorably or we fail to follow the directions of our conscience or our soul, we cause ourselves the pain of self-betrayal. Often we do this out of fear of what others will think—in other words, we fear humiliating ourselves. Self-betrayal can include anything great or small, from missing an opportunity to speak with someone who might have become a lifelong friend, to speaking up for someone who needed help, to sharing a creative idea at a business meeting or making a good business investment. If you continue to fear listening to your soul, you will be one of those people who recognizes soul guidance only after the fact. "I knew that would happen," is a common mantra for people who lack the courage to be present and receive guidance. Many people, in order to live with themselves after betraying their soul, blame others—parents, siblings, false friends, teachers, ex-lovers—for who they are today and what they have become. But once you undertake a journey into your soul, you see that who you are—and the source of much of the pain you are in—lies within you.

Soul Work: Dialogue with your soul about the opportunities you wish you had taken. List at least twenty. Of those twenty, ten should relate to regrets about strangers or situations that have nothing to do with your career. After listing these examples, go back over them and ask your soul for any images or information on what might have occurred had you acted on even one of those opportunities.

Ask your soul how and why you betrayed yourself. In what situations do you continue to betray yourself? Under what circumstances are you likely to betray yourself? Describe the process of self-betrayal. How can you change this? This is a good room to visit whenever you are struggling not to betray yourself again. It will help you build your soul to face and sort through the wreckage that previous betrayals created.

After you have recorded at least five instances of self-betrayal, close your journal and make your way through the clutter into the clean, well-lighted hallway again. Now, you're ready to move closer to your soul in the seventh room. Look around the hallway and find that seventh door.

THE SEVENTH ROOM:
Why Being Humble Is Difficult for You

This door opens a room lined with many closed closets, cupboards, and even armoires. One side of the room contains the reasons why you have a hard time being humble; the other side contains the soul characteristics of humility. In spite of teachings that humbleness protects and fortifies the soul, in spite of the examples of truly powerful humble people, you may still find that humbleness is difficult for you. Detaching from the controlling influence of others so that you adhere to the trust and humbleness you need in order to listen to divine instructions is difficult, but it is your task in this room. You might be surprised at how challenging it is for you to see yourself as both humbled and empowered. In this room, you will call forth resources you did not know you had.

Soul Work: Refer back to your list in the second room of humble people you admire and your negative and positive associations with humility. Now, ask your soul to reveal ten reasons why being humble is difficult. You might say that you cannot produce ten reasons, but you can. Try harder. Go deeper. Ask your soul to open the closet doors in this room where you can find aspects of yourself that you have not yet met. Do not list just the familiar reasons for being prideful, or for why you need to be right or in control.

You will need to return to this room as you work with the challenge of humility. You must take this challenge with you into your daily life. Observe yourself in action, noting whenever you respond negatively in a situation or relationship because you perceive that you are being humiliated or being asked or told to do something that is "beneath" you. What makes something beneath you? Where is the line between what is beneath you and what isn't? How did you determine that? Imagine this scenario: You are all dressed up for an evening out with friends, and as the group of you walk past a homeless person all of you try to ignore him, but you hear guidance instructing you: "Help that homeless person get something to eat. He's starving." What would you do in that situation? Would you just keep on going because your friends might say something to you? Or would you have the backbone to stop and follow that guidance immediately?

Ask your soul which qualities you have to refine in order to feel truly empowered and humble. For example, do you need personal integrity, or to detach from the need for approval to feel good about yourself? Teresa describes being nourished by God as an internal spring that never ceases to flow. True self-respect and personal integrity are like a spring that nourishes the power of humility.

Identify five qualities within your soul that you need to refine in order to serve the goal of humbleness. You need work on only one at a time, but identify five. Return to this room and note your progress, your struggles, your successes.

Now shut the doors and make your way back to the main hallway. You'll see a bright, shining door that you'll want to go through. If this is as much work as you wish to do for today, leave the Castle with a prayer of thanks and closure.

THE EIGHTH ROOM:
Acknowledge the Guidance You Are Receiving

You are always praying for guidance even when you are not consciously aware of it. And you are always receiving guidance—even now—though you may not hear or realize it. In this room, you'll take a seat across from your soul once again and open yourself to its voice and presence within you. This room is located with the rooms on humiliation, because divine guidance has several routes into your soul: your intuitive system (survival, "gut" intuitions, and organic or physical symptoms such as lower back pain, anxiety, ulcers, depression, sleep disorders, and various other chronic conditions that tell you something is wrong), dreams, and auditory and visual guidance (both of which are rare). In short, guidance always finds its way to you. The ques-

tion is, Why do you ignore it? No matter how many ways you answer that question, the basic truth is that you fear that it will ultimately lead to ruin and humiliation. Acknowledging guidance
means acknowledging the presence of God, the reality of God,
and it means acknowledging the reality of your interior world.
Acknowledging the divine means that you have to act when you
receive guidance, and action means change. Change means loss
of control, and loss of control can lead to . . . humiliation. Yet,
you cannot avoid the fact that, as long as you are breathing, you
are receiving guidance.

Soul Work: Do not assume that divine guidance flows only
when you are in need of help. Guidance continues to flow
whether or not you have problems. It transcends problems,
heartbreaks, and traumas, flowing through dreams and illuminations. This strikes many people as an entirely new concept
about their relationship to God. Whether guidance comes during times of tranquility or trauma, however, it is up to you to have
the courage to acknowledge it, to learn the systems through
which God reaches you, and to recognize when a physical stress
or symptom is, in fact, caused by repressed or misinterpreted intuitive guidance or simply by indigestion or nervousness about
some aspect of your daily life. You are the only one who can
clearly discern these signals, which you do in this way:

1. Review your prayers and your requests for guidance. Do
not pray casually, as prayers do not fall upon deaf ears. And do
not presume that your prayers are not answered, because they
are. It is up to you to receive and listen. Practice silence and contemplation as a means of continually attuning to the one clear
voice of the divine that is present within your soul.

2. Take time every day to review and interpret your intuitive information. What "hits" are you receiving? What intuitive information do you need to process and interpret?

3. Review your biological feedback. Do you feel stress around your stomach? Your lower back? Is depression or sleeplessness increasing? What life stresses are going on simultaneously and what guidance have you been asking to receive?

4. Presume that you have received the answer to your prayer. If you cannot clearly discern it, it is because *you do not want to.* The next step is for you to acknowledge what guidance you *least* want to hear right now.

Once you acknowledge guidance, you will always be shown pathways through whatever difficulties arise. You are never abandoned in the midst of a prayer.

These exercises open you gradually to the manner in which your intuitive channels work, but, more important, they slowly bring you around to realizing that you knew your intuitive channels worked all the time. With prayer and practice in this room, your capacity to look directly into the light will grow. And with it, you will gradually develop the stamina to act on the guidance you receive, confronting whatever fears surface along the way. You never free yourself completely from the fear of humiliation, and yet there comes a day, a moment, a point at which you *will* feel the power of your inner voice speaking to you with a commanding authority. This is its own mystical experience, because for the first time in your life, you will know beyond a shadow of a doubt that your soul's authority blends with God's instructions. It may occur over something very small or during a major crossroads in your life. But in that instance, a sense of knowingness will give you a direction that you will recognize as nonnegotiable. From that moment on, you know what it is to hear God. That doesn't, by the way, settle the challenge of whether you will follow this voice. It only increases the pressure.

THE NINTH ROOM:
Developing Soul Stamina; Challenging Contradictions

Becoming congruent means identifying your contradictions and then consciously working to bring your mind, heart, body, and soul into harmony. Becoming congruent is essential groundwork for developing a soul with stamina. Through the exercises in the previous rooms you have begun the excavation of your deep and vast interior self, discovering the challenges of conscience; the need to control others instead of being supportive of them; negative power plays; consciously choosing to harm others; maintaining an addiction; and ignoring guidance while continuing to pray for guidance. These exercises may strike you as extreme, but consider this: they are clues leading to the reasons why you have habits and patterns of incongruent behavior, inner reptiles that interfere with your capacity to love and be loved.

Soul Work: Name your contradictions. This room isn't about mastering or defeating them—just naming them. It is also about charting a course of action that brings harmony to your soul. And for God's sake—really, for God's sake—be compassionate with yourself. Let your soul empty itself. That is the task in this room. Empty yourself. Cleanse yourself. You won't finish this task in one visit, of course. Just begin it and then return to this room at another time. But begin it. And note in your journal how difficult it is to live a congruent life, to resolve your internal and external contradictions, to move past your regrets and on to consciously building up your soul. Your task is to make your Castle a spiritual reality, an inner sanctum of grace in which the sacred comes to meet you when you pray. Your task is to open yourself to the mystical expression of the divine, the strength to let your entire life change as a result of deepening your prayer life and self-examination. Your task, simply put, is to let your soul come into its highest potential.

Work with your contradictions in this way: Identify three or four contradictions among your thoughts, attitudes, and behaviors. Select one to work on. Contemplate how you contradict yourself and when, and how you justify your thoughts or actions. Observe yourself in your daily life—when you're tempted to act against your deeper nature do you consciously stop yourself? Recognize the roots of your actions and replace them with positive ones. Give up the license to act in negative ways that hurt and blame provide you. Work on each contradiction, one at a time.

For example, a woman had been in therapy for years because she felt that she had been betrayed by friends and family time and again. Then she saw that she was also a betrayer and had broken her word constantly to friends by breaking confidences. She contemplated the history of that pattern, recalling the many instances in which she had betrayed others, noting how she had justified her actions according to her own hurt feelings. Then, she took this into the field, observing herself in her daily life, noting when she felt tempted to act in the betrayer mode—to pass on gossip, for example—and instead she would hold a confidence. For her, this marked an achievement in becoming congruent. She had always seen herself as a loyal friend, but realized that she acted differently than she believed. This discovery was life-changing.

Does this become easier each time? Not necessarily. And you shouldn't look for tasks to become easier. Easier is not the goal. Stamina is your goal. Endurance is your goal. Health is your goal. Ease has nothing to do with it.

A Landing between Halls

You have come to the end of your first journey through the first hallway—a challenging suite of rooms. Yet, you never complete your struggle to become humble and maintain humility—never. There are rooms in the first hallway to which you will need to return again and again, as small and large challenges enter your life and threaten to knock you off balance. Going through an entire hallway of rooms opens up a place in your soul that will continue to speak to you, always reminding you to have courage, be fearless, and trust your guidance.

There are two more hallways in the First Mansion that will give you a strong foundation in your continuing soul work. Each is a passage into a deeper understanding of your soul, a path to divine guidance, and both give you basic ways to deal with life crises. You can return to them when you feel fragile or are in a situation that you fear will cause you humiliation. You merely open yourself to your Castle, get back in touch with your soul, and find a quiet place for reflection to address the challenge. The mansions are actually infinite in length and form and can contain many more halls and rooms than I have shown you. You can add as many as you want or need. It is your Castle.

In the next hallway you confront the pull of earthly and divine chaos in your life. Should you need to leave the Castle, however, say a closing or an exit prayer like the one on p. 162.

THE PULL OF TWO WORLDS: DIVINE GUIDANCE AND DIVINE CHAOS

You've put yourself through the preceding exercises in order to find your soul, your innermost self, at its most basic level. You've begun to illuminate the deepest kind of self-knowledge, shifting from an intellectual understanding of the nature of the soul to an experience of it. For instance, you know intellectually that you are made in the image and likeness of God, but when you experience the meaning of that teaching, you become illuminated by it. Yet, the experience of knowing—of becoming absorbed into the image and likeness of God—is not something that you can grasp through words. It becomes real only when it is illuminated from within, which you cannot generate—this mystical experience must be given to you by God. Until then, those words remain vague theological theory.

An example of illumination occurred to a man I know who, while working alone in his studio, was enveloped by a sense of tranquility. He stopped what he was doing, leaned back in his chair, and began to pray. He then felt light suffusing his body and soul. He could see the light shining within him. He was illuminated, and in that state of consciousness, he knew—not believed, but absolutely knew—what it meant to be made in the image and likeness of God. This kind of mystical experience and soul revelation is, Teresa writes, abundant in the Castle.

Even though the First Mansion holds the potential for illumination, it also contains darkness, because, at this ground-floor level, the soul is still so attached to earthly powers. The external world creates internal chaos and seduces the intellect, pulling it in two different directions, confronting it with two different value systems, two different devotions, two different loyalties, and an earthly and a divine reality. Seduction of the intellect, to Teresa, is the same as what the Buddha called "illusion."

The medieval mystics cloistered themselves and severed most ties to the outside world, but you will continue to live in the world, even as you maneuver through the rooms of your Castle. For this reason, the First Mansion is where you dialogue with your soul about the tension and chaos created by the pull of two worlds. How does this chaos control your life? How do you use it to your benefit and to others' detriment? For instance, people create chaos as a way to avoid hearing the truth. You may be one of these individuals or you may be in a relationship with such a person. One scenario goes like this: An alcoholic who is in denial is about to take a drink. You tell him that he doesn't drink just to relax but is in fact, an alcoholic. The truth is so painful, so powerfully painful that, if he managed to hear it, he would have to change. To prevent himself from hearing the truth, he uses chaos as a weapon. He screams, he yells, he blames you for even suggesting that he is an alcoholic. The chaos becomes unbearable, almost as unbearable as his drinking, so you back down. You will do anything to make the chaos stop—anything.

Chaos is a powerful weapon. And we all have our weapons for creating chaos. Teresa advises us to recognize chaos as a power we use too often and to recognize that each of us has an actual relationship to chaos. Chaos is, in fact, a force throughout the universe, its own entity, an archetype of destruction and transformation that operates in every life.

The word *chaos* derives from the Greek *khaos* and typically refers to a state of unorganization. In the metaphysical sense, it is the opposite of order, but it is both creative and destructive. In classical-period Greece, however, *khaos* meant "the primal emptiness, space" and derived from an Indo-European root meaning "gape, be wide open." Indeed, chaos requires that you be open to guidance. Some ancient philosophers believed chaos to be the primary source of all things. Mythologists wrote that Chaos gave birth (without a mate) to Gaia (Earth) and to Eros. Then Gaia gave birth to Uranus (heaven or sky). So, from Chaos came all that is, all other energies and archetypes, including Eros—divine love, divine seduction, divine order in all of creation.

To a mystic, chaos is an organic expression of the divine. The ancients believed that omens and visions emerged from chaos. Divine chaos cannot be stopped, manipulated, postponed, or bargained with. It is an impersonal yet very intimate force of seduction. It sweeps into your life, taking charge of your life path and redirecting you according to its own plan—not yours. You can perceive chaotic changes as cruel, unfair, or undeserved, or you can perceive them as benevolent, since chaos can bring death and life, endings and beginnings. For the divine, death is a part of life, not a tragedy. Life and death are one and the same. Yet, even though what happens to our bodies is impersonal, in the cosmic sense, to the divine, what happens to our souls is a matter of divine intimacy.

Everyone has experienced divine chaos, although you might not have called it that at the time. Perhaps you still do not see the hand of the divine in the rubble, particularly if you hold tightly to the view that events that happened to you were unfair or un- deserved. In order to glimpse the hand of God at work in your chaos, you must think beyond your personal view. What is right and wrong, fair and unjust, does not revolve around you. You have to be willing to consider that, regardless of the trauma, there is a divine purpose that moves in tandem with every event in your life, painful and joyful. (In fact, when you asked, "For what reason was I born?" *you invoked divine chaos—change.*) And then you have to work through the pull of two worlds. For exam- ple, one man realized, after an illuminating experience, that we are all equal and it is wrong to be judgmental of others, but he was not able to stop himself. I asked him if this contradiction was a source of stress and he replied, "When I think about what I claim to believe and how I really am, I feel like a spiritual fraud. I tell myself that I am doing the best that I can, but I know I'm not. And I know that the result of this little conversation I'm having right now is only going to add to my stress, because I have to con- front this contradiction even more directly."

Ultimately, we create our own chaos when we do not resolve these sorts of spiritual contradictions. We want to live in two worlds simultaneously—the external world and that of the soul. We want the divine to provide us with guidance to keep us safe in the physical world but we are not sure we are ready for a direct experience of the divine.

Many rooms in the First Mansion allow you to examine your relationship to chaos and change and the many ways you express personal power and powerlessness (fear of humiliation) in the physical world.

If you feel you need to center yourself before starting this new exploration, say the prayer of entry again. See yourself back in the beautiful, infinite hallway of the First Mansion. Perhaps you see a new hallway branching off, a safe, solid, well-lighted corridor, or you see a suite of rooms encircled by a hall. If it helps you, continue to visualize yourself entering and exiting each room. Do whatever helps you prepare to reflect on the questions and communicate with your soul, but always open and close each room with a prayer. Keep a journal of all the work you are doing.

Exploring Chaos in Your Soul

THE FIRST ROOM:
Describe Your Relationship to Chaos

Chaos can include subtle changes in a relationship as well as major life changes, such as a new job, job loss, retirement, or catastrophes like accidents or natural disasters. Positive changes can cause as much chaos as negative ones. You may get the new job you want but need to relocate to a new community. The birth of a child brings love as well as chaos to a home. Newly inherited wealth can turn a family against one another even as it puts an end to fears about having enough money to survive.

Change is constant, a fact of life. And your intuition alerts you when change is in the air. Often we get signals, warnings, dreams, hunches, or feelings that alert us to an inevitable period of change. Fighting change is the same as fighting your guidance. Instead, learn to listen, prepare, and act.

Soul Work: Ask your soul when it has warned you that change was coming. Follow that memory as closely as you can from start to finish, reliving the sensations of the changes in the atmosphere of your energy, body, psyche, and environment. Commit these signals to memory, for they represent communications from your soul. Now, go deeper into your thoughts and memories and recall what changes came about and why. What needed to leave your life and what needed to come in? Why? What growth did you need to experience at the time? Think even more deeply: Was chaos the only means for you to learn or expand your consciousness? Did you have other options but turned them down because you did not want to listen?

For example, one man was warned by friends, family, and his physician to monitor his diet because he had serious diabetes. No amount of affection could compete with his passion for food and his denial of the seriousness of his disease. Then one night he had a dream in which he was asked to dance by a lovely woman. The quintessential flirt, he was flattered even in his dream. When he stood up to accept this beauty's invitation, however, he fell on his face. Only then did he notice that both his legs had been amputated due to his diabetes. He woke from this dream in a state of complete terror. Was he about to lose his legs? Was this a done deal or just a warning? Feeling like Ebenezer Scrooge viewing his own gravestone with the ghost of Christmas Future, this man decided not to dismiss this dream as just one really bad nightmare. He believed his soul had reached out to him in an effort to avert what could have been a painful outcome. And while he considers his now very strict diabetic diet "chaotic for the hedonist" that he is, it is a chaos he can live with.

These exercises are essential to help you recognize when you are being alerted to change and when you blocked it or acted on it. Review the choices you made and the reasons you acted as you did in as many circumstances as you can. Do not blame anyone else for any of your actions in any exercise. No one but you is responsible for who you are and what you do.

Every time you ignore that "organic hunch" because you want to avoid change—which is futile—you need to return to this room, retrace your footsteps, and ask yourself:

1. What did I sense and when?
2. Why did I block my guidance?
3. At what point did I begin to block my guidance?
4. What changes did I sense were coming and why were they important?
5. If I had acknowledged the guidance at that time, could I have handled the process and people involved in a more positive way?
6. What did I learn about myself? How am I different now?
7. How has this helped my prayer life and my relationship with my soul?

THE SECOND ROOM:
Where Is Your Life in Chaos? What Is the Message?

The preceding room was about your past. This room is concerned with chaos in your life now. Some chaos is more emotional and psychological than physical, some creative and dynamic, but it is always brewing somewhere. Some part of your life will always be in chaos. For that reason, this room will become familiar to you.

Soul Work: Chaos is always a messenger. Sometimes its message is hugely significant; at other times it is a lesser but still valuable insight. Ask your soul how it communicates with you through chaos. Does it give you physical symptoms—a headache, for example, when you feel that a discussion has become unreasonable and things are about to get out of control? Or a stomachache, when you are waiting for information that can change your life? Potentially life-changing information is generally felt in the solar plexus. Do you get insomnia when you feel uncertain about what to do next? Your body has intuitive radar. Listen; prepare; act.

Settle quietly into a chair opposite your soul. What information are you receiving from your physical, emotional, and intuitive systems? What dreams and symbols are you receiving and what do they mean? What changes are going on in your external life and how do those changes reflect changes in your internal life? What significant spiritual questions are you working on that could be affecting your everyday life? Do you need to act on any of this information?

THE THIRD ROOM:
Which Areas of Your Life Do You Want to Keep in Chaos?

You may not want to admit that you deliberately maintain chaos in certain parts of your life, but you do. You do this, for example, in order to prevent having to make a final decision about something (nothing postpones decision making better than keeping a situation or a relationship in a mess). You keep your inner self in chaos, too, constantly rehashing the same problems without ever coming to a conclusion, constantly talking about a decision you need to make but never getting to the point of making that decision, and constantly complaining about the same person or situation without taking any action. You have a huge repertoire of songs for nurturing chaos in your life.

One woman, for example, always got involved in the chaos of her siblings' and parents' lives to postpone starting her own family with her husband. Because she was the only one in her family who spoke English, they did need her help, but she promised her husband that as soon as they got their lives together, she would become pregnant. The truth was she didn't want to have a child and used chaos as an excuse for not starting a family. A man I know kept his garage/workroom a complete mess, filled with parts, tires, dirty rags, and tools, all smelling of oil and gasoline. His wife would come out there on occasion and ask, "Sam, when are you going to clean this up? How can you stand it out here?" Then she would leave him alone, which is just what he wanted. He used the chaos of his garage to keep his wife away so that he did not have to go near the chaos in his heart.

Soul Work: Ask your soul for help in understanding which areas of your life you deliberately keep in chaos. Why? What are you afraid of? What are God and your soul communicating to you through this chaos even though you try not to hear them? In your journal describe three steps you will now take to resolve this chaotic situation. Do not leave this room without saying a prayer asking for courage, even if you don't see what you must do or how you can do it.

THE FOURTH ROOM:
Your Methods of Creating Chaos

One woman was a screamer—hysterical behavior was her way of creating chaos, controlling her family, and getting everyone to do what she wanted. Just the thought of her screaming was enough for her husband and kids to cave in to her demands. The thought of becoming rational was incomprehensible to this woman. She absolutely could not conceive of herself not screaming. She actually went "blank" right in front of me when I asked her to name an alternative behavior. She felt completely powerless—voiceless—without screaming, and she was not about to give it up.

You cling to your methods with the same tenacity. Some of the most common ploys are anger, pouting, hysteria, manipulation, gossip, lying, adultery, addiction, indecisiveness, chronic tardiness, always interrupting conversations, and never listening to others.

Paradoxically, you create chaos to attempt to maintain control and power over your world. Yet, creating chaos in your external life will always cause it within your soul. Ultimately, every act of divine chaos is an attempt to affirm that there is actually a plan for us on Earth. It is a method of getting us or keeping us on the right course. We want divine intervention to pull us out of our anger or indecision, but, without a divine guarantee to keep us safe, we keep trying to exert our own will.

Soul Work: Ask your soul how you create chaos. Whom do you control through chaos? What sets off your disruptive behaviors? Describe in detail why, amid chaos, you opt not to act from higher consciousness. In your journal, chart how you will stop trying to control your external world, one step at a time. Pay attention to when, how, and why you act out in chaotic patterns and when you catch yourself, say "I am resisting guidance. I will now listen deeply to the messages from my soul." Make that a habit. Close with a prayer asking for courage as you go out into the world.

THE FIFTH ROOM:
Where Do You Fear Divine Chaos in Your Life?

Where do you fear the force and presence of God the most? One person said, "I can take anything from God so long as 'he' doesn't touch my family." We are always bargaining with the divine, always imagining that we have more power and authority over our lives than we do. We are so deluded. We are in control of nothing whatsoever; not the weather, not the government, not the stock market, not traffic, barely our health and relationships, not the millions of decisions being made by people all over the world every second—all of which influence our lives in both unseen and all-too-apparent ways. We wake in chaos and we go to sleep in chaos. How can we possibly think that we can control or maneuver around the cosmic force of the divine?

Denial is a very potent force. Even when we *know* we are consciously denying something we need to look at, we continue to function in denial. Even when we receive guidance that we asked for, we sometimes regret it. But rejected guidance does not disappear: It gets repressed in unconscious fears, anxieties, and tensions. You are forming an internal partnership with the divine. The fear that God makes you pay a price for his intimacy, however, is centuries old, ingrained in your psyche. In this room, you have to unearth your fears of coming close to God.

Soul Work: Ask your soul what parts of your life you consider off-limits to God. Where do you fear that God will create chaos in your life? What is the worst that can happen to you? And if it does, then what? Why do you assume that the only type of chaos that God would bring into your life would be negative? You might say that you do not make only negative assumptions, but you do. You rarely think about positive chaos. Take that truth into your soul and dialogue in prayer about your fears of divine intimacy. Ask your soul, "What would it take for me not to fear God?"

THE SIXTH ROOM:
Fears You Nurture

Some fears you are born with; others you learn from family members or develop from personal experience. With faith, prayer, and conscious awareness (as well as counseling, if necessary), you should be able to dissolve many of your fears. An irrational fear of the dark, of course, will be easier to overcome than, say, a fear of rejection rooted in childhood trauma. If you don't work to overcome them, fears and anxiety can become part of you, ultimately controlling you and, in many cases, destroying the quality of your life. We often present our fears as if we were subject to them or possessed by them, as if they are in charge and we have no capacity whatsoever to stand up to them and their bullying on the playground of our psyche. But the truth is, some fears are habits that we nurture because we have become accustomed to them and we simply don't want to make the effort to overcome them. As one woman said, "I'm afraid to release that fear of being alone because then I might really be alone. My fear of being alone keeps me from being alone—I know it."

Fears cause chaos. Even if you cannot accept that you nurture fears, you *definitely* use at least some of them when you feel you need to. One evening after a workshop, for instance, a group of us were going out to dinner to a restaurant on the lower level of an old building. At the last moment, a woman tagged along uninvited. When we arrived at the restaurant, she announced, "I can't eat in this restaurant. I have a fear of basements." The woman who had made the dinner arrangements loved this restaurant and immediately recognized the other's behavior as a manipulative ploy for attention. So our hostess looked her square in the eye and graciously said, "And I have a fear of not eating here. So either we eat here or you have to find a take-out place and meet up with us later." Our tag along guest tucked her fear of basements right back into her bag of tricks and descended the stairs with the rest of us.

Soul Work: Ask your soul to help you identify the fears that you nurture (but could release) but which you do not want to lose because of the consequences. These fears represent power tools for you in the social arena. Setting them aside would change every relationship, including your relationship to God and your soul. Note in your journal the answer to the questions: Why do you nurture these fears? How do you use them to manipulate other people and circumstances? Are you afraid to appear to be strong and healthy? Are you afraid that people would not respond to you the same way if you were strong? As on ongoing practice, choose a fear and observe its influence in your everyday life. Your goal is to become aware—catch yourself in the act, so to speak—of using your fears for power and control. Following that, your next step is to consciously break that pattern, little by little, until you are free.

A Landing between Rooms

So far, you've been working in relative comfort through your fears in the safe, well-appointed rooms of your First Mansion. But now it's time to find the entrance to your Castle's dungeon. Everyone has a dungeon. It's where you hold your prisoners. You need to acknowledge their presence. In the words of Pope John Paul II, "The worst prison in the world would be a closed heart."

This journey into self-knowledge is necessary because the unknown self is unstable; it wanders aimlessly, subject to the whims of other people and to the controlling force of what Teresa called "the devil." We can name this dark force anything we want—the influence of others, the shadow—but in the end, without a true sense of your convictions, your honor and integrity, and an uncompromising foundation in your theology, you will find this world frightening, unsafe; you will never trust yourself to protect and take care of yourself; you will never trust yourself to keep your word when intimidated; you will tend to negotiate your honor and betray yourself in exchange for earthly security. You will keep yourself and others imprisoned in your dungeon.

We often build ferocious resentments as a result of our weaknesses because we counted on other people to protect us and be strong and courageous for us. Or we end up feeling victimized because we thought our goodness owed us protection in this world, believing that bad things should not happen to good people. The end result of all "unfair" pain and suffering is burning hurt and resentments fueled by righteousness. You have carried these resentments for years. To heal from them, you must forgive the individuals involved. Until you are *willing and able* to release and forgive fully, you weigh down your soul with these prisoners.

You are about to enter into what Jung called the "shadow"—the dark, unknown parts of yourself that function out of fear and self-serving intentions. Return to the courtyard of your Castle. Visualize walking across the courtyard toward a dark corner where there is a heavy, lead door. Say a prayer as you open yourself to the experience of entering your shadow.

THE SEVENTH ROOM:
The Dungeon

Haul open the heavy, lead door and walk down the damp, stone stairs. The atmosphere gets darker and colder as you descend. You are now in the dungeon of your soul. As you walk through, notice that there are cells for prisoners lining the walls. Everyone you cannot forgive or whom you resent or wish harm to is held by you in these cells. The parents you cannot forgive are in a cell; the business partner who cheated you and whom you still resent is in a cell; the ex-spouse is in a cell. Sometimes the people you keep in the dungeon are tortured by the power and negativity of your memories, because thoughts, just like prayers, travel. No doubt some of the people you hold prisoner are holding you prisoner as well.

Why do you keep prisoners? Pursue this question with your soul and, as always, record your response in your journal. Usually the answer is that you keep someone or something prisoner because you feel he has not yet been punished enough for the harm he did to you. You must have your pound of flesh; you still believe, or so you tell yourself here in the First Mansion, that you have a right to exact revenge.

Your soul, of course, is not, by nature, a warden. Your soul would say to you, "Do not imprison trauma and rage inside me. Do not lock up images of vengeance within me and believe you are being righteous. Do not try to justify yourself with self-pity and protestations of your innocence. Events happen as they do for reasons greater than your reason can comprehend. Your challenge is to develop the strength to accept things as they happen. Learn from them, and move on. You are not the Great Executioner." Imagine yourself in the prisons of others' Castles. This alone is a reason to release all prisoners from your dungeon.

Soul Work: With your soul, dialogue with each prisoner, one at a time. Recall why and for how long you have been holding each person in your dungeon. You are seeking to discover your need for vengeance and personal justice and your obstacles to forgiveness. Do not disguise your vengeful motives in phrases such as, "I simply need to bring this matter to closure." *Closure* is often just a soft word for "I simply need to fire the last bullet. I need to hurt that person—and that will close the book on this incident just fine." Review the quality of energy, emotions, and thoughts that you have generated within your soul as a result of holding this person in your dungeon. What do you need from each one to allow you to release him? Be honest—do you need to humiliate or hurt him? Do you need to punish him because he hurt you? What will it take for you to release these people? If you are waiting for them to admit that they harmed you, chances are that will never happen.

There comes a point at which you have to let go and forgive. You can start your prayer with, "Help me to forgive because I don't want to forgive. I feel entitled to be angry even though the anger is killing me, not them. And no one really cares that I'm angry. It's destroying my life, not theirs. I want to punish someone, so I punish my kids or I punish other innocent people who have never harmed me because it is my way of punishing them. So I really don't want to forgive because then I think all my hurt will be forgotten and that feels so unfair. But what is fair? No one's hurt is fair. I just think that justice should revolve around me. So, help me to forgive, one person at a time, beginning with———." That's your beginning. You take it from there until you have emptied your dungeon. Whenever you add new prisoners, you will have to revisit your dungeon.

THE EIGHTH ROOM:
Gratitude for Divine Chaos

Accepting the changes that divine chaos has brought into your life includes being grateful for difficulties and loss, as well as for plans that don't work out as anticipated. For example, a man got a new job and decided to treat himself to a vacation before starting. Feeling jubilant and full of life, he resigned the next day and left shortly thereafter, missing the phone call that his new position had fallen through. On returning home, having effectively emptied his bank account on his vacation, he learned that he was unemployed. At first he sat in his kitchen and stared out the window, thinking what a fool he had been. And then he thought, Well, if I am such a fool, what is the most foolish thing I could do right now to get out of this situation? In that moment, he took a deep breath and thought back on his dreams, when he wasn't so fearful of what other people thought. Now that he had lost just the right job and confronted humiliation, the worst was over. He was free to do what he wanted, so he decided to follow his passion and become a chef. He sold his belongings and turned divine chaos into a new life.

In the acceptance comes the gift—always look for the gift. Always pray for the grace to see the gift, even in your darkest moments.

Soul Work: Ask your soul for insights into why you battle with accepting the choices God has made for you. Bring your arguments with God into your consciousness. Let go of the route you had in mind for yourself and felt so sure was right for you. Identify the choices you have made out of insecurities and fear; notice when you have closed yourself off from your soul's and other people's wisdom. Sometimes the only way to get through to you has been for the winds of divine chaos to sweep through your life.

When divine chaos comes through personal crisis—the death of a loved one, the diagnosis of a serious or terminal illness, the breakup of a family through divorce—you must still find a way to gratitude through prayer and endurance, if not for the event then for the support system that is sent to you or for the insights that arise when you need them.

DIVINE SEDUCTION

In spite of your fear of divine intimacy—and in spite of the many ways you use chaos to create guidance "blackouts"—you have a biological and spiritual need to experience the awe of the sacred. That is why we put sacred objects on our desks and night-stands, perform rituals, and travel to ancient temples, ashrams, and churches where saints are buried. We want to touch the sa-cred and feel its energy, to connect to it personally and to con-nect to it through our purpose. The divine calls to us through these places, actions, and objects, constantly seducing us. Even as our rational, security-oriented selves create ways to distance ourselves from God, divine seduction still occurs through our hearts, our need for comfort, love, and healing.

But beyond that, we also need to experience transcendent truth and consciousness, to know what fearlessness feels like—to know that it is possible to break free from the iron shackles of fear that hold us to dense, heavy, earthly illusions. This *is* what it means to discover the mystical experience of God. This is your mystical self. The mystical state of consciousness is not a dream or fantasy; it is a reality. As you go mansion by mansion, room by room in your Castle, you are making this reality more manifest, more a part of you. Even so, it is a mistake to expect that God will give you a mystical experience. Few if any occur in the First Man-sion, as here you have not yet committed to the journey with your whole heart. God does not tempt you or reward you with mystical experiences, but gives them without warning, just like that, but rarely to the pilgrim in the First Mansion. Teresa con-tinually reminded her nuns of this, always adding that in spite of the absence of the mystical experience, God was everywhere and in every detail of the First Mansion.

In the Castle, you become increasingly conscious of the grace in which your soul lives, and you give form to your soul, its challenges and joys. Even though your soul reflects the image and likeness of God, the God we know in the First Mansion is half real and half a product of your imagination and faith, which is sometimes firm and sometimes uncertain.

Here in your First Mansion, you start to identify divine love. Here you identify "organic divinity"—that is, the many ways God is present in your life and always has been, and not just when you are looking in that direction for help. The divine within the details of your life is present in every second, every motion, every thought. To recognize this is a profound mystical experience. Such intimacy with the divine in the "earth of your life" is what the mystics identify as love. The spiritual paradox is that we can exist in a universe so vast and impersonal yet be so intimately known to this divine being that every detail of our lives somehow matter.

So, as a part of your mystical awakening, you must come to treasure every detail of your life as significant, vital, and sacred, from the most obvious and beautiful, to the most seemingly inconsequential, to the most painful. Seeing God in the details is not just a working order for your First Mansion, it is a lifetime devotion. It takes great courage to look for God. It takes even more courage to find God.

In this next suite of rooms, you encounter the light and beauty of the First Mansion and the divine within yourself. In previous hallways, you found contradictions and sources of chaos, but in these rooms, you find God and the exquisite beauty of your own being. Do not rush through these rooms. Go deeply, as slowly as you can. Try to stay in your heart and soul rather than your mind, but if your mind takes over, use prayer to return to the First Mansion.

Rooms for Finding God

THE FIRST ROOM:
Silence

To work with silence is to work with the language of God. We often don't know what to do with silence because, in our everyday world, silence means that no one is listening or responding. We can mistakenly think silence means that we are alone rather than that we are finally "alone to be together with God." Silence is the discipline of the mystic, the way you come to know your nature and the content of your soul. Falling in love with silence is essential for serious prayer and contemplation.

Soul Work: First, be within the energy of your soul in complete silence and contemplate this: Be still and know that I am God. How long can you wait for God? How impatient are you? How difficult is it for you to maintain a silent mind, a mind that does not drift? And how difficult is it for you to go beyond your mind, into an interior of no thought? Why is silence difficult? These questions require hours of contemplation. Note your insights in your journal.

Here, in undisturbed silence, you need also to dwell on these two questions that draw you beyond your cluttered mind and into the quietude of the soul, as Teresa calls it: "What is God to me?" and "What am I to God?"

THE SECOND ROOM:
God Is Here / God Loves You

The divine is always present—always. Few thoughts are as comforting but even fewer are more difficult to comprehend. What does God's love *feel* like? How can you *experience* divine love so thoroughly that you can say without hesitation, "The one thing that I am sure of in this life is that I am loved by God"? Mystics have often expressed their experience of divine love through poetry, as the senses and the intellect cannot comprehend the sensual presence of God as love. The thirteenth-century mystic Mechthilde of Magdeburg was a Beguine, an unusual, radical type of Catholic mystic. She wrote some of the most extraordinary poetry that captured the union of the human and the divine heart. Her poetry may inspire you to come close to this love within your own soul.

HOW THE SOUL SPEAKS TO GOD

Lord, you are my lover,
My desire,
My flowing fount,
My sun,
And I am your reflection.

HOW GOD RESPONDS TO THE SOUL

That I love you passionately comes from my nature,
For I am love itself.
That I love you often comes from my desire,
For I desire to be loved passionately.
That I love you long comes from my being eternal,
For I am without an end and without a beginning.

$\mathcal{S}$*oul Work:* Pray to be open to the experience of divine love. Ask that you be made aware of the grace that comes from God, that you be allowed to feel it, to sense it, to know that this force is active within your body, mind, and emotions. Divine love is a mystery that you pray to have revealed to you.

Take special notice if this dialogue is a struggle. If so, ask to be shown the reptiles that prevent you from embracing the love of God. Are you working at the mental level to come up with places instead of allowing yourself to receive impressions from your soul—feelings, intuitive hits, images, and even absurd associations that may at first mean nothing, but let their significance come through. Become poetry itself.

THE THIRD ROOM:
God, Where Were You When . . . ? Why Did Bad Things Happen to Me?

Difficult experiences can make you feel that God has abandoned you. Prayers seem to go unanswered; sacred rituals seem to lose their ability to comfort you. The heavens seem to have no compassion. What are your memories? One woman wondered, Where was God for me when my parents were getting divorced and I was all alone? She still is angry with God, a typical reaction to the feeling of abandonment, to the death or prolonged suffering of a loved one, or to an ordeal perceived as undeserved.

The word *deserve* causes immeasurable pain. Beliefs about what we deserve are rooted in a social-superstitious creed that suggests bad things should only happen to bad people. Most people believe that if they are good, God will reward them with protection from all undeserved suffering. This is human logic, but not divine logic. Pain and pleasure, suffering and abundance, are two sides of the coin of life experience. The divine asks you to learn through your life experiences. Yet we struggle with the concept of deserving because we continually strive to see the logic behind events that occur to us. We cling to the belief that goodness is a shield of protection against having to experience the injustice or unfairness. But all sides of life are expressions of the divine; the unjust side tests our capacity to trust in a wisdom greater than our own. Without that trust, we often end up holding on to the memories of feeling betrayed by God, believing that somehow the wrong things happened to us. Such illusions give rise to bitterness and an inability to forgive.

*S*oul Work: Ask your soul for guidance in understanding the gifts within any tragedies or crises in your life. You are to pray for grace, wait, and receive. Do not let your mind feel pressured to answer; keep soul dialogue gentle, flowing like dream imagery. Do not expect or seek rational explanations. Note any symbolic impressions or single words that come to you: Often, these are messengers.

You are seeking the roots of your struggle with God that goes deep into your bones. For all of the many sufferings you have in your life, resentments over coping with undeserved pain are among the most difficult to heal. And transforming the creed of "deserve" into one of trusting in the wisdom of God, coping through prayer, self-reflection, and faith, requires devotion, for you are breaking through a pattern of thought that holds your world together, including your idea of a just and fair God. To release the image of a God who works within the code of human justice is to break free of a limiting mindset, which allows you to embrace a cosmic figure of the divine who is not contained within the parameters of human law and order. This marks a major transformation of fear to faith and is no simple task.

The following poem, "Fringe," by the great thirteenth-century Muslim mystic Rumi, is a perfect inspiration for your reflection in this room.

FRINGE

You wreck my shop and my house and now my heart, but
How can I run from what

Gives me life? I'm weary of personal worrying, in love
With the art of madness!

Tear open my shame and show the mystery. How much longer
    do I have to fret with

Self-restraint and fear? Friends, this is how it is:
We are fringe sewn inside

The lining of a robe. Soon we'll be loosened, the binding
  threads torn out. The beloved

Is a lion. We're the lame deer in his paws. Consider what
  choices we have! Acquiesce

When the Friend says, *Come into me. Let me show my face.*
You saw it once in preexistence,

Now you want to be quickened and quickened again. We have been
  secretly fed

from beyond space and time. That's why we look for something
  more than this.

(*The Soul of Rumi*, translated by Coleman Barks,

HarperSanFrancisco, 2001)

THE FOURTH ROOM:
God, Give Me the Grace to Endure

Endurance is an essential quality of a soul with stamina. Without
endurance, you cannot wait for God, or for anything else. Without the capacity to endure, you are impatient, demanding,
short-tempered, and you tend to abandon projects that you are
meant to complete because you cannot immediately see their
significance. With endurance, you know that you can survive
anything that is asked of you, whether by a friend or by God. Endurance enables you spiritually to listen better to God, to follow
your inner compass. You know you can manage the consequences of courageous personal decisions. Endurance means
that your soul can confront enormous odds and accomplish
great and powerful tasks, alone if necessary. Only by having
something to endure can you develop trust in God's reasons for
giving you challenges as you must be able to see them through,
realizing only at the end the blessings hidden in the journey.

S*oul Work:* Consider this room a sacred place for nourishing your soul and receiving grace. In your journal, reflect with your soul on what you have been given to endure and how you feel about these challenges. Do not answer quickly and dismissively or deny your true feelings. Is your challenge an illness? A relationship? When is your challenge most difficult to endure? What are you learning from it? Have you thought of it as unfair or undeserved? Do you turn to prayer to help you and do you ask God, "Why me?" If so, on what are you basing your scale of fairness? If you believe that only good things should happen to good people, ask why you *need* to believe that. Work on getting free of this superstition. How has endurance built your character? What are your strengths? Accepting that which you have been given to endure takes prayer. You must practice letting go of the belief that your life should have been different. It won't be easy. Ask your soul for the grace of acceptance.

The following excerpt from the lovely poem "You Ask," by the Hindu mystic Rabindranath Tagore, captures the essence of mystical endurance in its give and take between a person and God.

"What comes from your willing hands I take. I beg for nothing
      more."
"Yes, yes, I know you, modest mendicant, you ask for all that one
      has."

"If there be a stray flower for me I will wear it in my heart."
"But if there be thorns?"

"I will endure them."

"Yes, yes, I know you, modest mendicant, you ask for all that one
has."

(*Tagore: The Mystic Poets,* SkyLight Paths Publishing,
Woodstock, 2004) by Rabindranath Tagore

THE FIFTH ROOM:
Who Is a Gift in My Life?

Do you consider just the people you love to be gifts? Everyone is
in your life for a purpose. Appreciating the people who appreciate you is effortless. You have to learn to appreciate the reptiles
in your soul as well. It is very, very difficult to find a divine purpose for people in your life who have harmed you, but consider
that you yourself have harmed people who were busy trying to
figure out why you came into their lives. Underneath it all, there
is a purpose. You can choose to be defeated by adversity or cru-
elty or choose to keep going and never to be cruel. These are
gifts, great gifts, in fact. But of all the many gifts in life that bring
joy and grace to the soul, among the greatest is the choice to see
the people in our lives as gifts from God.

Soul Work: Ask your soul to show you the essence of each person whom you keep in your life. How you think of these people,
how you feel about them, and how you remember them are re-
flected in the health of your soul. Dialogue with your soul until
you see how each person is a gift. This is an intense practice because so many relationships are contaminated with power struggles—but identifying that struggle is precisely the purpose of the
work in this room. Few relationships are easy, and you can suffer
immense pain when you are unable to acknowledge the good in
another. It is all the more difficult to see someone else's good-

ness when he cannot see the goodness in you—but this work is your journey, no one else's.

THE SIXTH ROOM:
Expressing Divine Love

If you truly believe that God loves you, you act accordingly. Divine love is compassionate and accepting, silent and healing, nonjudgmental. How does divine love influence your everyday life, including your thoughts, actions, emotions, and how you treat others? How often and in what circumstances do you *consciously* act without love? Divine love is the most difficult love to put into practice on Earth, and yet, if you believe in the power of divine love what other choice do you really have? Anything else you do will create chaos and contaminate the rooms of your Castle—which you've just begun to clean out!

Soul Work: We are not Jesus or Buddha; we all prefer to love within our comfort zone, but that is not what is asked of those who seek to know the deeper nature of the soul. The soul is essentially a vessel of love. As a channel for love, you cannot hold expectations that you will be loved in return or appreciated for your efforts. You cannot judge yourself for not being able to act out of love. Rather, your task is just to love, again and again.

In this room, dialogue with your soul—recording your dialogues in your journal—about the challenge of divine love. Examine in each instance why a loving response was difficult or why you may have expected gratitude from another for acting out of love and not receiving the same response. Divine love is a quality of grace to be given freely from your soul, released like a dove from a cage.

THE SEVENTH ROOM:
Surrendering to God, Finding Awe

Surrendering your all to God is the final act of trust. You surrender not your earthly belongings but rather your trust and allegiance to your earthly senses and logical mind as your system for understanding the nature of God. Consider that in the Garden of Gethsemane, Jesus surrendered his life to God after first pleading with the divine to *not* have to endure the brutal suffering of a death by crucifixion. He wanted to know *why* he had to go through that misery, but when a logical reason was not forthcoming, he finally said, "Thy will be done." He transcended the need for earthly reasons and trusted the divine, surrendering his life to a plan that he feared.

Buddha, Muhammad, and other great enlightened beings all faced the same test—surrender is the initiation into the mystical life. In your work in this room in the First Mansion, you begin your encounters with acts of personal surrender.

Soul Work: In this room, pray and be present with the divine. With your soul, contemplate what it means to surrender your fears to God and put your life in divine hands. Why would you fear that? Write extensively about your fears about surrender in your journal. Let go of the superstition that, because you do not surrender, you can prevent the divine from creating chaos in your life. Feel the awe that illuminates you where fear once lived.

THE EIGHTH ROOM:
A Time For Prayer

In order to grow your soul, look at how you pray. In the content of your prayers is your personal agenda with God. Within the

First Mansion, your agenda has tended to focus on your needs, fears, health, and family, with occasional prayers of gratitude. Begin to dedicate daily prayer to those who have harmed you, to those who do not pray for themselves, and to the well-being of the human community. Begin that practice now; it becomes a devotion unto itself within the Fourth Mansion.

Soul Work: Note in your journal your struggles with prayer. Do you find it difficult to be present with God unless you have an agenda? Note what it is like for you to make praying for others a part of your daily life. Find time to pray every day. Find time for silence every day. Carry silence within you. Be still and know that you are divine.

A *Moment of Contemplation*

Your soul is your most powerful and certainly most intimate companion. Why would you not want to trust your companion? Nothing is as comforting as knowing that you can enter your Castle at will. Your Castle is real, a place of divine presence, activity, guidance, contemplation, prayer, and grace. The work you do in the First Mansion is arduous. You are, as Teresa noted, still half in the world of reptiles while also in the Castle with God. Consider, however, that you have always lived in these two worlds. The only difference now is that you have chosen to become aware of this truth. You must now strengthen your soul in order to live at a higher level of consciousness. But you have begun a relationship with your soul that is genuine and deepening. It takes great courage to accept humility as a soul practice, it requires constant attention to manage your relationship to chaos, and it takes pure devotion to continue toward God when, as Teresa so aptly noted, the rewards in the First Mansion are few and far between. But how blessed you are to have discovered that your Castle is hidden within your soul.

LEAVING THE CASTLE

You must not simply open your eyes and exit your Castle. You are deep within a field of grace, even if your five senses are fully active. You have a spiritual energy field around you that has been heightened by prayer, by contemplation, by the quality of thought in which you have been engaged. Now you need to withdraw gradually from your Castle. Think of your soul as if it has been deep under water with you and you are both now adjusting the oxygen content in your bloodstream as you ascend back to the surface, the external world.

Exit Prayer

I am a channel of grace. As I leave my Castle, grace surrounds me and grace protects me. I enter my life under the blessing of God and I remain open to receive guidance from my soul.

THE SECOND MANSION

God in the Details: Inner Vision and Soul Companions

You are holy, Lord,
The only God,
And Your deeds are wonderful.
You are strong.
You are love.
You are wisdom.
You are humility.
You are endurance.

—Francis of Assisi

I N 1881, the great Hindu mystic Ramakrishna was asked by the young man who eventually became Swami Vivekananda (the teacher who introduced Hinduism to the West) if he had seen God. Ramakrishna answered, "Yes, I see God, just as I see you here, only in a much more intense sense." Ramakrishna was renowned for his visions, and his life was devoted to a continual contemplation of God—a God that transcends all time and place and is present in all religions. Later, when his student Swami Vivekananda left India for America, he is said to have had the Bhagavad Gita in one pocket and Thomas à Kempis's *Imitation of Christ* in another. That fif-

teenth-century text appeals to seekers of all religions and reminds us of the need for daily commitment to spiritual practice
and awareness. As the poet Tagore wrote, "[O]ur daily worship
of God is not really the process of gradual acquisition of him, but
the daily process of surrendering ourselves, removing all obstacles to union and extending our consciousness of him in devotion and service, in goodness and in love."

One obstacle is lack of self-knowledge. Indeed, the mystical
path is a journey toward illumination through self-knowledge. In
the First Mansion, you uncovered and faced your struggles with
power, control, and humility. In the Second Mansion, you strive
to illuminate the conflicts, darkness, and fears within your soul,
purifying them. *The Cloud of Unknowing* affirms that "through
contemplation a person is purified." You sharpen your observa-
tional skills in order to identify the indirect ways in which you lose
your center of spiritual gravity. This can sometimes feel as if
everything broken in your life is being pulled through your guts,
and you may wonder, What is the point of this and what kind of
God would want a human being to suffer such pain? The answer
is another divine paradox. Simply put, the purpose of purification is to empty you of the sources of suffering—fears, attachments, and doubt. This requires personal experiences that make
you face your fears, your inner demons and shadow.

Toward that end, the soul provides you with experiences
that are necessary, that purge or cleanse you. There is no such
thing as a frivolous cleansing, and such experiences can take
many familiar forms, such as illnesses or persistent inner sufferings. Others may be more spontaneous, the result of a sudden
"aha" that hits home when you least expect it. For example, a
man who rose very rapidly in the corporate world was enormously successful, but his arrogance, insecurity, and need for approval and attention made him unbearable to be around. Once
his bank account was overflowing, he declared that he was being
called by God to do good in the world, informed everyone that
he was now a mystic, and set up a foundation to do good. But he

went about all this with his old, bullish, corporate style. He had not changed inside, but would not admit that he was still a greedy, controlling creature in spite of his declaration that he was now a mystic. Eventually, however, he met his match in a woman involved in a global project who told him that he did not qualify as a contributor, because, "You have an untrustworthy soul and until your soul is cleansed, we cannot have you sit among us. You will do more harm than good, in spite of your full wallet." He was stunned, but eventually admitted he had had an agenda behind his charity work and began the process of purification.

In the Second Mansion, you aim to become more discerning about your thoughts, motivations, and personal companions. We all need to be more discriminating about whom we allow into the circles that influence our souls. Beyond your friendships and social interactions, you need to become aware of how your psyche and soul are changing, of their shifts in perceptions. As you become more awakened, you may become psychically hypersensitive and reactive to other people's emotional energy, to highly charged negative atmospheres, to stresses in people around you, or even to the great tensions of the planet. Teresa warned her nuns that as they progressed in their Castles, they would become vulnerable in some way to other people's emotional, psychological, mental, and spiritual debris. You need to learn, as an emerging mystic, how to protect your energy field.

This hypersensitivity can be brought on by spending too much time alone in retreat or by opening up too many interior rooms too rapidly. In rare cases, achieving a blissful state of consciousness can result in a sense of ungroundedness and disorientation. A more common experience is that reading sacred literature and doing other soul work can shift your values and make you feel very detached from your familiar world. In these states, you require serious hand-holding and the companionship of someone who understands the journey of the soul. You will always need to maintain a solitary, silent prayer life and time for reflection, but you will also need to reach out to at least one other person to share your experience of God.

Teresa herself was starved for such companionship, especially when her mystical experiences of God reached a cosmic level to which no one else could relate. It is a great comfort to be understood by others who trust and *believe* in the personal experiences that we share with them, especially those for which there are no witnesses. There is no such thing as a mystical experience that can be proven. Even though Teresa's levitations, for instance, were witnessed by the nuns in her community, she could not *offer them proof* that, during those experiences, she was in conversation with Jesus. They had to take her word for that. When Teresa was fifty-two years old, she met John of the Cross, who was then only twenty-five. After they exchanged their experiences of God, they recognized each other as soul companions. In John, Teresa finally found someone with whom she could share the mystery of her life with God. After they met, she no longer needed to prove or defend the experiences of her soul. (Sadly, John burned all their correspondence shortly before his death.)

Teresa emphasized the need for companions on the spiritual journey. No one should travel through her Castle alone, she wrote again and again. Teresa knew firsthand the difficulty of the inner work required of the soul pilgrim, who was as likely to experience a dark night of the soul, to borrow a phrase from John of the Cross, as she was to experience the light and grace of liberation.

One of the most famous spiritual friendships was between Shams Tabrizi and the great thirteenth-century mystic poet Rumi. Shams traveled throughout the Middle East, searching and praying for someone who could endure his company, when a voice told him to seek out Rumi. Shams spent several years with Rumi, whose love for him he recorded in a great outpouring of poetry after Shams's death. Eventually, Rumi received the insight that he and Shams were one being, one soul, and elevated Shams in his poetry to a symbol of God's love for mankind.

Shams, which means "sun" in Arabic, came to mean the "Light of God" to one of the greatest poets of illumination.

Another way to describe the changes that mystics can undergo is that their psychic wiring is upgraded or expanded in order to accommodate infusions of divine light. Both the physical body and the psyche seem to need to adjust to its force, and sometimes this inner light has to be ministered to by another person who understands its power. For instance, in the story of Saul on the road to Damascus, to persecute Christians, Saul was blinded for three days by divine light, which knocked him to the ground. Then he heard the voice of the Lord command him to go into the city, where he would learn what he needed to do. Saul's traveling companions saw him fall but did not hear the voice, but at the same time, a Christian in Damascus, Ananias, had a vision that he must go out to find Saul and restore his vision. For three days Saul waited and did not eat or drink. After Ananias found him and restored his sight, Saul was baptized Paul, recovered his strength, and began a new life.

The effects of the sudden presence of God as light are meant to be overwhelming. Divine light is also reported frequently in near-death experiences. Thousands of people describe entering a tunnel of light in which they meet family members and friends who have gone before them and feel the presence of the divine, which radiates love and tenderness of a conscious, transcendent nature. This light is God, they say, and many report that they wanted to remain in its embrace. But they were commanded to return to their physical lives, after which they were compelled to make profound changes and seek a path back to that divine light.

Revelations of self-knowledge can also be emotionally and physically exhausting. During this process, you can—emphasis on *can*—develop a physical illness, for example, such as extreme fatigue, depression, a cold, or even more extreme or chronic conditions such as arthritis. Many people have told me that they believe their cancer or other serious diseases were, in fact, rooted in their spiritual transformation. From a mystical perspective, these physical conditions result from the shift in your relationship to power, as you withdraw from earthly authority and build your faith in divine authority. Just as dietary change and cleansing can make you feel worse before you feel better, a cleansing of your spirit and a new way of standing in your skin sometimes can bring on an actual illness.

Lest this information about mystical sensitivity alarm you, let me tell you that you are already familiar with this dynamic of light. In fact, you have been living with it for a long time. You already know that when you realize you have a problem—say, in your marriage or job—that realization is like a light going on. We use that metaphor because intuitively we know that divine light does alert us when negative situations can impair our health and well-being. You know that a physical illness is likely to develop if you do not follow inner guidance. How many times have you said, "I should have followed my gut?"

Many medieval mystics became ill, which was due to more than ordinary job stress. Part of the reason for their illnesses was their extraordinary relationship with God, but let us also remember that illnesses and injuries were common—they did not occur just to mystics or to people devoted to the spiritual path. Until the modern era, effective treatment of most illnesses did not exist. If medicine and effective treatments had been available, no doubt the mystics would have made use of them, as many, Teresa included, taught that it is important to care for your physical body.

Spiritual transitions are transitions of consciousness, and, just like finally awakening to the seriousness of certain problems at home or in a relationship, that awakening causes pain. Yet, it also immediately begins a healing because it ends a period of denial. It's common to say that our eyes are wide open now after a shocking realization that we had not wanted to see before. Perceiving the truth is painful, but it's more painful to tell yourself that lies are truth. The soul will not let you get away with such a betrayal. After you open to the truth, after you have expanded your perception of reality, you can never close that lens again. The world will never look the same, and even everything familiar will look entirely different. Truth is so healing and so liberating that, regardless of how stressful a revelation might be, the healing that follows is extraordinary because you feel free.

For instance, a woman discovered that her husband was cheating on her. Most of her friends knew but none wanted to tell her. She had prayed for guidance: "I no longer care what the truth is or how bad it is. Just show it to me. I can't take the lies anymore." Shortly after that, her husband told her he was involved with another woman. Then, all the odd behaviors, late-night delays, and personality changes, including her own constant gut feelings, made sense. Everything in her life that hadn't made sense instantly reordered itself into a huge, crystal-clear window through which she saw that everything in her life had changed while she had been living in denial. Breaking through that denial felt as if she had lanced an infected blister. She was still in pain, but it was a healing, liberating pain that came from facing, and not fearing, the truth.

Just as this woman had to go through a withdrawal from her personal illusions, mystics have to move beyond their personal illusions and go on to confront their greater illusions about God and the universe. These "heavenly" breakthroughs can be even more painful than earthly ones, but their consequences are wider reaching. Think about this: Every time you shed an illusion and see something clearly for the first time, you burst with a need to share that life-changing truth with someone. And in the sharing of a genuine truth, you in turn change that person's life. Mystics—genuine mystics—are called to share truth. It can be painful but it is healing. Preparing to be a channel for truth and for grace sometimes can take down the body, but prayer and grace have the force to lift it up again.

One of my students remarked casually to me after a Castle workshop on the Second Mansion, "I could just avoid all this by stopping this Castle work."

I looked at her for a moment and thought, Could you? Is it possible to walk away from the spiritual life because you want to avoid the challenges that come with it?

Then I asked her, "Well, tell me, then, how will you go about becoming unaware again? Tell me how you intend to stop thinking about your soul's purpose. How do you plan to silence your soul's voice? If you can do that, if you can figure out a way to go backward and be content with a life of ordinary troubles as opposed to divine chaos—because you will always have chaos, that is a given—then I'll take *your* workshop." She laughed and decided not to turn back.

Understanding how your awakening soul begins to affect your psychic field is a priority in this mansion. You practice heightening your awareness of the presence of God in the mundane details of your life. You make a practice of seeing God everywhere, in every thing, small and large, in every conversation, and in all the activities of your life. The divine does not intervene only in dramatic acts of healing or in eleventh-hour interventions or only in situations that make sense to you. After all, who are you that the world should make sense to you? What if that meant the world would baffle someone else?

Another practice in the Second Mansion is to trap the reptiles that are here. We all have personal challenges, or active reptiles, but the more subtle reptiles are shadow aspects buried within our unconscious minds. Each of us has shadow ego patterns to which we do not want to admit, such as being manipulative. A man I knew was a compulsive liar. After I caught him in two lies and told him that he was deceitful, he responded that I should be more understanding because he needed to lie at this stage of his life because he suffered from low self-esteem. *Right.*

You need to bring your shadow into view in order to sever its authority over you. That's purification, and it's not easy. Teresa spent years doing it. The search for your subtle reptiles will lead you into hidden rooms and one room will lead to another. Let me encourage you to add on to the rooms that I show you in this mansion. Your intention should be to excavate the dark states that contaminate your soul and cause you pain—despair, depression, anger, jealousy—any and all of them.

The Second Mansion, like the First, still contains these temptations, vermin, and reptiles because the ego self still has more authority over you than your soul does. At this point, you still doubt that you are on a divinely guided path. Your faith is still building and you still find it difficult to utter a prayer of complete soul surrender. So, in this Second Mansion, you are working to excavate the shadow aspects of your ego and understand the subtle ways they control you and support illusions about God.

Our preconceptions and expectations of God are mental and practical because our Western spiritual traditions are, too. When we work for a day, we expect a day's wages. When we pray for a day, we expect a day-size miracle. If we pray for nine days, we expect a bigger miracle. We expect a great deal from God. We expect God to cover our physical needs. We expect the guidance we receive to be practical. For some people, it's not enough to receive the blessing of a mystical experience of peace, whose divine message might mean, "I've heard your prayer. All is well. You have nothing to worry about." They want God to spell out the answer: "Okay then, I heard you. You need a job. Here's the address. Here's your salary. Here's your pension plan, health and dental insurance. Good enough? *Now will you believe?*"

Our contemporary cultural feelings of entitlement often contaminate our experience of God. The truth is that you are not entitled to anything, including a mystical experience or a healing. Everything is a blessing. The soul knows that to be a divine truth, even though the ego finds that difficult to accept. We *want and hope* that God will respond to us in reasonable, practical terms because we want to feel that we have some authority over

our fates and we are always looking for proof. We also want to believe there is some order to our universe. This is one of the greatest challenges you will face in the Second Mansion: giving up
this false image of God, your need to control God's behavior,
and the illusion that the divine operates by *your* rules. This is
more difficult that you might think, because this myth is in your
bones and in your blood.

A woman who survived a car accident said, "I know there is
some reason why this happened to me and I am just waiting to
find out what that is." She lifted her eyes toward heaven as she
said this, revealing her hope that God was going to send her a
telegram or an e-mail that read, "And now that I saved your life,
you know for a fact that you are not just special, but *very, very* special. And now, because your ego needs to believe you are so special, you now want to be rewarded for having your life saved with
an incredible calling. How special you are!" She wanted me to re-
inforce this notion that God must have something *really* extraordinary in mind for her. Otherwise, obviously, she would have
died. That is how her God works.

How does your God work? In this mansion, you have to investigate your myths of the divine. I can assure you that they are
many and are thick in your system. (I can also assure you that if
God wanted your money, there is nothing you could do to prevent that from happening, regardless of whether you pursued a
deeper spiritual life.)

In this mansion, you will also be tempted to quit your journey into the Castle. Your excavation of self-knowledge here becomes more challenging, and mystical experiences remain rare.
It's as if you are putting small amounts of money into a savings
account each week, yet the account seems hardly to be growing;
and you can't really do anything significant with the little savings
you have accumulated. The wise move would be to stop checking your balance each week and just continue to make your deposits. Ignore your balance sheet and wait awhile. Then, after a
long period of time during which you have not broken your dis-

cipline of weekly deposits, check your balance. You will now have accumulated enough to change your life.

You cannot treat this soul work as if your effort entitles you to a reward. You must not ever think that you are entitled to intimacy with God or to any other type of mystical experience. You journey into your soul for the sake of inner truth, not inner rewards. If you are going to become distracted on your journey into the Castle, it will occur here, because the demands on you become greater. Yet, your inner vision does begin to open up in this mansion as God initiates the beginnings of intimacy. God allows you brief entries into blissful states of quietude, which are breakthrough mystical experiences. Therein lies the paradoxical nature of God. Just as you release the divine from your expectations, all is given to you. That is a truth that you will come to experience in the Second Mansion. These states of quietude, which begin in this mansion, eclipse what you may have experienced in any meditation. Although such experiences tend to be short-lived, their intensity and mystical authenticity are just enough to break through your doubts so that you commit to continuing your journey into the Castle.

THE PRACTICE OF ILLUMINATION

When you notice God in the details, you are practicing illumination, which you use repeatedly in the Second Mansion. Pause and observe with appreciation all the so-called small things of the world around you. Put all your perceptual senses into slow motion. As you observe and appreciate, you are looking for the hand of God at work within every single particle, object, and conversation. Everything in your life is present because of divine intention.

You animate an internal theology and say, "I am exactly where I am supposed to be. All is as it should be. The divine is active within every detail. Therefore, every detail is serving a divine purpose and influencing my life in this moment. God is speaking to me through every detail." Then, breathe, relax, hold your focus, and receive impressions. Your mind will start making things up, because you will want answers or responses immediately. But quiet your mind and put your attention back on your breath and your intention on receiving rather than reasoning.

The practice of illumination sets the stage for awakening your inner vision, which is the first experience of mysticism in this mansion. Practicing God-in-the-details is harder than it may at first seem, because you must slow down. You have to pause in your perceptions, observe, and consciously appreciate what you are seeing, doing, hearing, thinking, and speaking. You have to learn to slow down your habit of looking at everything while asking, "Is this safe?"; "Is this mine?"; "Is this comfortable?"; "Is this valuable?"; "Is this attractive?"; "Is this powerful?" You practice approaching every person, place, flower, or crack in the wall as if it were there just for you to appreciate. And if you cannot see value in what you are looking at, then that itself is a meditation, as you must ask yourself, "Why is it that I cannot see value in this person or in this task or in this moment of my life?" Every moment of your life has value. As you have to *slow down* your perceptions and senses and shift gears to become receptive, you learn how to enter mystery itself. The practice of illumination is the practice of entering into mystery. Today, with the infusion of Eastern wisdom, we might call Teresa's recommendations the practice of mindfulness, of being present to every moment and all sensations. Inner vision, as she calls it, is a mystical practice, mysticism in action.

Entry Prayer

I cross the bridge into the silent bliss of my Castle. I close the drawbridge and forbid all outside influences from entry into this holy place that is my soul. Here in my Castle, I am alone with God. Under God's light and companionship I discover the depth and beauty of my soul. I embrace the power of prayer. I open myself to divine guidance. I surrender myself to become as a channel for grace, healing, and service as God directs my life.

The Stirrings of Inner Vision

Here in the Second Mansion, inner visions begin to stir as you grow more comfortable with your interior life. The soul begins to rise and make its presence and power known to both your intuitive and your conscious mind. In a sense, you develop your "mystical sea legs" in this mansion.

Inner visions and quietude are gifts from God. One might even call them visitations. Being enveloped in a state of quietude is unlike ordinary silence. Mystical quiet is like a soft dream that flows into every cell, transcending ordinary relaxation. You feel as if you are suspended within the soothing sensation of silence as it draws out of you all the scars and bruises created by the loud, harsh sounds of life. You return to your five senses, renewed.

Spontaneous experiences of bliss may also overtake you at this stage, creating the sensation that your soul has temporarily been separated from your body. You may feel replenished with boundless hope, compassion, and unconditional love. Problems feel insignificant in those moments when you are fully in your soul. And from that place of mystical insight and perspective, you realize the gift that is your life, and you want to embrace every second with your full consciousness.

Inner visions are very different from intuitions. Intuition is a gut-focused self-protective sense. An experience of inner vision, however, is an act of grace that is given to you. A genuine state of illumination cannot be self-induced. Yet, after I described in a workshop some ways in which an inner vision can manifest, one person asked me, "Tell me how to do that," as if she could bring on a mystical state at will. Inner visions, like all mystical states, are spontaneous gifts from God, not rewards for long hours of prayer or good behavior. I cannot emphasize that enough.

Teresa mentions a state of consciousness called spiritual sleep, in which her nuns claimed that their souls were "intoxicated" by God and their bodies became languid and weak. Perhaps this was a form of spiritual hysteria, an etheric version of girls who faint over rock bands or movie stars. Teresa wrote, "They fancy this is a trance; I call it nonsense. It does nothing but waste their time and injure their health." And we thought we invented tough love in the twentieth century. . . .

There is no pattern of human logic behind how or why the divine begins to communicate with you. Your job is to build your spiritual stamina, for in the Second Mansion you still have much work to do to be ready for these gifts of inner visions and other states. You need to continue to confront the darkness and reptiles that can waste your time and keep your soul from God. And you need to grow in confidence so that your light—your gifts of the soul—can emerge.

Inner vision is a way of perceiving the grander purpose of life and the divine mechanics that operate behind the scenes. The cosmic design includes an entire cast of invisible divine characters: angels, saints, the Divine Mother, Buddha, Shiva, and our dearly departed. They may all be aspects of a single divine source, of course; regardless, we love the cast of characters that live on the "light" side of the tracks. But you cannot accept a pantheon of light-life and not have the "night-life" that goes with it. If there are angels, then you must presume—like it or not—that there are demons. So, from a practical point of view, here in your Second Mansion, Teresa directs you to consider that reptiles and destructive temptations (which she called demons) orbit your soul.

As you come into your inner life, you attract temptations. That is not so difficult to understand, as you know that opposites attract. Goodness attracts evil, light attracts darkness—an interior as well as an exterior force. Inner darkness is your shadow—your reptiles; external darkness takes many forms.

To protect yourself, as you begin to act as a channel of grace and walk this world as a mystic outside a monastery, do not succumb to the ego temptation to tell people about your inner life in order to get their approval or impress them with your spiritual life. You are only asking for trouble and, at the very least, criticism. Practice silence and fly under the radar. Depend on your soul companions for spiritual support. Teresa would call the need to impress others with your spiritual life a temptation of the devil, an act of pride, evidence of a lack of humility. Be aware of this tendency; purify the need within you to evangelize or judge others or to assume an attitude of superiority. Heighten your senses to the presence of darkness and negativity as it exists in the world and in your personal energy field. I marvel at how people recoil from any mention of demons or negativity while draping themselves in protective crystals and amulets so that negative forces don't come near them.

Another form of temptation—a devil that comes to your door—is to make public a spiritual activity—for example, fasting or doing charitable work. These should remain private, between you and God. Broadcasting such activities will always draw criticism or envy. Many people become jealous of someone who is doing something that just may result in genuine empowerment. When they sense that there is even the slightest chance that this person could surface from his fast or her charitable work happier or healthier than they were, then chances are they will look for a flaw in that good intention, consciously or unconsciously. As the great Sufi poet Hafiz wrote, "Don't surrender your loneliness / So quickly. / Let it cut more deep."

Teresa believed that the devil knows exactly when to press your buttons of insecurity, for example always having to be first or neediness for approval. It doesn't matter if your world allows only angels and forbids demons. It does matter that you recognize that mystical empowerment is the most prized possession of all, beyond wealth, beyond anything you can own. This is why the greatest souls who walked the Earth—Jesus, Buddha, and other holy masters—were visited by demons upon their enlightenment or shortly thereafter. The demons wanted to prevent such great light from coming to Earth, for they knew that the power of the soul was far greater than their physical powers. Mystical empowerment liberates us from all our earthly fears. To *know and see and experience* the power of truth and the soul *frees* you from the fears that drive others to sell their souls for illusory safety nets—for money, security, jobs, or companionship. In the center of truth is the nature of mystical illumination.

Rooms of Inner Vision and Purification

THE FIRST ROOM:
Discerning Intuition

Intuition is not a higher power. It is organic divinity—God in your bowels and gut. Gut instincts are attuned to protect you; they are survival mechanisms, fight-or-flight, trust-or-suspicion responses. You likely spend more time blocking your intuition than you do honoring your hunches. Most of your pain comes from acting against the personal guidance you receive because you are afraid of how it will affect your personal and professional lives. Intuition is a constant guiding voice that tells you to speak honestly, to act with integrity, to live consciously, and to act in good conscience. The more you betray your intuitive voice, the more you will come to fear it. You need to clear a channel to your intuitive voice so that you cannot deny or ignore it. This exercise takes practice. You need to apply it in your everyday life and refer to it in every decision you make.

Soul Work: Reading poetry, such as that of Rumi or Yeats or other inspirational authors, can help center you as you prepare for an intuitive exercise. Deep breathing and stretching are also excellent. Any practice that gets your attention into the present moment will serve you well in this room. Use your journal to describe your intuitive voice. What does it feel like? How do you distinguish it from your imagination? Does your intuition speak through your biology? Does it come through your gut, head, neck, or back? Recall instances in which you have had intuitive hits; describe them in detail, recalling the sensations psychically and biologically. In what circumstances have you acted on your intuition and when have you repressed it? Do you associate your intuition with a warning system as opposed to a channel for guidance? Describe in detail the reasons for your different reactions.

Now, pause for a moment and listen to your intuition. What are you sensing now? If there is a situation in your life that requires intuitive guidance, request it and open yourself to receive the response. Intuitive information comes immediately. Are you open to intuitive guidance about your health or a talent you should pursue? Can you sense your intuition encouraging you to expand your creativity? It is instantaneous and objective. Emotional content is added to it once the information gets routed through your mind.

THE SECOND ROOM:
Private Agendas Versus Intuitive Guidance

Your intuition can often become confused with the voice of your ego and its private agendas. Why do you make the choices that you do? This question takes on far greater significance within the Castle as you must now assume that the active voice of God is constantly coming through your intuition. The challenge within the Second Mansion is to discern that clear intuitive voice from private agendas that are often fueled by fear or other negative emotions.

Many times I am asked how to tell the difference between the voices of the imagination versus the ego versus the soul— could they all sound the same? How do you know which voice is truly the right one? Actually, it's not difficult at all. In fact, it's easy. Your intuition is relentless and cannot be budged from its position whereas the ego can be talked into or out of anything. For example, if your intuition tells you that you *must* pursue training as a healer, no human being on this earth could truly talk you out of that feeling. You could be talked out of *following* that feeling, but never out of recognizing that feeling. Self-reflection is the essential practice of evaluating your choices against a standard of absolute inner knowing that has feelings and sensations that go along with it. You know what that standard within you feels like because you know exactly what it is like to receive a pure intuitive hit about your life. And you know when you have betrayed that feeling.

Soul Work: Assume that half of your intuitive hits are directly from God and half are fear-based. To discern the one clear voice, you have to commit to observing yourself in action from the time you awaken. Follow this practice:

1. Begin your day with prayer, receiving and noting any relevant guidance for the day.

2. Pause every few hours during the day to reflect upon the choices you have made so far and your motivations for making those choices. Are you following through on the morning's guidance? Are any choices compromising your honor? Your integrity? Your self-esteem? Are you entering into power plays even though you are now able to recognize the nonsense of such interpersonal dynamics? What are you telling yourself in order to allow yourself to get away with that behavior?

3. At the end of the day, review your day in prayer. Read an inspirational text. And then dwell on what a lovely journey it is to walk through life surrounded by God and grace.

THE THIRD ROOM:
Temptations

One of the most well-known prayers in the world is, "Lead us not into temptation but deliver us from evil." Any number of temptations surround you. It would be easier to answer the question, "What *isn't* a temptation?" But in this room, you dialogue with your soul on the subject of temptations, which are far more than just a word in a prayer; a temptation is an archetype familiar to the soul. The soul expects to be tempted literally and symbolically; perhaps in the desert, perhaps in the bar, perhaps in the bedroom. Who knows where your vulnerability is? The truth is— and that's the point of this quest—do you know where you can be tempted? Do you know your own vulnerabilities? Do we attack people who are different than we are, perhaps too wild or too sensual, because they represent ways we *want* to be tempted but dare not admit? This is a room for rich inner work and self-reflection.

Soul Work: What tempts you to compromise your soul? What are your temptations? What do you fear you cannot go too near because your soul is not yet strong enough to hold its center? What are the root causes of your temptations? Which ones do you want to keep in your life because they are thrilling even if they are destructive? Which of your temptations cause you to lead a double life? Practice illuminating these demons by journaling or sharing with soul companions. This usually requires the support of soul companions.

THE FOURTH ROOM:
Recognizing Your Light

Out of the work of excavating the reptiles hidden within your soul comes your light. You learn to love more deeply by discovering why you were afraid to love; you learn to appreciate the beauty in others by overcoming the fear that their beauty somehow diminishes your own; and you learn to hear the voice of God by overcoming your fear that profound guidance will lead you into darkness instead of into the light.

All mystics discovered profound inner resources of the soul as they grew in their trust of God. Yet people fear their lives will change if they really follow their passions. Soul passions are a powerful grace. Knowing that you have such a force within you begs the question, "How can you *not* release your light?" What would that be like?

I know a woman who lived the first half of her life in five square miles of her hometown in Ireland. Then one day she gathered the courage to venture beyond, traveling first through her native country and then to the Middle East. After that, she could hardly contain her new self. She enrolled in classes to learn computer skills and she got involved in organizations in communities around her hometown. She began to teach computer skills to other women and has since become an activist for social change. She is now someone she could never have imagined becoming five years ago, but she felt her passion and she knew that she had to "give her soul a chance," as she put it. I love that phrase as much as I admire her courage. For all of the difficult work that must be done within these many rooms of the first three mansions, you are working to give your soul a chance to emerge and take charge of your life.

Soul Work: The capacity to see goodness in another person reflects a light in your soul, as does the capacity to be compassionate, generous, understanding, and gentle. What light do you hold in your soul? Your particular light is your charism, a type of grace unique to every person that embodies his or her spiritual essence. Name your light. What is the essence of the grace that is you? Listen and look deeply into your soul and identify its forces of light. You have boundless qualities that make up the complexity of who you are, I assure you. You have never encountered most of them.

Your charism directs your life path, so you need to know what it is. Life moves through passages that can be confusing, difficult, and painful or outrageously abundant, lavish, and happy. You can lose yourself to achieving abundance as easily as you can to starvation. You can rely on your charism—your essential self—to guide you, however. You know when you have compromised yourself just a bit too much, when you are not the real you. Follow your charism and you will inevitably find your soul.

THE FIFTH ROOM:
Your Darkness Attracts Light

Life is a constant dance of light and darkness. Your goodness attracts darkness; your darkness attracts the light. That is the divine design, which you must learn to recognize as an active principle in your life, like cause and effect or magnetic attraction. You can never be too sure of yourself, too sure that you are above temptation or above seduction, but nor should you ever doubt the power of your inner light to protect you no matter what the circumstance. The emphasis that all spiritual masters place upon humility reminds us that we are never beyond the power of our own shadow. The practice of self-reflection and prayer must remain a constant in your life to feed your need for the right of wisdom and truth.

*S*oul Work: In order to build your appreciation for how much light is continually sent into your life, you will want to practice this many times to learn about the power of your grace and your shadow in action.

1. Choose one positive quality, for example, humor or patience or compassionate listening, and think of that quality as a channel for grace. Observe how that quality affects the lives of the people around you. Pay attention to who is drawn to you and why. Observe any mood swings you might experience or shifts in your attitude; that is, at what point does it become difficult for you to maintain that positive quality? Note any changes in your environment that may have contributed to that, including shifts in your own attitude. For example, a woman known for her outrageous sense of humor and for always lightening an atmosphere frequently drew to herself the one person in the office who was known to be an unredeemable pessimist. Invariably he sought her out to attack her optimism. His darkness was determined to shatter her light. Some days he succeeded in making a dent in her life force but that was rare. She had too much to be grateful for to let his negativity contaminate her—but oh how he tried.

2. Now choose one negative quality that you have, for example, the habit of judging another person or needing to be right. Pay special attention to that behavior for one or two days, watching how it influences you and the people around you. Do you avoid the people you judge? Do you gossip about them? Knowing that you could be kind, at least in thought, about them, why would you choose to be judgmental? And in the midst of a negative action or thought about another person, notice the immedi-

ate infusion of light, because it is immediate. Notice, for example, that the instant that you judge a person, you become saturated with the question, "Are you sure you want to hold that judgment?" As if giving you a chance to erase the effects of a negative judgment against another human being, a light-filled question always follows a negative thought about another human being. Divine light is instantly present the second we slip into darkness.

THE SIXTH ROOM:
Resisting Quietude; Waiting for God

It makes no sense to resist quietude, yet we create distractions all the time because we fear the consequences of guidance. Paradoxically, we pray for stillness and seek it because we yearn to quiet our distractions.

Soul Work: Listen to your distractions. Observe the noise in your mind. What thoughts do you hear when you take time to be conscious of them? Is stress your default setting, your automatic place of attention? Is your unconscious constantly filled with fearful messages? What makes you uncomfortable about waiting for God? Take thirty minutes in which you wait for God and note where your mind wanders. Just follow your mind as it waits for God. Afterward, sit back, breathe, close your eyes, and open to the grace of quietude. Return to this room regularly and practice waiting for God, observing how much your mind needs to be entertained, amused, and stuffed full of thoughts. Use your spiritual journal to empty, empty, empty your mind.

THE SEVENTH ROOM:
Fearless Bliss

Imagine not fearing your life. Imagine being free of all of your survival worries. Imagine being satisfied with your life, and even more than satisfied, elated. Imagine having the courage to live your life fully, to live beyond needs and wounds but rather through the power and energy of your creativity. Imagine having the courage to take a risk, play the odds, be the person who invests in the unknown and ends up winning. These are descriptions of fearless bliss, a state of consciousness that you attain gradually as you shed your fears about how an intimate relationship with your soul will change your life. A deeply active soul life does not mean the end of a normal physical life. By shedding fear, you gain bliss—not perfection, not the end of problems or strife or difficulties, because those come with life. But even in the midst of all the problems that embody the business of life, you can know bliss, you can be fearless.

Soul Work: What would equal bliss for you? When you imagine yourself fearless, how does your life's compass shift? Examine the hold that survival fears have on you. Do you even fear bliss and perhaps think of it as being out of control? Do you fear discovering the many limitations that you have placed on yourself? List these limitations—emotional, intellectual, psychological, physical, sexual, creative, and spiritual. You are now the only one who is keeping you down.

THE EIGHTH ROOM:
Meeting the Demon

Evil exists in many forms. However you refer to a dark force, the fact is that energy fields of negativity or evil are real. Spiritual masters have always trained their students in arts of protection, from smudging to keeping candles lighted to the use of holy water and oil. All spiritual traditions have prayers for protection because wisdom dictates that light attracts shadow and that shadow comes in many forms.

Soul Work: Meet with your soul and ask it to help you recall times when you felt a presence or force of extreme negativity or evil. That sensation is real. Pay attention to it. Have you felt it in a moment of weakness, vulnerability, or temptation? Have you ever felt that something negative or evil has penetrated your energy field, such as someone's anger?

Now breathe deeply and invoke the presence of light and grace. Feel the walls of your Castle surround you immediately. Evil cannot penetrate your Castle. Maintain time every day for prayer, and invoke the grace of protection.

THE NINTH ROOM:
Purification

Purification of the soul is a part of the mystic's journey. To purify your soul means to cleanse it of all the earthly debris and shadow energies on your path to illumination. Purification is a process so natural to the soul that even without setting your foot upon a spiritual path, your soul would maintain its own dynamic of purification through stirrings of conscience or through posing questions about the meaning of your life. For the conscious sojourner, the task of purification becomes more rigorous yet more satisfying and uplifting, as if you have been released from a small, dark space where you have been confined for years. Use the practice of purification as a healing ritual or use it whenever you feel the need to work through problems, like reptiles entering your Castle.

Soul Work: Consider the experience of purification as being like a sauna for the soul. Imagine that you are releasing all the toxins from every negative emotion. Imagine the fragrances of lemongrass or jasmine flushing out all your worries and fears. Let the heat melt through any physical pain or illness that you are suffering.

THE TENTH ROOM:
The Sanctuary

Imagine that you are entering a room that is filled only with light. This is a sacred sanctuary, a room for prayer and contemplation only. You are meeting God in this room. No work needs to be done here; you need only to rest. Be still, be present, be open to the grace of illumination.

SOUL COMPANIONS

An ancient Hindu story in the Mahabharata tells of a group of men searching for the road to heaven. Over the years, all but one died on the journey, so the last man had to continue with only a stray dog to keep him company. They traveled together, sharing whatever food and water they found, helping each other over rough places in the road. After some years, they came to the gate to paradise. The gatekeeper greeted the tired holy man and invited him in but refused to allow the dog to enter, telling the man to drive it away. The holy man would have to enter alone. The man looked at his dog and then at paradise, and he remembered all that he and his dog had been through together, the dangers they'd faced, the distance they had traveled. He turned away, saying that paradise was not worth the price of betraying a companion who had stood by him. As the pair started back down the mountain, the dog revealed himself to be the god Dharma, who thanked the man for his friendship and care and granted him admission to heaven.

Dharma is also the everyday practice of spiritual values, so, in other words, the spiritual journey requires a soul companion to help you both with bliss and with difficulty. God is in this spiritual companion and on the quest with you. Sacred literature, myths, and legends are full of stories of the gods testing our human capacity for compassion, for acknowledging the divinity in others, in strangers and unfortunates whom we meet unexpectedly. Ovid recorded the beautiful myth of Baucis and Philemon, a poor, elderly, rural couple who welcomed two ragged, exhausted travelers into their hut to share their small meal. All their neighbors, rich or poor, had refused to help the wayfarers, who were actually the gods Jupiter and Mercury in disguise. As a reward, the gods of course offered the couple whatever they wished, and the couple asked only to serve as the gods' priests and to continue living together, until they died, because they had never lived alone and delighted in each other's company. All this was granted, and the gods also installed them in a beautiful castle for the rest of their years, their souls ministering to each other as well as the divine.

Teresa encouraged her nuns to share their experiences of the divine with one another and to consider themselves companions on the journey. To share our experiences of God, we need the blessing of a spiritual community of like-minded souls around us. We need a place where we belong spiritually as well as physically, but not necessarily as a part of a traditional religion. In Teresa's day, of course, that meant a convent for the women and a monastery for the men. Yet, today's emerging mystics without monasteries also need others for soul support. Spiritual life is not supposed to be lonely, celibate, poverty-stricken, or full of suffering. The early mystics endured their sufferings as gifts from God as a way of coping with physical ailments for which there were no treatments. Through that choice they developed the stamina of their souls. You, however, can live today as a mystic in this world and you can pursue being an artist, singer, actor, entrepreneur, doctor, lawyer, pilot, mother, father, teacher, salesman, or computer expert. And you can marry and have a family and take vacations—and channel grace.

This is not an either/or world anymore. You have both a body and a soul and don't choose to have one or the other. You don't choose to acknowledge your soul in your health care and then leave it at home when you go to work, do you? Your soul, too, requires both solitary time for prayer and companions of the soul. You need community around you and with you because, as your interior world becomes more alive, you will want to be with people who understand the journey—not *your* journey, but the *soul's* journey. Such a community is not an emotional support group modeled on sharing wounds and addictions, nor does it need to be all men or all women. If you need a healing support group, then seek out a healing support group. A soul group gathers for the purpose of sharing mystical awakenings and experiences of God, for the celebration of the blessings in one another's lives, for exploring ways of being of service, and for supporting one another in that goal.

A soul companion is not a soul mate but a person with whom you share a bond of reverence for the spiritual journey you are both on and for how you have chosen to walk on this Earth. Soul companions discuss topics that nourish each other's spirits and help each other appreciate the divine gifts in their lives including building friendship networks that support each other's creativity and work in the world. Soul companions use their inner light to illuminate the light in each other. You utilize the gifts of your soul to bring as much truth and wisdom into each other's lives as possible. You are spiritual mirrors for each other, witnesses to each other's sacred experiences, just as Ananias restored Paul's sight, helping him transit into a new faith.

Imagine gathering to share your life with people who accept the existence of God, angels, saints, and miracles, who understand the practice of healing and channeling grace, who take seriously their practice as mystics in the world. That is a bit of heaven on Earth. It would be divinely ordinary to be a part of a circle of mystics and share the gift of illumination.

Teresa noted that God was especially fond of choosing the books that we read and of slipping into our everyday conversations unexpectedly. God is perfectly capable of sending guidance through your companions to help you just as you help them with your insights. Today, we often call such spontaneous answering of a need with a solution "synchronicity," which is just an intellectual code word for divine action behind the scenes. Synchronicity appears in anecdotes of so-called parking angels, who find you just the right parking spot when you're running late; synchronicity is also at work when a book with information you need falls off a shelf in front of you, or a friend mentions just the right doctor for your mother or the right therapist, school program, or camp for your child. So, certainly words of divine guidance can slip into your conversations with a dear friend.

With your soul companions, practice receptivity and silence. Together, channel quietude to people in need of it, such as people with psychological trauma, people who are facing difficulties, people with whom you have adversarial relationships, and to the global community for peace. One of the first circles of grace I helped form was for families with autistic children. Every member of that circle has an autistic child. Although many do not live in the same area, they have agreed to pray together at a certain time each day and to share information via the Internet.

They keep one another hopeful and filled with optimism and a sense of humor. This is the practice of mystical illumination.

In addition to the blessings of friendship and support, a circle of soul companions keeps you from becoming emotionally and psychically isolated. Your work in the Castle is a higher state of consciousness that would not be real for most people, and you shouldn't attempt to share your intense personal work or mystical experiences with just anyone. You need to share them with others who are on the same path and who are not afraid of it. In short, you need *someone who believes you* when you have a mystical experience. Finding the right words to describe an ineffable encounter with divine illumination is beyond difficult. You need to know at least one individual who recognizes the *truth* in your experience.

You also need companions of the soul because mystical experiences can be difficult to bear, particularly if you are given a vision or a revelation that elevates your understanding but also contradicts commonly held beliefs. For instance, imagine that your mother, brother, husband, or child has been diagnosed with a potentially terminal illness. Your family gathers around, holding tight to one another, sharing a combination of fear, hope, and faith. Although you have sought out the best possible medical care, the doctors have given you very little realistic hope. Fear and exhaustion take their toll on all of you. Then, one night, you have a vision and you see that your sick loved one is going to recover. You are not told how, only that he will pull through his disease and that it will take five long years. And then you are told in this moment of illumination that you are not to say a thing to anyone in your family. They must endure these five years not knowing whether this loved one is going to make it. You now know he is, but you are to keep this revelation to yourself. You are not told why; you are only given those directions to follow.

The next morning you return to the hospital. Your family is losing faith, weeping, and breaking down. You now hold the news that could release their suffering because you have "seen" what is to come. Yet, you cannot—you must not—reveal one word. Maybe you could tell just one person, you think to yourself. Would this person even believe you? Would it be worth risking the promise you made to heaven, only to discover that the person with whom you shared this revelation would *not* believe you? He would ask you, again and again, "Are you sure? Did that *really* happen?" You would betray your instructions and help no one by doing so.

In this situation, you would be burdened by two realities. You have to contain your interior life, in which experiences of illumination and revelation occur. You also have to live with your family's reality, which is filled with doubt, despair, and fear. You have to contain the outcome of this situation, revealing to no one that your loved one is going to heal. You have to contain your deeply intimate relationship with God and the sacred, beautiful, healing secret, because those were your instructions. How typical of God to ask something so unreasonable and not explain why you would be given such a profound gift and not allowed to share it. What on earth is heaven up to?

Keeping silent and following those instructions would be enormously difficult. Most people would implode from having been given an illumination that could alleviate pain for people they love but that they have to keep to themselves. Few can carry the burden of the light of the "unreasonable mind of God" alone. Being in the company of soul companions who themselves have sacred secrets will help you bear up under the weight of these multiple realities.

A Moment of Contemplation

We are creatures of community. We seek out one another's company because we are compelled to share our lives, to give of ourselves, and to be there for one another. Even if you were not on a journey into your Castle, you would still reach a point in your life in which chatter about the neighborhood and family dynamics, while still being of interest, is not enough. Once you are on a spiritual path, you begin to yearn for a spiritual community, for a gathering of soul companions with whom you can share meaningful, nourishing exchanges of truth and conversations that lift you up into a mystical perspective that helps make sense of your relationships, your life, and the world.

You want to see life through your soul, with your soul, in your soul. You want to *use* your soul to reshape the world you live in, to help make sense of the great and small madness in your life—and the madness that may surface in the life of a dear friend. You realize that life isn't rational, and your mind is limited in its ability to understand it. When the invisible becomes as real as the visible, you must seek out companions for your soul. As you sojourn into the invisible domain of the spirit, they can help you keep both feet on the ground. A circle of soul companions with whom you can share the unimaginable power of grace is mystical community at its best; that is home.

Exploring Spiritual Companionships

THE FIRST ROOM:
Loneliness

Being alone and isolated is a core human fear that can be so overwhelming that it controls your life choices. We fear that we will be alone if we follow spiritual guidance, like medieval hermits and other renunciates. While this outcome is unlikely, if you do *not* follow the guidance you receive, you *will* end up lonely, because, even if you surround yourself with people you love, your soul will be empty. Soul loneliness can also stem from the fear that when you encounter God or discover your most authentic feelings, you will no longer be able to relate to your life. Often, you are not as frightened of God as you are frightened about coming closer to owning deeper truths about yourself.

Most traditional mystics were alone for only brief periods of time, and you think you fear this archetypal aloneness, but in truth you fear the journey into your self, which only you can do.

Soul Work: What causes you to feel lonely—even among friends and family? How does the fear of loneliness control you and your life choices? Have you compromised a soul calling because you feared that it would isolate you? How many times have you not followed divine guidance out of the fear of being lonely? What specifically was that guidance? Can you see yourself able to respond to that calling now? Practice discovering how the fear of loneliness distracts you from surrendering to God. Record in your journal how much this fear causes you to negotiate away your inner guidance. Pray for guidance, listen, and respond. Return to this room often to work on these insights. Be compassionate with yourself. This is a very difficult room.

THE SECOND ROOM:
Are New Thoughts Stirring within Your Soul?

Entering your Castle is the same as perceiving the universe through the lens of your soul. As you pursue an inner life, you develop new insights about your world that can be challenging to incorporate into your old worldview. When you discard belief patterns that you finally recognize as false, obsolete, or burdensome, you leave yourself wide open for new, fresh perceptions. Some can be quite startling, some richly insightful, and some so profound that they can redirect the course of your life. One person might say, "This is hopeless," but you see that there is always hope, and grace and hope always go together. Another person might ask, "Do negative attitudes cause negative actions?" but you see clearly that they are one and the same thing. Be still, listen, observe, pray. Prepare to enter into the newness of your own soul.

Soul Work: In the silence of this room, ask your soul what is fresh, inspired, and new within it. What have you never thought about before? Let newness in. Newness can arrive as words, images, or symbols and not necessarily be related to anything going on in your life at the moment. Be open to wonderful insights. Were you praying about anything special? Open yourself to any response from God. Are there responses that are confusing or uncomfortable? Become attuned to your soul. Attunement to new perspectives is your discipline in this room. Return whenever you need to illuminate new beginnings or recognize that something new has been sent into your soul.

THE THIRD ROOM:
What Unknown Territory Could Soul Companions Help You Explore?

Soul companions can provide a structure to your spiritual practice. They inspire you to keep your commitment to a practice that you might otherwise drop if left on your own. Would you go to a yoga class—or take up dream work, for example, if you had someone to go with you? Or form a mysticism study group?

Soul Work: How many times have you been drawn to try something new in a spiritual or consciousness field but decided not to because you didn't want to go it alone? What were you attracted to? And now? Your attraction to that activity may be your soul telling you what it needs. Find soul companions, even one or two. This is essential as you continue your journey through the Castle. Keep a list of all that you would like to share. You can begin by sharing this material with a couple of trusted friends. Honor your journey by honoring your process.

THE FOURTH ROOM:
You Can Be Difficult

Admit it. Like everyone else, you have defense mechanisms that make you difficult to get to know. Defensiveness is a protection against humiliation and criticism, a way of trying to control your environment. Behind your defense mechanisms is a desire to be comfortable with other people, but rather than risk rejection, you push others away. Shoring up your defenses will not help you find a soul companion.

You cannot shed the difficult, stubborn aspects of your nature in one visit to this room. Deeper than the surface reasons for your behavior are the soul reasons, all of which have to do with your relationship to God and power. Digging your heels deep into the ground and screaming, "I'm not moving, so the world has to move around me," is just a way of taking out your frustration at God on your friends, family, and anyone else who crosses your path. You want more control over your life but you can't have it, so you become difficult personally. As one very stubborn man reminded his children every autumn, "I may not be able to control the weather or the cost of fuel, but, by God, I can certainly control the temperature in my house and the gas bill." Regardless of how cold the weather became in the fall in the Midwest, he did not turn on the heat until November 15, and the thermostat never read higher than sixty-five degrees.

Soul Work: What makes you difficult to get to know? What role do you need to play in a friendship? Is it important for you to be the know-it-all? Is it important for you always to be in charge? Even if you are open and warm, this does not mean you are easy to get to know. Examine how you set up your relationships and the rules you require in order to make friendships work. How difficult is it for you to relinquish control? Can you see yourself opening up and allowing another person to channel grace or guidance for you? Take note of your stubborn and difficult patterns. Choose one to work with and observe yourself in action when that pattern asserts itself. Note to yourself, "I am now deliberately behaving in a stubborn or difficult way. Why? What is my private power agenda? Am I seeking attention? Do I want to control this situation? Do I need to be seen as the winner or right about something?" Holding yourself accountable for your actions means more than recognizing them. It means modifying your behavior consciously, little by little.

Remind yourself that contradictions are the design of this universe. You can be very stubborn and very loving. You can be both—most people are. Being difficult or stubborn does not serve you or anyone else. Intimacy and soul companionship are built on mutual give and take, trust, humor, and enjoyment of each other's gifts. Take your conflicts about your nature into this room and work with them. Dwell on love and all the good that you do to help you investigate why you are stubborn.

THE FIFTH ROOM:
Enter the Mystery of the Unknown

Every second of our lives is filled with unknown possibilities. You wake up living one life and go to bed in an entirely new world. A pregnant woman becomes a mother with a child in her arms; a man with a modest income buys a lotto ticket and goes to bed a multimillionaire. A man walks into a funeral parlor to say a prayer for the deceased just because the parlor was empty and he felt someone should say at least one prayer; he signed his name to the visitors' register and learned later that he had inherited the decedent's fortune, as his will read that anyone who prayed for him at his funeral would inherit his wealth.

What do we *really* know for certain about our lives? What and who can we *really* count on to be there for us tomorrow when we wake up? The truth is, tomorrow morning is an unknown. The joy in this truth is that you never know how problems will be worked out for you. You never know when you might meet someone special. You never know when just the right circumstances will be set into motion that will trigger your creativity.

Soul Work: Start with this truth: the unknown represents God. Entering into the mystery of the unknown is entering into the mystery of God. Imagine yourself in a dialogue with God in which you must tell the divine all that you know for certain about your life. Write this dialogue in your journal. In addition, do the following journal exercise, which is a rich and delightful way of learning to see God in the details of your life.

1. First thing in the morning, write five things that you are absolutely certain will happen on this day. Then, write what would happen if these things did not occur.
2. How much control did you have in organizing these five events?
3. At the end of the day, evaluate how well the "known" did that day. Did everything come off as planned?
4. Make note of all the unknown or unplanned events that happened that day and the impact

      they had on your life, such as meeting a new person, going to a new place, a new crisis occurring.

5. Look at all of these planned and unplanned events and see if you can imagine which will ultimately have the most effect on your life. Will it be your list or God's?—the known or the unknown?

6. Do this exercise on several different days.

THE SIXTH ROOM:
Illuminate Who and What You Judge

Judgmentalism is an aggressive act of your ego, a need to be superior. A judgment blocks your ability to receive insight about anything. You do not want to be judged by others; in fact, you resent those who have judged you harshly. Illuminate the darkness of your judgments, including those about your challenges, experiences, life circumstances, and other people in your life. Quick judgments cause you to devalue or miss countless gifts that come into your life, whereas bringing light to bear upon each circumstance, illuminating it, allows its greater significance, divine purpose, and direction to come through.

Soul Work: Pray and begin to illuminate who and what you habitually judge, including significant and insignificant events and challenges. When you come down to it, few things pass before your eyes without your passing judgment of some sort. As the Buddhists teach, all judgments reshape the moment or event. To judge means that you are already anticipating being disappointed or defeated. Think of whom you judge and illuminate and melt that harsh tendency. To be without judgment and to know how to dissolve judgmentalism is one of the finest skills you can offer a soul companion and one of the most gracious gifts you can receive.

THE SEVENTH ROOM:
Illuminate Your Fear of Losing an Ordinary Life

Even though you have entered the Castle, you still fear that a mystical life will keep you from having an ordinary life. It will, but you really don't want an ordinary life. You want a safe life, perhaps, but certainly not an ordinary life—whatever that is. What you actually fear is that you will no longer find your familiar life attractive or interesting. You fear that you will lose interest in living on Earth if, in fact, you realize that your soul can channel grace, heal others, and talk with God. That would change your world to something quite unordinary, indeed. But now that you know that could be you, would you really want to go back to being ordinary?

Soul Work: What is your definition of an ordinary life? Using your spiritual journal, go back to your earliest recollections, decade by decade. Describe in detail what you wanted out of life then and what you settled for because you were afraid to change or to trust that change would be for the good. Imagine yourself assigned now to a fully ordinary but safe life—is that your vision of contentment and fulfillment of your soul's highest potential?

THE EIGHTH ROOM:
Practice Illumination in the Moment

Every day brings something that can allow a reptile into your soul. Practice illumination—bring light onto that which appears dark—until it becomes as natural as breathing. Be a source of illumination for a soul companion. You have many gifts in your soul, one of which is to help another see what he or she cannot because of fear of loneliness. Practice illumination in the moment: pause and consciously reframe what you are looking at in a window of light. Find God in the details in conversations, passages in literature, vistas in nature, and difficult situations.

Soul Work: Practice on a situation that caused you to lose power today. Stay with it until the reptile is gone from your Castle. Find the hand of the divine, the gift in the event. Even if the event is brutal, imagine that, on some level beyond which your mind can reach, the laws of the universe promise that all will come into balance. Then think of something insignificant, like a stranger you may have noticed at a restaurant. Recall that stranger now and illuminate his face. Shine your grace upon him and think, "I do not know who you are and I may never see you again, but today I did see you. We shared the same space and I am sending you grace." You will delight in such a practice as the grace will fill you as well.

COMMITMENT TO GOD

Imagine that you are a trainer at a gym who is meeting with a new group of enthusiastic individuals, all of them novices at fitness training. They, of course, notice that you are in perfect physical condition, because you long ago mastered the discipline of the daily workout. In fact, you no longer consider your daily workout a discipline at all. It has become simply a way of life that maintains your vitality and stamina. As you prepare to give your new trainees an introduction into how demanding a body fitness program really is, you study their faces and wonder who among them is going to go the distance. You know that each one wants a beautiful, healthy body that will not break under pressure and can endure strenuous demands. But not everyone has what it takes to make the commitment.

The first thing you tell your trainees is that the most difficult part of developing body fitness is committing to a daily routine. If they take even one day off—just one—they'll need a week's recovery time. "Suffer not one exception," wrote William James. Do not stray from the path or stop the motion under any circumstances, for you will find it all the more difficult to start again and again and again. You warn them that the early days of the commitment are the most difficult, as expected, because they will want to see the results of their efforts immediately—weight loss, better muscle tone, and greater physical strength. But they have to be willing to put time into the program without seeing results in the early days. Genuine transformations do not come easily. Success in anything has a very simple formula: commitment to the goal, faith in the outcome, and trust in the trainer.

Watching their faces as you brace them for the long journey ahead, you wish you could find a way to let them step inside your body to sample, just for a minute, how extraordinary a perfect body feels. One minute, or even thirty seconds, or even less than that in your body would be enough to convince them that showing up at the gym each day and going through their daily routine is going to pay off.

Teresa herself struggled to explain the mystical reality of the soul and its journey on a path of prayer until she found the perfect metaphor in the Castle. Even so, she knew that her nuns, and all people on the mystical path, would find it extremely challenging to make the commitment to enter their Castle each day, because the First and Second Mansions are, in her language, "arid." In the initial weeks if not months of self-exploration, after numerous instructions about self-examination, after constantly setting traps for your reptiles, you may feel as if you're undergoing a daily dose of self-torture. Instead, think of your work in the Castle as setting time aside each day to enter into another reality. Don't think of your Castle as a discipline. Remove that association from the Castle and make entering it one of the most pleasurable parts of your daily life—even when you are searching for your reptiles. If searching and destroying or purifying doesn't please you, think of it as capturing and releasing. Imagine that you are discussing the subject matter of each room directly with the divine, allowing all your senses to participate fully in the conversation. Let the communication take all forms: energetic, multisensory, imaginative. What a precious gift you are giving to yourself. Open yourself to quietude and, above all, prepare with prayer for all dialogues with God.

A Moment of Contemplation

Think of your journey into the first mansions of your Castle as ascending from relying on simple intuition to receiving grace and illumination. Dismiss your old, illusory fears about isolation, alienation, and not being able to survive in the everyday world. All of that is your mind creating reasons for you not to pursue a genuine spiritual life.

Think of your life as it is now. What would you like to change about it? What would you release from your past? What fears would you let go and what negative attitudes or jealousies would you exorcise if you had the chance? Would your life be better or worse if you were free of your fears? Whether or not you continue on to meet God, your life would be much richer without the reptiles in your soul.

One way or the other, you are destined to make this journey—that is the divine paradox. You cannot avoid confronting yourself, no matter which path in life you take. Your only real choice is whether you walk that path as a lonely body or as a body with a soul.

Exploring Your Commitment to the Divine

THE FIRST ROOM:
My Expectations of God

Everyone carries expectations of God. You expect God to answer your prayers. You expect a miracle if you pray long enough or light enough candles or make a pilgrimage to a sacred spot. You expect God to provide an abundant life for you. You expect God to be fair, to be just, and to follow the rules of earthly law and order. You expect God to be a benevolent employer, and when things do not go as expected, you expect God to provide you with an explanation. You expect to see meaning and purpose in everything you do. Your expectations of God are endless, a reflection of the expectations we project onto one another—an ego spirituality.

Soul Work: Expectations are the ego's way of holding God accountable. They block surrender and trust. What do you expect from God? Do you feel entitled to a job? To a home? To good health? Do you expect protection? Physical abundance? Physical healing? Purpose and meaning in all that happens to you?

Visit this room to examine and process your disappointments when your expectations are not met. What did you expect from God whenever you were disappointed?

Pray for guidance in approaching all that comes in each new day without expectations. When you are disappointed, come to this room and pray to release your expectations of God. Leave this room when you feel that you are once again centered in the truth that all expectations are a projection of the ego and an act of fear.

THE SECOND ROOM:
A Spiritual Journey Is Irrational

Perhaps some part of you is fighting the whole notion of a devoted spiritual path precisely because you are a logical, rational individual in a modern world. In a spiritual journey, you use irrational, invisible means to search for an even more invisible soul. You are operating on faith that there is something inside you other than your imagination—something beyond your mind, beyond your body, beyond your emotions, beyond your ego.

Soul Work: What sabotages your spiritual journey? How do you generally sabotage yourself? Why does a spiritual commitment not make any sense to you in terms of the life you lead? Identify the voice of self-sabotage, of self-defeating thoughts and behaviors. This is the archetype of the inner saboteur, who is a formidable opponent on your path. You need to learn its methods, its way of attempting to exhaust you and distract you from your commitment. Be alert in this room.

THE THIRD ROOM:
Do You Feel Called to a Mystical Path?

Only you can decide if you feel called to a mystical path. You can ask, as many have, "But how do I know for sure and what do I do about it?" but my answer is always the same. If you said yes, I do believe I am a mystic in the world, or if you said, no, that's not me—what would change about your life? Would you pray any less? Would you be any less kind? Would you feel that your physical world and all its goods would be more secure? Your physical world would not change at all, whether you answer yes or no to that question. Or would it?

Soul Work: The defining question that says it all is: Do you want to read about God or do you want to *experience* God? If you are seeking the *experience* of God, then you have crossed the spiritual Rubicon. If you are still content to read about God, you are but sitting on the riverbank. In this room, dialogue with your soul on what experiencing God means to you. To do this, you must go beyond a quick definition and image the *experience* of God. Drift into that thought, pray into that thought, let yourself meditate on that image, moving your understanding of experiencing God throughout every cell of your body.

THE FOURTH ROOM:
Committing to the Divine

In this final room, the dialogue is between you and God. You enter this room to dwell on surrender and commitment to the divine. If you are able to make this leap, release your life into the embrace of the divine. Do not give up even if you cannot do it. Keep praying. The door to the soul is prayer.

Teresa was extremely compassionate in her understanding of how difficult it is to utter the prayer of unconditional surrender. You know in your soul that prayer is difficult because it is so powerful. You know it will shift the direction of your life. People hold back on that prayer as if they are withholding a cosmic permission slip that will prevent God from tampering with their lives. They cling to the illusion that somehow in this wildly chaotic world where nothing is stable, they are still in charge of at least one thing because they haven't uttered that prayer—they think they are in charge of God.

A Moment of Contemplation

Soul companionship, inner vision, the practice of illumination, and commitment to the divine create an extraordinarily rich texture for the soul in the Second Mansion. Practice illumination as part of your daily life. Look for God in the details and shed light on darkness at every opportunity. Take time in prayer so that you can open to and consciously receive grace. Imagine yourself surrounded by a community of soul companions. Just as like-minded people are drawn to one another, so are light-minded. Trust in the workings of the divine behind the scenes of your life.

Exit Prayer

I am a channel of grace. As I leave my Castle, grace surrounds me and protects me. I enter my life under the blessing of God and I remain open to receive guidance from my soul.

THE THIRD MANSION

Surrender: The Defeat of Reason/The Presence of God

Oh, humility, humility! . . . whenever I hear people making so much of their times of aridity, I cannot help thinking that they are somewhat lacking in [humility].

—*The Interior Castle*, Peers

No outward trial really matters. We should become stronger and stronger through our experiences, until we are able to stand among those of whom it may be said that their conquest of self has been final, needing no further testing.

—*Sri Gyanamata* ("Mother of Wisdom")

G OD MUST HAVE A REASON for everything," said one woman to me during a workshop. I said, "Really? Why?" My response baffled her, frightened her, and then finally she decided I was teasing her.

"Oh, come on, you know God does everything for a reason. I mean, how else could he run this universe? Nothing would make sense otherwise. We just have to have enough faith to figure out what those reasons are."

I looked at her and realized that she was under a kind of spell, the enchantment of reason, and the God of reason. She relies on a God who orders this universe according to a map of very specific personal plans for every single person. Her adoration of reason was her means of counteracting the forces of random chaos or a more mechanical view of the universe and its natural systems. If you are in the path of a storm and your boat sinks, is the reason the boat sank due to the storm, or was it divine planning that made you take the boat out that day, ignoring the warnings that the weather was unsuitable for sailing? This woman would say that God had made the man do an unreasonable thing and take the boat out because that rationale is the only "reasonable" one that fits her theology of the nature of God.

In the Third Mansion, it is essential that you come to understand how you perceive the nature of reality, because that reflects the content of your mind—your beliefs, perceptions, and prejudices. Teresa of Ávila lived long before the Age of Reason, so, in her time, the soul was immanent—constantly present and active within the individual body, community, and nature. The divine, too, was a constant companion that infiltrated the whole of life, whether you were in a conversation with a friend, in a public meeting place, or in private thought and prayer. It was impossible to keep secrets from the active—though invisible—God in Teresa's theology. The reality of God was everywhere.

Since then, however, masters of logic and reason—Descartes, Locke, Hobbes, and others—broke the shackles of superstitions and Church influence. The scientific, empirical method came into its golden age, and rapidly changed the way everyone viewed reality and what is and is not true. Faith in personal perceptions and insights was no longer sufficient—those perceptions had to be reproducible or observable by others. Individual spiritual insights were not as valued as the mechanical and scientific breakthroughs that propelled European culture into global exploration, conquest, and industry. The official spiritual Trinity of the Church—love, compassion, and faith—was gradually replaced with the scientific trinity of logic, reason, and practicality. You and I are offspring of this later world and our minds and beliefs reflect these attitudes. The God of reason and reward reigns supreme. Believe me when I say that most people, including you, *need a reason for everything*—a reward in the equation—or else they consider a task hardly worth the effort and they won't budge. This is the myth of God that keeps you in an earth-based mental-spiritual life.

Many use the male pronoun for God because we actually believe that God is male. He is just like us only in larger proportions; for instance, we are loving creatures, so God is *all-loving*. We have a system of justice, so God must have an even more powerful system of justice on a cosmic scale. How could it be otherwise? This myth-based view of reality is spiritually immature, stuck in a vision of organic divinity and a child-father relationship. This is the kind of attitude to which Dante refers when he writes in *Paradiso,* "The senses [the mind] only can apprehend / what then becomes fit for intellect. / And this is why the Bible condescends / to human powers, assigning feet and hands / to God, but meaning something else instead."

It is not a simple matter to investigate the contents of your reality and to dismantle your myths, even when you *know* they may not actually be true. We cling to our myths because either we fear what will happen to us if we release them—our superstitious tendencies—or because we draw power from them—our need to have faith.

In the sixteenth-century Catholic world, theological debates were rampant. A rationalist tradition had been enormously influential for centuries, as was its opposite, the passionate pursuit of faith, the love of God-seeking. In the thirteenth century, Aquinas charted "the erotics of knowing," wedding intellect and affect, but Dante himself rebelled against intellectual theology, writing of "that collision with mystery, the dissatisfaction of the mind."

Teresa, too, grappled with the influence that the mind and its perceptions have over the soul. In the Third Mansion, Teresa envisions a last series of ego obstacles that you must face before you break through into mystical consciousness. Here you aim to understand how your mind perceives the nature of reality, since that reflects your mental attitudes about the universe—your world and the way it is—and about God. This is the final mansion of the earthly plane or material world, before you move into the Fourth Mansion, the turning point of your journey.

Teresa continually urges her readers to let go of the rational mind, to "leave our reason and our fears" and surrender to divine love, but she does so even more passionately in this mansion. Many mystics agreed with Teresa in that the "simplicity of contemplation [inner connection with God] may not be acquired through knowledge or imagination," as the author of *The Cloud of Unknowing* wrote. Even so, Teresa's description of God is less mystical in the Third Mansion than in the preceding two. Here, she describes God as "arid," dry, nearly absent, almost unavailable, but always present. In the Third Mansion, God is waiting for you to come closer; in the Fourth Mansion, God will meet you—and greet you—with mystical embraces at the door. Perhaps this aridity in the Third Mansion is because this is where you learn the limits of your intellectual perceptions and conceptions of God—their own aridity—and get beyond them to a fuller understanding.

A Moment of Contemplation

Again and again, you feel the mystery. Surrender is the ultimate test of the human experience. What are you actually surrendering to? How is a prayer of surrender supposed to change your life? What does it feel like to abandon yourself into the mystical arms of the divine? Christ Consciousness is a universal force, the energy of spiritual evolution, the realization within the individual soul that power, wisdom, and love must be balanced in the mind. With Christ Consciousness, you experience the unity of all the universe—yourself as part of a greater awakening to God as the universe and the universe as God. Christ Consciousness means that you empty yourself of ego so that the spirit can come in; as Jesus said, "Empty thyself and I shall fill thee." This is the consciousness of the third eye, the spiritual eye, which identifies the vision of the inner mind and receives information from higher sources. This is the consciousness you want to embrace in your Third Mansion, a consciousness that surpasses the rational mind.

In surrendering to God, you enter a state of consciousness in which you engage fully in your life. You are fearless, full of faith, and possessed by an active, mystical purpose. You live in the present moment. You follow guidance, releasing your expectations of what the outcome will be. You live with great faith but continue your devotion to inner work and evicting reptiles. Abraham, the Buddha, Jesus, Muhammad, and many others underwent profound transformations upon complete release of their "right" to direct their lives, when they gave up their illusions that they had a choice to follow or not to follow higher, divine directives. Your surrender tells God that you are ready for experiences that few others would understand and that you yourself may not understand. How much of your life do you really understand, anyway? Experiences that are not of this world are difficult to describe with the language of reason, but you, too, may have these experiences, and feel how they displace the lesser tensions, fears, and illusions of life.

Having mystical experiences, moments of quietude and illumination, has only enhanced my life, not detracted from it. As I wrestle with my journey through the Castle, I would rather be swept away into the embrace of a divine vision than left behind with those who wonder whether there is a God, whether their life choices matter. It fills me with great contentment to know that I do matter, and you matter, and each prayer matters—and I delight in surrendering to that truth. If experiences of mystical illumination reorder my life and priorities, and position the numinous before the rational, then I see no other direction ahead of me.

Many of Teresa's nuns did not proceed further than the Third Mansion in their spiritual lives, even with her—a living saint—residing among them to help them. Teresa does not reveal that directly; she praises the soulfulness of those who take their spiritual practice out into the world, living exemplary lives and practicing acts of charity. What good is faith without good works? she asks. To serve God by serving others is a worthy life purpose.

Still, your soul may not be satisfied with living a good life in the world. A soul that is driven toward mystical illumination will not stop its quest just because the mind cannot comprehend or process the journey. The soul will find its way. As Teresa noted, "How I wish ours [our reason] would make us dissatisfied with this habit of always serving God at a snail's pace! As long as we do that we shall never get to the end of the road. And as we seem to be walking along and getting fatigued all the time, for believe me, it is an exhausting road, we shall be very lucky if we escape getting lost. Do you think, daughters, if we could get from one country to another in a week, it would be advisable, with all the winds and snow and floods and bad roads, to take a year over it? Would it not be better to get the journey over and done with?" (*The Interior Castle,* Peers)

Enlightenment is the only authentic path—as it was for Teresa, the Buddha, Jesus, and other saints and spiritual masters of all traditions. Everything else is a detour. You are already on this path. Why not become conscious of it? Why not participate in your soul's life?

Perhaps you have yet to convince yourself of the logic of falling deeper and deeper into the mystical gravity field of your Castle. But your soul will still determine what occurs within you and around you. All your fears and all your denials will not change the fact that your life serves the needs of your soul and your soul's only pursuit is active illumination—not poverty, not chastity, not suffering, not isolation, but conscious, active illumination while you are in Earth School, in the physical world. Decide not to fear illumination.

Decide you will trust God. The alternative—to trust nothing at all, not your God, not your world, not your relationships, not growing older—is so desperately bleak. Openly declare your loyalty to the expansion of your consciousness. You have no other choice but to pursue your mystical awakening.

THE DEFEAT OF REASON

The pilgrimage into your Castle is not logical, since we can't prove that there is a soul. And by the same token, it isn't logically reasonable to pursue a mystical life. Nonetheless, it is still in your best interests to examine your attachment to the power of reason and logic and the ways in which they fuel arrogance, hubris, greed, self-righteousness, and anger. For instance, when you feel that bad things happen to you undeservedly, your mind wants to strike back. When your pride has been injured, you rationalize, making excuses for saying and doing what you want. A mind fueled by hurt pride will never stop harming other people until its owner develops a spirit strong enough to see beyond personal anger, so the challenge here is about becoming more conscious of what connects us all, rather than what divides us.

The logical mind asks, "Just tell me what to do to make a breakthrough into mystical consciousness. Surely there must be a simple method." Teresa would respond: Go back and start again from the First Mansion. I just told you what to do: Stop looking for a short cut. Stop always trying to beat the system. Instead, you need to beat that voice within you that continues to want to beat the system.

The logical mind is impatient. It wants the way to be clear, obvious, and simple. It wants results and thrives on guarantees. Logic and reason have shaped your God and your theology, a combination of a strong work ethic and an expectant prayer ethic of entitlement: If I pray hard enough and sacrifice enough, I deserve to have my prayers answered. If I'm a good person, I deserve not to suffer. If I do good in my life and pray, I deserve to be rewarded here on Earth with earthly rewards and in heaven with divine favors.

We relate to the cosmos as something we must constantly try to manipulate and outsmart. Books and seminars instruct people to focus, focus, focus their thoughts and their positive energies on simple seven-step or three-step or one-step methods that guarantee financial success, finding a soul mate, and recovering health. We're told that anything we want can be ours if we find the right mental alchemical formula. Even though many thousands of people—if not millions at this point—have tried to create their own universes through easy steps or positive attitudes, I've not seen evidence that they succeeded. The popularity of such teachings is a testimony to the fact that our culture practices "psychic narcissism," which has become an obsession.

The rational mind not only questions the soul's existence, it views faith as a liability, so it will try to impede your spiritual journey with one obstacle after another. Your mind demands a logical reason for surrender and also wants a guarantee that such an act of spiritual alchemy will not lead you to financial loss or ruin. Individuals who awaken to a thirst for God after having been brought up with an arid, logical, punitive God will have trouble surrendering. Such a mystical act is anathema to most Westerners' basic theology, which sees human beings as having dominion—rather than stewardship—over all other life. To the rational Western mind, no form of life but the human being has consciousness, and all was created to serve us or to be exploited by us. Even the God of this Western worldview falls into submission to the individual who maintains the God-given right to determine—according to his view of what God can and cannot do—which form of life has consciousness, which is worthy of protection, which is "higher" and which "lower."

The God of this rational world cannot conduct mystical acts

of illumination, miracles, apparitions, acts of inner revelations, and healings—only emotional, hysterical people would believe that such things are possible. Scientists since Descartes have denied even vestiges of emotion in animals—in spite of primates' bonding with their offspring—and intelligence—in spite of the fact that dolphins and whales do communicate. They test and retest animals and still only a handful of scientists will allow the (obvious) conclusion that animals do have intelligence. If reason works overtime to deny that any other life on Earth has attributes similar or common to us humans, in order to keep humans in a superior position, it follows that reason would also deny the soul a journey that begins in humility.

Reason can't comprehend the mystic's vision of the world— that the divine comprises the collective soul of humanity and all life. Such a view is a paradigm shift, dismantling the rationalist's entire scheme of reality. Could a lover of law and reason live in accord with the mystical truth that every single action generated by every life form affects the whole of the universe, from the subtle movement of a butterfly's wing, to the explosion of a bomb, to the grace released from a prayer said in the privacy of his bedroom?

The rational mind dictates that you cannot trust anyone, that this isn't a safe world, and that you must save for rainy days and retirement, put things under mattresses and in security boxes. Your mind will consider any inner guidance an emotional overreaction. It wants to study, strategize. It never wants to relinquish control to anyone or anything else without a guarantee that an act of surrender will pay off. Better to err on the side of caution and take the obvious, reasonable path: follow what you can see, touch, feel, hear, and smell. Everything else is illusion and foolishness, for who will protect you? Ultimately, the motivation of the rationalist is to be safe in a finely decorated bunker when the golden years finally arrive.

For the mystic, this is folly—divine paradox at its best—because what appears to be the safe, practical route is illusion; that path is the one you take when motivated by fear. The choices you make are always and only motivated by either faith or fear. To God, the choices you make are not as important as your motivations.

And Now You

Here in the Third Mansion, you must finally confront your core beliefs, your view of the world. Do you need a God that is logical, reasonable, and scientific—a God of law and order, right and wrong, good and bad, reward and punishment? When scientific rules fail to help you, do you then and *only then* turn to faith? Your mind may still need to cling to this image of a well-behaved God whose task it is to keep your life in order whether or not you want to enter the Castle. Many people need to believe in this God. I have addressed many audiences and heard one person after another—sometimes entire audiences—claim that they *know* that their God is fully contrived—that he can't be rational, well behaved, and follow a reward-and-punishment system based on their personal views of justice—and yet *they need to believe in that God*. In other words, they are consciously maintaining a made-up God. But they are unable to let go of that God and move on because they are not yet ready to let God become irrational, mystical, and spontaneous. To them, this would mean that God would also become unreliable and untrustworthy.

One man summarized the challenge quite well: "So long as I need God to play fair, I'll see God that way. If I'm a good person, then bad things won't happen to me. I need to believe that because it gives me some measure of control over my life and the things that might happen to me. If bad things do happen, then I'll deal with them. But I am not prepared to unscrew the bolts that hold the ground level of my world together by thinking about my relationship with God and my inner thoughts. I like my world simple. I like the rules simple. I do this; God does that. If I don't do this, God won't do that. That's enough for me. I can't go any further than that because I just don't want God to notice me. I look at it this way: God is like a landlord. If I pay my rent on time each month, there is no need to see the landlord and no chance of getting evicted. What's the advantage to changing that?"

People like this dear and very good man, who practice a fear-based faith with great devotion, do not realize that they are not able to control God. They basically don't trust God and so consciously put their faith in a God who plays by the "rules." They believe they're holding God to an arrangement that restricts the divine from conducting any outlandish apparitions, Lazarus-type resurrections, random partings of the Red Sea, or unannounced archangel-messenger deliveries—in short, any and all forms of divine interference that could possibly challenge their rational view of the world, except of course for emergency family miracles, which are allowed in cases where healings are required, especially for children. As a result of these common misconceptions of God's behavior, a culture of doubt arose around the domain of the soul, which gradually became the receptacle of superstitious, psychic waste material filled with anemic rituals, icon worship, and negative fundamentalist teachings about the end of the world.

So where are you in all this? You have your rational, grounded, left-brained relationship to the world, but you are also in the thick of a spiritual search, already making an exodus from the left-brained, locked-down reality. You have obviously established eye contact with the vast field of consciousness, but now you need to explore your construction of God. In the First and Second Mansions, you entered rooms in which you examined your behavior and your power struggles, your ego issues and your humiliated tender spots. But none of those rooms or their questions challenged you to examine the roots of your God myth and whether you can pull up those roots once and for all.

I don't want you to think that science and its pursuit of

knowledge are the enemy of the mystic. There is no enemy here, though it can seem that way. The pursuit of knowledge is as much a divinely ordained journey as is the pursuit of the soul. But the power of reason should not be pursued at the expense of the power of the soul. Some rationalists view the mystical realm as immaterial, insignificant, powerless, because they can't measure it. Mystical power can do little in the way of guaranteeing your physical comfort. In fact, mystical power cannot guarantee that it can move even one particle on Earth. But mystical power transcends all the fears that control the material world and frees you of your illusions. In the end, the God you believe in—*even if you don't want to believe in this God*—is a reflection of your power myths about the world.

Your mind, ego, and personality may not like even to admit, for example, that your loyalties are to a path of logic and reason. You may *want to* want to pursue a more mystical relationship to the divine, but when it comes to day-to-day decision making, you find that you simply cannot detach from an allegiance to the so-called facts on the table. You may even have prayed for guidance, and been shown what path to take in a dream or in an image or through intuitions, but when it came to actually taking action on intuitive guidance, you still couldn't make that leap into the unknown. This is exactly the type of crisis—the halting point—that the Third Mansion represents.

To be sure, this position of being half in one world and half in the other—having your soul at the door of mystical flight and your mind clinging to Earth with all its might—is a spiritual crisis. In the Third Mansion, you are neither a resident of the rational world nor yet fully in your soul. You are neither a believer nor a nonbeliever. You are living in a type of superstitious safe house where you can gain access to the divine when you need to but return to your old views and life in order to survive. But to enter into a mystical relationship with God means that you finally must let go of superstitious spirituality. You must let go of private agendas for personal safety and rituals of protection rooted in fear. You step out of the irrational attitude that you can control God and the world around you—and everyone in it. Finally, you can stop being afraid of your life and your world. Finally, you can learn about prayer and how to pray, move beyond praying for protection, for explanations of why things happen as they do, for the acquisition and protection of earthly goods. Mysticism in the Third Mansion is liberation.

But first you have to defeat the power that reason has over your life and bring it into line with your soul. The great scientist Blaise Pascal wrote, "Faith certainly tells us what the senses do not, but not the contrary of what they see; it is above them, not against them." And from *The Cloud of Unknowing*: "We begin to understand the spiritual where our sense-knowledge ends. . . . We most easily come to the highest understanding of God possible in this life with the help of grace, where our spiritual knowledge ends."

As you enter into the rooms that belong to this mansion, you are shifting your life's direction a few degrees simply by approaching a dialogue with your soul. But, even as you read this, you can feel that old gravitational pull of reason dragging at your feet.

A Moment of Contemplation

Take a moment to breathe into the image of the Castle and to rise out of the heavy, mental plane. Breathe your awareness out of your mind and throughout the full energy field of your body. Feel the power your mind has over you, how much authority that rational voice carries within you. It can drown the softer whisper of your soul. But your mind is a precious gift. Imagine its energy aligned with the vision of your soul.

Breathe easily. Be still. Remind yourself that you are in the Third Mansion of your Castle. You are preparing for mystical consciousness. Know that you can limit the influence of reason and logic over you. You can experience a transcendent force of love that embraces the whole of humanity, transforming the individual heart into the heart of the sacred. Do not fear the loss of familiar ground beneath your feet. You never lose ground through mystical vision. You only see more and become more. This is the nature of the illuminated path.

Entry Prayer

I cross the bridge into the silent bliss of my Castle. I close the drawbridge and forbid all outside influences from entry into this holy place that is my soul. Here in my Castle, I am alone with God. Under God's light and companionship I discover the depth and beauty of my soul. I embrace the power of prayer. I open myself to divine guidance. I surrender myself to become as a channel for grace, healing, and service as God directs my life.

The Rooms of Reason

THE FIRST ROOM:
Awakening to Discernment

Everyone is quick to judge, which is why it is essential to develop discernment, the refined capacity of reason. Discernment opens a channel for grace. Negative judgments come from fear and insecurity, from not wanting another to be your equal, from not wanting to acknowledge someone else's accomplishments, or from not wanting something new to initiate change. With discernment, you practice detachment. Instead of looking through the lens of your personal vulnerabilities, the discerning eye is objective. You gain discernment by becoming aware of the reasons why you judge and why you fear what is new and different. Since the divine only speaks to you through new perceptions, you need discernment in order to recognize when and how you are being guided.

S*oul Work:* Developing discernment takes work. Being discerning is not just about not judging others or being more open to change. Practicing discernment represents a commitment to the practice of wisdom—a way of thinking that relies upon truth as its foundation. Your decisions and choices are anchored in truth and in principle. A wise life is a simple life, as many spiritual traditions have taught.

In this room, you are asked to reflect upon wisdom teachings and apply them to your life. You may choose from any tradition. Select one teaching and work it into the daily activity of your life, and bring it to mind particularly whenever your judgmental nature surfaces. Apply wisdom instead of judgment. Afterward, return to this room and note in your journal the difference between viewing life judgmentally and with the help of discernment. This practice will change your life.

THE SECOND ROOM:
The Power of Reason versus Forgiveness

Of the many challenges for the reasonable mind, few are more difficult than forgiveness. For a culture that believes in law and order, it is difficult to accept the spiritual imperative to forgive. Forgiveness is, in fact, the most irrational spiritual task you could be given because it stands in direct opposition to all that you have been taught about fairness and justice. And of all the many injuries that are difficult to forgive, among the most difficult is being humiliated. But forgiveness is a mystical necessity. The mind cannot fulfill such a divine order and in fact rebels against it, tossing out justifications for remaining unforgiving while telling us we *should* be forgiving. A true act of forgiveness is a leap into mystical consciousness, an initiation by choice into divine trust.

Soul Work: Your soul is inherently forgiving. We struggle with forgiveness because we *want* to forgive. It is an effort to be bitter and unforgiving. Such negativity does not come naturally; it has to be fueled and the source of that fuel is your mind. You must continually give yourself reasons to remain angry. You have to re-live memories and traumas in order to keep the fires of rage burning. Granted, some traumas are so deep that they pursue you and require special healing; but even these enormous wounds need to be released. At some point, you need to silence your reasons for not forgiving and turn toward the mystery of forgiveness.

In this room, reflect on the difficulties you face with this challenge. With each act of forgiveness, your mind will produce a list of pro's and con's. Pride always plays a role. It is for you to examine each situation and decide for yourself whether you are prepared to withdraw your soul from the battlefield and enter into the healing mystery of forgiveness.

THE THIRD ROOM:
You Create Your Reality: Illusions, Superstitions, and Spells

In order to survive mentally and physically, you have organized an archive of how things are and how they should be in your universe—that is, what can and cannot happen; what is true and what is not true; what should and should not happen; what you can tolerate and what you cannot endure. In your mind you have an entire worldview about reality. Many of your beliefs qualify more as superstitions; for example, you add phrases such as *God forbid,* or *God willing,* or *knock on wood* at the end of sentences. Superstitions and spells are reptiles of the mind. They compete with divine guidance. They control your consciousness and unconscious and can outrun even the sharpest intellect. To admit to being superstitious is difficult for an educated mind. You are caught between worlds: The mind longs to be rational, yet it must contend with an instinctual spirituality.

By now, you recognize beliefs that are illusions but that actively choreograph events or relationships in your life. For example, a phrase such as, *If he ever leaves me, I'll just die,* qualifies as an emotional illusion. You won't die if someone leaves you. You may *want* to die, or you may want to make that other person think you are going to die, but you won't die. "I must earn at least $250,000 per year in order to live comfortably. I don't know how people make it on less than that," one woman said to me. That is an illusion; she could live on $25,000 a year, or even less, *if she had to.* People do this all the time. "I simply have to live by the ocean in order to be peaceful." Again, this is a preference, an illusion. You do not *need* the ocean for tranquility. You may *want* to live near the ocean, but do not tell yourself that your soul requires the ocean in order to reach enlightenment. You attain enlightenment by detaching from the burden of such illusions.

Soul Work: Respect your mind's intellectual capacity, but recognize its capacity to manufacture illusion. The mind will cling to irrational ideas and false beliefs in order to *prevent* the expansion of its own field of vision. Examine how you do this with the illusions, superstitions, and spells you nurture within your mind, knowing full well that none qualifies as *truth.* On your soul's journey, you are in pursuit of truth. You must be dedicated to dismantling illusions—the reptiles that consume you from within and cause you to negotiate and compromise the guidance you receive from your soul.

Do you listen to your soul and respond to its guidance? Which controls you, truth or illusion? Identify ten illusions—ten active, powerful, self-imposed beliefs that you treat as truth but know are illusions. Describe how their authority influences your life. Then detail how your life would change if you dismantled those illusions.

Grapple with this challenge: Even though illusions control you, do you still consider yourself rational? How do you reconcile being a reasonable person with your superstitions?

In this room, describe in detail the beliefs out of which you create your own reality. This exercise will take you days if not weeks of observation, prayer, and contemplation. You need to observe the way you structure your thoughts; the way you see the world; the manner in which you have to have the world operate. Make this a regular practice. For example, I often hear people dismiss the mounting evidence of the drastic effects that global warming is having on the environment. In their reality, the environment is just fine and will always be just fine. They dismiss the bad news coming from environmentalists as just liberal political hype—or are the facts simply too painful for them to consider?

To begin this practice, take one illusion and "live" its dismantling. Bring it into the public arena of your life and break it down as your mystical practice in the world. For example, one person came to terms with the fact that she felt entitled to a much better life than she had. She believed she was entitled to more money, to a better marriage, to a better home—to *more*. Dismantling the myth of entitlement became her practice. She took it into the streets of her life and began observing when this myth was animated in her psyche—that is, when she became envious of what others had or angry because she felt entitled to something that was lacking in her life. She unraveled one realization about herself after another, but she bravely stuck to her commitment because she did not want to suffer from this inner demon any longer. As she said to me in an extraordinary moment, "You know, I have never truly been happy for anyone else. No kidding. I have no idea what it feels like to celebrate joy for anyone else because I have always felt that until I get what I feel I am entitled to, I refuse to be happy for anyone else. I was this angry girl pouting at God. I can tell you that it is a great burden to not feel joy for others and that is a suffering few people ever talk about. It's a ferocious way of being selfish. I needed to be done with that and I was determined to rid myself of this demon, of this reptile, if it was the last thing I did on this Earth."

Observe and then take action on your personal myths. Observe how your life changes. When do you interfere with allowing the old to die and the new to come forward? Pay attention to whether you do more to keep your illusions alive or to dismantle them. You always want your choices to make more room for the power of truth. Nothing changes, nothing heals, if you don't take action. All the insights in the world will not further your awakening if you don't act on them.

THE FOURTH ROOM:
Your God Is Better Than Any Other God Because . . .

Even though we have taken the template of the Castle from a Catholic mystic as a map, our journey is not about becoming Christian or Catholic. It is about finding our soul, the universal soul, and God.

Competition in the God marketplace is a primary cause of war and of personal conflicts. "My God is better and more powerful than yours." You may not want to admit that you hold such a thought, and yet you must examine your belief patterns for your particular illusions about your particular God. After all, few grow up in a religion that promotes the equality of all the faiths in the world. Quite the contrary; everyone who grows up in a religion grows up in prejudice. Several people I know saw themselves as being above conflicts such as religious differences— until they got married and had a child. Then religious war broke out between families as both sides fought over which religion would gain custody of the newborn's soul. Let's face it, it is difficult to stay rational when discussing God as your primary base of power.

Soul Work: God has many expressions, many teachers, and many scriptures. The entire world is a divine scripture, unfolding like cosmic prayer. Mystics can perceive such a universe and some wrote about such visions. In one line from the poem, "True Wealth," the poet Tagore describes cosmic wealth as, "the simple blade of grass sits on the same carpet with the sunbeam and the stars of midnight." In other words, each of us is enriched by the presence of God everywhere, in every blade of grass, in every beam of light, in every prayer, and in every truth in every scripture.

Are you able to see the truth in all scriptures? Are you able to see God in all teachings and religions, not from a distance, but through reading the various teachings to appreciate the many languages of the divine? This is a room for the rich work of coming to know the God of other traditions. Select various sacred texts and use them for study and reflection. Write down the wisdom each tradition has in common, that is, the universal voice of God. Ask yourself how you feel about the tradition you are studying compared with your own. If there is even the slightest feeling of superiority, then "you have miles to go before you sleep."

THE FIFTH ROOM:
My Power Myths and Rituals of God

Everyone has power myths about God. You have power objects—rosaries and prayer beads, medals and rituals—that you believe influence the divine's actions and behavior. This isn't rational, of course, but a combination of attachment, habit, superstition, and faith. Yet, these myths can influence you more than the guidance of your soul. Such rituals that ask for divine influence beg the question, "Are you trying to control heaven?"

Soul Work: Identify a minimum of five power myths and rituals related to how you believe you influence the divine and keep your personal cosmos in order. For example, one person carries a holy card of a painting of Jesus in his wallet for protection against "financial ruin, illness, accidents, and bad luck." He believes that as long as he keeps that holy card on him as a show of faith, God will prevent any of those catastrophes from happening to him. Rational? Not at all; but our minds believe what we program them to believe. When I asked him what would happen if he "surrendered" his holy card as an act of faith, he turned pale and said, "I do have faith. I have faith in this holy card and I am not giving it up for anything." This man could not even discuss the idea of mystical surrender.

When do you turn to your power myths and rituals out of faith and when do you turn to them out of fear? Describe the difference between your feelings and your inner dialogue when you are responding with faith and when with fear. What would it mean, what would happen, if you surrendered your power myths and rituals? Can you see yourself finally tossing aside these illusions? Can you see yourself releasing your irrational illusions of God?

THE SIXTH ROOM:
Your Struggle with Doubt

Doubt is an ever-present force with which we must contend all the days of our lives. Even the great mystics suffered through periods of doubt and despair. One day we feel so secure on our path, and within an instant—one phone call, one letter—that security is shattered. Doubt influences the rational mind, causing indecisiveness, depression, procrastination, and illness. Doubt is often self-generated, a convenient way to avoid making a decision and to hold your life in suspended animation. You seem to be making a choice; you are almost to the point of choice; just a few more details; you'll get there soon. You recognized the best route for your soul within seconds of arriving at the crossroads. "First thought—best thought" is a Zen attitude that is good to recall when listening for the soul's voice. Your soul is faster with its guidance than you are with manufacturing doubt. Doubt is a result of receiving guidance, not a method of preventing it. But you do not always want to act on that guidance. How can you surrender your need to feed your doubts?

Soul Work: Describe your struggle with doubt. What do you doubt about God and the purpose of your life? What brings you to moments of doubt in your everyday life? What do you need to experience to alleviate doubt? In the past, when you were plagued with doubts and then those doubts and fears were lifted from your life, was your first thought that God had intervened? Or was that a later thought? How often does your doubt-to-faith pendulum swing? How easily is doubt activated for you?

Enter deeply into prayer and contemplation to examine the doubts you hold about surrendering. What doubts do you have about yourself within the mystical experience? What do you fear? Where do you feel you will lose control of your life? Do you doubt that you can return to your ordinary life and assume "normalcy" while nurturing a mystic's soul?

THE SEVENTH ROOM:
Faith versus Reason: Your Castle Library

To have faith is a struggle—period. Even Jesus lost faith momentarily while dying on the cross, crying out, "Father, why have you abandoned me?" Faith is unreasonable and our rational minds are skilled at "proving" with facts that faith is foolish. In the face of a diagnosis of terminal cancer, for instance, how can one have faith in the healing power of prayer and grace, given the scientific statistics? But spontaneous remissions and remarkable recoveries do occur.

In your Castle library, you keep a small notebook that contains beliefs that you very much want to animate with faith but have not yet been able to. You want to be like the mystics, like young Bernadette, who were given divine visions or audible messages and followed their instructions without asking, "But why?" We all want to believe more than what we do believe. We want to have faith in our guidance. And the mystics reassure us, as the Buddha taught, "On life's journey, faith is nourishment and virtuous deeds a shelter."

Soul Work: Think deeply about the many tributaries to the divine that you would love to follow unconditionally. Include among them divine instructions that seem simply unreasonable, such as forgiving people who have offended or harmed you and turning the other cheek. Contemplate the mystical meaning of forgiveness and turning the other cheek, which help you manage the power of your soul so that you do not waste it on an illusion or in contending with the negative force of another person. You *must* have faith in order to act on these instructions precisely because they are *unreasonable.*

You cannot excavate all the many memories and conflicts of faith and reason that you carry within you in one visit to this room. Observe your actions in your outside life for conflicts that surface now that you have given them permission to appear.

THE EIGHTH ROOM:
Your Call to Service / Your Struggle with Service

Service takes many forms, as I learned when I wrote *Invisible Acts of Power*. It can include community service, working on behalf of the homeless, attending to the needs of your family with more compassion, putting aside ten minutes a day or an hour a week to pray for others. Service requires that you give of yourself in a way that stretches you beyond your comfort zone and improves the lives of one or even many others. As I emphasized in the beginning of this book, mystics changed the world and many never left their monasteries, or left only for very brief intervals. The power of their souls and their faith did most of their work in the world for them. Service at the mystical level is about devotion, dedication, and maintaining faith in the governing laws of the universe, pouring grace and praying into the world. As the author of *The Cloud of Unknowing* wrote, "Your fellow men are marvelously enriched by the work of yours, even if you may not fully understand how."

Being of service in the world is an expression of your soul's purpose—your purpose. Service to one is service to life. People who cannot become fully devoted to the mystic path must still put their awakened souls to work, and can choose lives of service in the world.

You have already begun an active service in your life if you are on a spiritual path. You are already attuned to the needs of people around you and to the environment. Your sensibilities have already expanded. But your soul will never let you rest— never. It will never be content with becoming comfortable. Your soul will always lead you into situations where you would rather not be because that is the means through which your soul expands its skills in the physical world. Your rational mind will fight those soul instructions; you probably are already fighting instructions to venture into new territory.

Soul Work: What and where can you serve and where would you draw the line? Are you conscious of having interfered with guidance that told you to serve because you did not like the instructions you received? And the reason? Were they too humbling? Do you think of service as something that must be convenient? Do you see service as having to be physical or action-oriented?

Enter into a deep state of prayer. Listen to your soul instruct you about its capacity to serve. What are your soul gifts, the gifts of service you have yet to discover? Return to this meditation until you uncover ten gifts within you that you have never, ever identified before. These can be gifts inherent in your personality or talents—a gift for listening and empathy, for instance, or for music or art or cooking or sewing. You must identify and describe them using three full sentences per gift. This will ground them and bring them into your consciousness.

THE NINTH ROOM:
An Unreasonable Prayer: A Mystic's Bliss

Your soul long ago took the lead on your life's journey and is pulling you toward the divine. But at this point, you must give the reins of power over to your soul. See yourself moving from your rational mind to the center of your being—your inner chamber—and consciously, fully enter your soul.

Soul Work: Go into your soul and visualize yourself as a mystic. Breathe into that imagery. Turn off the sounds and power of your rational mind. Enough of that distraction. Enough. Simply pray. Release your soul. Imagine yourself beyond your body, beyond this Earth, beyond this life. Pray without effort into a mystic's bliss.

THE ARCHETYPAL DESERT IN THE SOUL

An arid God is associated with the desert, where Jesus wandered for forty days and the Jews for forty years. The archetypal struggle of those sent to the desert is simple: Not my will, but thine. You are left to wander for as long as is necessary until you finally are able to relinquish control over the path of your life.

But what does that mean? Surrender is a mystical, archetypal ritual of transformation. In it and through it the authority of your life shifts from your ego-rational mind to your soul-mystical vision. Individuals who have undergone complete journeys of transformation are always renamed, given a spirit name. No longer are they addressed by the name of their ego identities. Jesus is the man: Christ is the soul. Siddhartha is the man: Buddha is the soul. The mystical act of surrender repositions the compass of your life's journey, pointing you away from the plans you had in your mind to the plans most suited to the capacities and talents of your soul. Of course, your life changes completely whenever you make any significant life choice, mystical or otherwise, but the difference here is that in your archetypal surrender to the divine, you give up what human beings cherish most: control and (the illusion of) power. In *The Imitation of Christ,* Thomas à Kempis wrote, "The road a man must walk is not always of his own choosing. It belongs to God."

Imagine that you are alone in a desert. Or go into a desert if you can, or a forest, or any other place where you can be completely alone, without the distraction of cell phones, computers, or people. Feel, imagine, sense your soul expanding outward— larger and larger—until the Earth is so small that it can fit in your hand. And now wait for the divine to come find you. Contemplate the fact that this life is so brief, so quick. It is gone "in the swish of a horse's tail," as Confucius wrote. The planet is so small. And you are so grand, so eternal, and have so much to give. Into whose hands shall you place your spirit—those of the people on this tiny planet or those of the divine, who has sent you here for a higher purpose?

Here in your Third Mansion, you must decide whether you are ready to contain mystical consciousness. In the words of the artist Charles Dubois, "The important thing is to be able at any moment to sacrifice what we are for what we can become." Do you really want to return to the temporary comforts of an ordinary life? Imagine a life without mysticism, mystical vision, and divine mystery. Imagine a life without miracles. Imagine a life without divine intervention. Imagine a life in which higher purpose and meaning mean nothing; imagine a life devoid of your Castle, in which you are soulless. If you can go deeply enough into your Castle, you can liberate yourself from your fears and truly come to know that you are watched over and guided down to the smallest detail of your life. The rational mind cannot comprehend this mystical truth, but once you accept it fully, you will have gone far enough to cross the desert.

Teresa would tell you, as she told her nuns, to go further. Do not rest. This journey is inevitable. There comes a point when resting becomes more difficult than keeping on the journey itself, for you know what you are giving up. Cross the mystical Rubicon. Surrender and let God reorder the flow of your life. You aren't leaving your life; you are reentering your life . . . soul first.

A Moment of Contemplation

Teresa did not have to struggle to make a case for the existence of the soul. It was already a living companion for people of her time. Teresa also used words that belong to the soul, that stir the soul, wake it up and bring it to attention, invite it in to give counsel. We have dismissed or retired much of the soul's vocabulary, putting our souls under a gag order.

Words such as *miracle, grace,* and *prayer* are part of a sacred, potent, alchemical language that awakens the soul. Words are power. They are the conduits of consciousness and the building blocks of reality. The ancient mystics knew the power that the words *in each prayer* contained to open their souls to divine consciousness. To understand the language of the soul and to know how to use that vocabulary in prayer, in healing, and in channeling grace is to truly unlock the power of your soul. For example, the prayer of surrender, "Thy Will Be Done," can be translated to mean, "I ask for the courage to step out of my own way, to not interfere with Your plans so that Your grace and love can pour through my actions, words, and deeds this day. Let me see each person as a vital and blessed part of my life. Let every action and thought I have today serve all."

The following prayer, from *The Cloud of Unknowing,* may be helpful:

> When you feel utterly exhausted from fighting your thoughts, say to yourself: "It is futile to contend with them any longer." . . . In doing this you commend yourself to God . . . You make yourself completely supple in God's hands . . . When this attitude is authentic, it is the same as self-knowledge, because you have seen yourself as you really are . . . less than nothing without God. This is, indeed, experiential humility. When God beholds you standing alone in this truth he cannot refrain from hastening to you. . . . Like a father rescuing his small child from the jaws of wild swine or savage bears, he will stoop to you and, gathering you in his arms, tenderly brush away your spiritual tears.

Contemplations in the Desert

THE FIRST ROOM:
Into the Desert

You know what it is to feel alone and that you have been abandoned by God. You know what that arid presence feels like, the despair and doubt. Describe your desert. Walk into the boundless, open horizon of a dry, hot desert. Describe being overwhelmed by your isolation. As you imagine this desert, do other arid experiences of your life occur to you, times that led you to feel you were alone, without any support? There is nothing to fear in this desert but the voice of the mind. This desert is the prelude to surrender, a physical breakdown before a mystical breakthrough.

THE SECOND ROOM:
Keeping Silence: I Recognize Your Voice, O God

Silence is the practice of holding grace within your soul. Contemplate where you feel grace being distributed to you. Follow the flow of grace to where it leads: What part of your inner life is being illuminated for you to examine? What is being asked of you? You are receiving guidance. Identify it here. Consciously recognize it in every part of your being, every sense, mind and body. For every prayer, there is a response. For every thought, there is a counterthought. For every action, there is a ruling of your conscience. You are never without divine guidance; you are never outside the orbit of divine sight. You have only to pay attention, to observe, to listen, to feel, and to respond. Responding heightens your senses and attunes you to your soul. Pay attention. You received it. Now accept it. Be quick. Respond from within your Castle.

THE THIRD ROOM:
Impatience

Everyone wants an immediate answer to a prayer. Everyone wants the answer to be obvious and safe. God is hidden, obscure, symbolic. You have to look for God. The more impatient you are, the more it seems that God is nowhere to be found. But "Nowhere spatially is everywhere spiritually," says *The Cloud of Unknowing.* You want your life to change, but not really. You want your life to change but only if someone else takes the risk for you, with you, on your behalf. You are impatient with the way life is and with yourself and your own nature. Why has God given you the blessings that you have as well as the challenges? Why do you have the talents that you have? And why do you lack others? Why are you not making the most of your abilities? Were you impatient when you were a child, a teenager, a young adult, middle-aged? Is it difficult for you to let God work out the details of your life?

THE FOURTH ROOM:
Your Mind Won't Stop Talking to You

You want to be quiet, to listen, to wait to receive the grace of quietude, but your mind won't stop chattering. Notice what your mind uses to distract you. When you turn your attention to God, what does your mind do to interfere? How does it compete with God? The *Book of Privy Counseling* recommends, "See that nothing remains in your conscious mind save a naked intent stretching out toward God. Leave it stripped of every particular idea about God (what he is like in Himself or in His works) and keeping the simple awareness that *he is as he is.*"

Visualize yourself in your Castle in a lovely setting—and see when your mind shows up to disturb that image. Whenever the mind distracts you, enter into prayer and withdraw from that distraction. Become stronger than the distraction. Practice this again and again, for your mind has had far more experience at getting your attention than has your soul.

THE FIFTH ROOM:
The God You Fear

You are now about to leave the Third Mansion and enter the Fourth, where the divine comes to you, calling you by name. Imagine that experience. Imagine not being able to run and hide behind a fear or a ritual or a distraction. Imagine having to admit that you recognize a mystical encounter with God. Imagine how that would change your life: Without doubt as a shield, you would have to become more conscious. Without doubt you would know that every one of your choices matters, that every action makes a difference to the quality of life on this Earth. To realize that your power is contained within God's power is frightening. To be called to live with a divinity so close at hand, so invisibly involved in the details of everyday life, is awe inspiring. But you have been called. How challenging is it to be unable to hide?

You are so near to crossing into mystical reality, but you still feel compelled to ask God, "Can I trust you to be fair with me?" If you come over to heaven's side of the bridge, if you surrender to a mystical path for the rest of your life, is there at least some reward? Can God be trusted to be fair? After all, you are considering giving it your "all," right? Ask yourself how you still bargain with God: Enter your soul and seek your need for rewards for being special or gifted. Bargaining with God is a reptile. Be conscious of it, as it can halt your soul's journey completely.

THE SIXTH ROOM:
Why Is This Life So Difficult?

Life is difficult—period. Whether you pursue a mystical path or not, you cannot avoid the challenges that life brings. Why life is difficult is a mystical question and the rational mind would never be content with a mystical response. Difficulties are created, in part, when the ego self and the soul do not communicate and work together. When you are living two lives—one for your ego and one for your soul—you are not congruent. Neither life is functional, neither life is complete or healthy. Where are you on this spectrum of congruence? How far apart is your ego self from your soul and your mind from your heart?

THE SEVENTH ROOM:
You Need God's Grace

You may wish to set up an actual space in your house as a physical representation of this particular room. In this room, you prepare for the mystical act of surrender. As you set up this room, whether physically or inwardly, your intention is to prepare for unconditional surrender to mystical consciousness. You are now at the door of the Fourth Mansion. In the next room is the meditation of surrender. To prepare, gather the sacred texts and inspirational literature you love. Read and write in your journal as you prepare for the most important mystical ritual of your journey. Your preparation may take weeks or even months. Before you go on to the Fourth Room, you may need to return to other mansions and go through them again. Open yourself to gifts of grace.

THE EIGHTH ROOM:
I Surrender

> Dear God:
> There is only one thing that I need to say. I surrender my life into your love and trust. My life has always been in your hands; how could it be otherwise? You could call me home to you now but you have kept me here on this Earth because I have work yet to do. I embrace this

mystical path. I release the illusion that I direct my life's path. I am ready to let my soul lead the way. I surrender.

A Moment of Contemplation

With your surrender, you mark a turning point in your soul's journey. Your entry into the Fourth Mansion is a transitional passage in your consciousness. Your interior life will deepen and your exterior life will change. Your soul will call you more deeply inward as its presence, its voice, and its grace become ever more tangible.

Exit Prayer

I am a channel of grace. As I leave my Castle, grace surrounds me and protects me. I enter my life and the world under the blessing of God and I remain open to receive guidance from my soul.

THE FOURTH MANSION

The Mystical Heart

Remember: if you want to make progress on the path and ascend to the places you have longed for, the important thing is not to think much but to love much, and so to do whatever best awakens you to love.

—*The Interior Castle*, Starr

THE CATHOLIC TRADITION has many icons and images of Jesus. One of them, the Sacred Heart of Jesus, shows Jesus revealing his heart wrapped in a crown of thorns. For most of my life, I found this particular image, and most other bleeding icons, to be hideous, but for some reason this one made me especially uncomfortable. Many people can just walk away from their early religious instruction and get on with their lives, but I am not one of them. That image stayed with me, and every time I met someone who had a devotion to the Sacred Heart of Jesus, I would wonder, What on earth are you devoted to? A heart with thorns? Why? I simply didn't get it. To worship a bleeding figure hanging on a cross was more than uncomfortable for me: It was visually so painful. I could handle the theology of the cosmic Christ, but not the bleeding, tortured Jesus. No, thanks.

Shortly before writing this book, I had a mystical vision. I saw an image of the sacred heart and watched it change into the mystical heart of the sacred. I had finally been shown a glimpse—just a glimpse—of the deeper, cosmic meaning of the mystical force of love, the Christ Consciousness, or greater consciousness. I had just the briefest moment of illumination in which I understood that, if that quality of love—transcendent, mystical, sacred love— could be channeled through human beings, so much of the madness in the world would be healed before our eyes.

INTO THE HEART OF THE SACRED

Mystical love is unleashed in your soul in the Fourth Mansion. We call this power love, but it is grander than love. Love is usually a very conditional emotion, but how many people have ever truly loved anyone without conditions? We speak of a love of humanity, but it's incomprehensible to love all of humanity. The personal heart is much too small a container for mystical love, which would shatter its walls. People actually fear becoming a channel of cosmic love, for fear of being asked to love too much and too many. Your soul knows exactly what I am describing. Pause for a moment. Take a deep breath and ask your soul how it would handle a transcendent love. Should an impersonal stream of love open up, would you still be able to love on a personal level, still be able to take care of your family, or would mystical love eclipse that? Many people fear this.

To be exposed to mystical love is the same as to be called to serve as a channel for that love. Mystical love cannot be contained within you. It bursts through you like bright light through a clean window. You simply cannot stop its force from changing the world. Yet, to describe mystical love as simply "love" is inadequate: It is an illuminated state of consciousness through which you comprehend the whole of life as a unified collective soul. Imagine—just imagine—being able to know that one of your prayers or a single loving thought affected all of life. That is the nature of mystical love—it transcends personal boundaries and forms a current that flows through you. Here in the Fourth Mansion, you are in the heart of the sacred, the mystical heart of the cosmos.

Entry Prayer

I cross the bridge into the silent bliss of my Castle. I close the drawbridge and forbid all outside influences from entry into this holy place that is my soul. Here in my Castle, I am alone with God. Under God's light and companionship I discover the depth and beauty of my soul. I embrace the power of prayer. I open myself to divine guidance. I surrender myself to become as a channel for grace, healing, and service as God directs my life.

For Teresa, entering the Fourth Mansion represented crossing yet another bridge, but this time it is inside the Castle, where you enter what she called "the realm of the supernatural." Finding words to convey adequately the experience of cosmic consciousness was frustrating for Teresa. Even today, with a sophisticated psychological and theological vocabulary, we still cannot convey the stratospheric ecstasies reported by mystics who have attained transcendence. Teresa, like most mystics, relied on the use of metaphors to communicate profound insights. To her, this state was as if a heavenly water began to flow from a deep inner spring, a source that has always been there. "As this heavenly water begins to flow from our very depths—[it] produces ineffable blessings, so that the soul itself cannot understand all that it receives . . . Very often . . . the effects extend even to the body." (*The Interior Castle*, Peers)

How will you enter the Fourth Mansion? You have gone deep in excavating your lower nature, expelling reptiles, discovering obstacles of earthly attachments to power and reason that lock

you outside your Castle. You have made your way through difficult passageways to a field of grace, preparing to receive God.

In the previous mansions, you were seeking God and had to
shore up yourself and your soul to remain on that quest. Now
you are ready to receive God. God is waiting for you in this mansion, waiting to fill your soul with luminous light that melts the
walls of the mortal heart, exposing you to the mystery of cosmic
love, cosmic consciousness that transcends any earthly form.
Love beyond the personal, beyond the self, beyond form and
name and place—love as an eternal conscious force that floods
through your being comes when God chooses to give it to you.
St. Augustine wrote, "Love made me what I am, that I may be
what I was not before." You must live *ready* to receive this love.
How do you do that? How do you live in readiness for cosmic
mysteries to envelop you spontaneously?

There's the proverbial wrong way and the right way. The
more you consciously prepare for God, paradoxically, the more
the ego gets in the way. You can begin to think you deserve a mystical experience because you've done all the exercises in all the
rooms, which is exactly what one woman told me: "I went
through all these exercises, just like you told me, and nothing
happened."

"Nothing happened? What were you expecting?"

"Well, I thought I at least deserved a healing or something."

The work undertaken in these rooms requires months of devotion work. Perhaps years. The mystical life is not a race to the
finish line.

Living in readiness for God in the "right way" means to live
within God consciousness, but without expectations of God.
This is the very definition of the conscious and humble life. One
man I know whose life embodies humility and divine awareness
sells home entertainment centers, a job that brings him into
contact with dozens of people each week. He envisions these
people as blessings that have come into his life to help him, and,
in return, he visualizes grace moving through all the compo-

nents that he sells to these people. He begins his day in prayer and ends his day that way and consciously but quietly works to bring peacefulness into his environment. "This requires that I always maintain a devotion toward maintaining my interior peace, so I live with one foot in the world and one within my soul." He expects constant guidance and love from the divine, "which is what everyone should expect," he says, and in fact what the divine provides, but nothing else. He lives in readiness to receive God.

There is no way to anticipate to whom God will come. You can attempt to describe who is most likely ready, willing, and able, but in the end, only God decides who and when and why. One man I know quite well would have been considered godless on the very day that he had his mystical awakening. He was a drug dealer and a thug who beat up people and collected money. While driving his car one day, he heard the voice of Jesus calling to him. He kept changing the radio stations, but Jesus came through each station. He ended up in a rented room in a dive hotel for three days, where he wept as he came to terms with how he had been living his life. He is very much a mystic in the world today, working as a personal fitness trainer and deeply devoted to his spiritual life. You can never, ever anticipate the actions of God, nor can you manipulate them by any actions of your own.

The images of walls, doors, and drawbridges serve as a full-sensory substitute for the soul. The physical image of the Castle can represent the soul until the soul itself becomes real. But in the Fourth Mansion, the image of the Castle itself evolves from that of a physical building to a metaphor of power and mystical authority. This is the seat of a celestial king and majestic cosmic presence—the divine in the center of your soul. The state of consciousness of the Fourth Mansion is where the power of your soul merges with the cosmic presence of God in a supernatural union, above and beyond earthly relationships. The Fourth Mansion represents your soul's integration into divine consciousness. Here, you are no longer consumed by mental chaos or distracted by earthly reptiles. In fact, reptiles cannot get into the Fourth Mansion. You have shifted your power from the external world in front of your eyes to the interior world of your Castle.

Yet, you can't stay in this Fourth Mansion state of consciousness full-time. In your inner dialogues with your soul, your focus now shifts from excavation to discovery. And you can now encounter the divine from within your Castle walls. Here in the realm of the supernatural, your mystical directive is, Prepare to receive God.

PREPARE TO RECEIVE GOD

Teresa describes patterns in human behavior that emerge around the business of God that are as true today as they were in her time. For instance, some aspiring medieval mystics would pray for days on end, fast, and do penance in an effort to make God come to them, but instead of entering a mystical state, they ended up collapsing from starvation or hysteria. Personal motives underlay these extreme behaviors; these aspirants were looking for favors from God, sacrificing themselves on their own altars in the hope that God would grant their petitions. Today, we have the same expectations, if not the same behaviors.

To God, she writes as a prayer, "Bear in mind what anguish we have to suffer on this path through lack of knowing the truth. The trouble is that since we think all we have to do is concentrate our thoughts on you, we can't even . . . comprehend how to frame the question in the first place. We suffer terrible trials because we do not understand ourselves. We worry about things that we think are bad but which are actually good things . . . This lack of knowledge afflicts many people who practice prayer. They complain of interior trials, grow depressed, and their health declines. They may even abandon prayer altogether.

These are people who have not learned to look inside them-selves and discover the inner world there. Can we stop the stars from hurtling across the heavens? No. We cannot stop the mind, either." (*The Interior Castle,* Starr)

Teresa is astutely aware of the relationship between the inte-rior life and health. She recognizes that we are prone to need to know too much too soon from God, which has emotional, physi-cal, and psychological risks. In my work, I have encountered countless people who are frustrated and even angry over a lack of response from heaven. One woman said, "I have lit dozens of candles, fasted, and said countless prayers and still I have no idea what to do with my life. I just don't get an answer from heaven or a sign or anything." Other people feel abandoned by God, hav-ing sought direction and heard nothing. "What should I do?" they ask me. Should they go on a pilgrimage? Should they quit drinking? What is the secret to making God come into your life when you call?

These people didn't doubt the presence of God *in general,* but they wanted to know how to call God *specifically in moments of need.* You cannot induce God to appear. At the same time, even though you may not think you see or hear him, God is always present. Even though you cannot invoke a mystical encounter, in the Fourth Mansion you are in an elevated state of consciousness that allows you to be present enough, courageous enough, to re-ceive the divine when it arrives. In this consciousness you live with an open heart, ready for a mystical encounter. Just as Teresa distinguishes between authentic and automatic prayer, she dis-tinguishes between the "consolations" and "spiritual sweetness" that result from prayer. We can be consoled through our medita-tions and supplications to God, or our actions, but this consola-tion is self-generated. Writes Teresa, "Solace arises from the virtuous acts we perform. It feels like we've earned it [our good feelings] through our own efforts. It is correct for us to feel con-soled when we act righteously."

But "spiritual sweetness [or grace] begins in God and makes

its way into our human nature where we delight in it far more than we enjoy the worldly kind of gratification." (*The Interior Castle*, Starr).

Spiritual consolations are like aqueducts, manmade waterways. Spiritual sweetness flows eternally from a divine source, requiring no human engineering. The water is abundant and endlessly fills the basin—meaning you.

Centering Prayer

Centering prayer is another Western contemplative practice that is very accessible and very similar to Eastern meditation techniques that use mantras, which are repeated words or sounds to focus the mind. Teresa of Ávila as well as the anonymous author of the great mystical classic *The Cloud of Unknowing* recommend a centering prayer practice to free the mind from all thoughts except those of God—and even from all your preconceived notions of God. *The Cloud of Unknowing* particularly recommends silently focusing on a one-syllable word, to exclude other thoughts or questions that arise while praying. *God* or *love* is best. But choose one that is meaningful to you. Then fix it in your mind so that it will remain there, come what may. This word will be your defense in conflict and in peace. If some thoughts just won't go away and persist in annoying you, just keep answering it with this one word. "Do this and I assure you these thoughts will vanish. Why? Because you have refused to develop them with arguing." Other words that are useful are *peace, Om, and one*. They carve a focus through your thoughts and create a deep peace and center of stillness into which the gift of God's presence— grace, divine love, and light—can flow. Scripture says, "A short prayer pierces the heavens," and *The Cloud of Unknowing* explains that this is "because it is the prayer of a man's whole being." Virtually every religion has such a practice, from Islam and Judaism to Buddhism and Taoism, and it works because you are praying with all the "height, depth, length, and breadth" of your spirit.

The stillness of mind and body that results from centering prayer allows you to connect with the mystery of God, beyond thought. It is a way to prepare to receive God.

A Moment of Contemplation

In a mystical experience, you are absorbed into the fullness of the moment, of the now, of eternity. You transcend the psychic weight of mortality and are lifted beyond time, beyond the restrictive boundaries of this life, and into the domain of timelessness *(kairos)* or the realm of the supernatural.

Each exercise you performed in the lower mansions helped you retrieve the fragments of your spirit that were scattered over the years and decades of your life. You retrieved them so that you can be whole and fully present in the moment, divested of the weight of your history, ready to receive the divine. The divine is timeless, the force of life in the fullness of the moment. The mystery of healing, the mystery of transformation, and the mystery of the mystical experience lie in understanding this essential truth: Empty your soul of its history. Retain love, wisdom, goodness, truth, as all these energies carry within them the people you love and the memories that make you who you are. Shed everything that leads nowhere and everything that continually repeats itself but serves nothing at all.

And then—prepare to receive God.

THE POWER OF YOUR COSMIC SOUL

Here in the Fourth Mansion, your cosmic faculties—the perceptual abilities of your soul—open and hold sway over your rational mind. As you become more conscious, your intuitive skills mature and begin to channel spiritual guidance. That is as far as your intuitive skills can take you until the opening of your cosmic faculties, which transcend personal matters and fears.

Cosmic perceptual faculties are the ability to receive—again, the operative word is *receive*—direct instruction, guidance, revelation, or a vision from the divine. Julian of Norwich saw beautiful images, for example. Hildegard of Bingen heard music, which she then put on paper. Francis of Assisi heard a voice speak to him. More contemporary mystics, such as Helen Schuckman, the late author of *A Course in Miracles,* heard a voice that identified itself as Jesus and took dictation from that voice for seven years. A perfect example of a mystic without a monastery, Helen was chosen by God to receive that very profound work on Jesus, even though she was a Jewish agnostic. The details of your earthly identity don't matter—God will grant favors to anyone he chooses, for that is the nature of God. "He knows what is best," says Teresa.

Your ordinary skills can be transformed into cosmic ones. A former nurse named Karen loved to sing but did not have a beautiful voice (she barely had a voice at all, in fact). She was at the hospital visiting her daughter who had just given birth to her first grandchild when she was quite taken by a desire to walk around that hospital floor and check out the other babies. She came upon a very young woman by herself with her newborn, obviously terrified of being a new mother. The woman was panicking because she could not calm her infant and was convincing herself that her baby was not bonding to her. Karen walked into the room and asked if she could help. Immediately the young mother turned over her infant to her, saying, "He won't stop crying. He hates me."

"Oh, he doesn't hate you," Karen said. "He's just trying to get his bearings. He just got here. This is a big world to get used to," she told her while she, a well-seasoned mother turned grandmother, began to rock the baby and softly sing a lullaby. The baby relaxed into the soothing rhythm of her voice and the gentle rocking. "Does singing work?" asked the young mother.

"I guess it must," Karen laughed, thinking that only an infant is too young to be a critic. Something about that experience, however, stayed with her. Months later, Karen went back to the hospital to check out the nursery again and to see the head nurse to ask if there were any openings for nurses who wanted to work with newborns. By "coincidence," this hospital was desperate for nurses. She started the next week in the nursery, holding emergency-care infants and singing to them. Karen told me, "I realized as soon as I walked into that nursery that I was called by God to be there and that I was meant to use my voice to channel grace into these newborns. They find my voice soothing and healing and perhaps grounding." Karen received God in her way and in God's way. She was not looking for an experience of God; God came calling for her. At one time she'd had fantasies about a singing career, but when the time was right, her very ordinary voice became a channel for some very extraordinary cosmic grace.

Cosmic perception enables you to absorb a mystical experience into your life without losing your footing. It is not easy to have your reality stretched to the boundaries of the cosmos and then squeezed back into your physical body. Think of how much support you need when something that's not even that extraordinary happens to you, a headache perhaps, or an argument with someone, or a traffic ticket. These events can be upsetting and may require an aspirin or a shoulder to cry on, but they are common and believable.

Hearing an inner voice for the first time, on the other hand, can be awesome, blessed, and very startling. In your first mystical communication, you sense an immediate familiarity, and a warmth illuminates your heart and you become aware of a profound feeling of love for something that you absolutely know is visiting you but is not you. What if, on top of this, you were given instructions to follow, as was Helen Schuckman, who took dictation for seven years from an invisible teacher named Jesus, for whom she had no devotion whatsoever?

In such a situation, you would have to acknowledge that your inner life—that is, your mystical spiritual life—was about to change your outer life. No one may be able to validate your experiences (although, once again, I recommend that you reveal them only to a soul companion or spiritual adviser). Yet, Helen Schuckman's mystical encounter became a channel of grace for millions of people around the world. No one who has been "used" by God saw it coming or had any idea he had the skill or talent that God required of him. They are more like Karen, who knew she liked singing but didn't realize that her unsuitability as a public performer made her perfect as a private channel.

Imagine yourself, in the quiet of your Castle, receiving God. Can you see yourself go beyond your initial surprise, go into stillness and say, "I'm here. I'm listening"? You do not know until the moment happens. But you do know, now, that you can live in readiness and awareness that God will come to you when the time is right.

Rooms for Receiving God

THE FIRST ROOM:
Ascending into the Supernatural

The supernatural is beyond our physical world but is completely natural to the soul's world. You are already familiar with the supernatural realm; you enter it when you dream, and you slip in and out of it occasionally through daydreams or when you actively imagine situations. When you daydream, you automatically withdraw from your senses. You slip into the realm of the supernatural and timelessness quite unconsciously—indeed, effortlessly.

The exercise below will help make the supernatural real for you. It may not be fully effective the first time or even the second or third. The intention is to help you achieve one thing—an experience of transcending your five senses, if only for a few seconds:

Remember that you are in the Fourth Mansion of your Castle and that you have crossed over into the realm of the supernatural. Focus your attention and gather your soul into present time. Then, imagine that your soul slips effortlessly out of your body and float with it, as if you are a bird gliding on a soft wind current. Travel away, always rising higher and higher above the ground. You're safe, you're secure, alone with your soul. Allow your soul to speak to you. What does it say? Do other interior senses awaken as you're floating? What do they feel like? Anytime one of your five senses attempts to reengage with your body, withdraw from it so that you keep your soul above your body. When you're ready, allow your soul to slip back into your center and resume what you were doing.

Practice this many times. Caring for your inner life requires practice, just as care of the body requires daily attention. As *The Cloud of Unknowing* recommends, be moderate in everything but love—love of God. This work demands a healthy and vigorous disposition of both body and spirit.

THE SECOND ROOM:
The Sensation of Mystical Water

The sound of water was "spiritual sweetness," or grace itself, for Teresa. Imagine the sound of mystical water running within your soul. Imagine it running through your entire body, beginning at the top of your head and flowing through your torso, down your arms, legs, and out through the bottom of your feet. Imagine this crystal-clear, sparkling mystical water flushing out all the debris from your body, mind, and emotions. Imagine that it is cleansing you of your history, of physical pain, of stiffness, of sadness. Now, pause and breathe in a wonderful sensation of mystical lightness.

Practice this exercise regularly. You may even want to practice it around water or add music to it. This is a brilliant exercise to distract your senses and delve deeper into your soul.

THE THIRD ROOM:
Entering the Heart of the Sacred

Here in the Fourth Mansion, you are in the realm of the sacred, the domain of the cosmic heart. Imagine that you are in your soul, detached from your physical form, viewing Earth from space, out among the stars and the planets. You can see that the Earth is tiny, spinning within a limitless universe of billions of stars and planets. You are illuminated with the mystical truths that life is so very brief and that the only true purpose is measured in how much love and grace we allow to flow through our souls during our lifetime.

Open yourself to feeling mystical love. Do not imagine it . . . do not think it, for this is not a quality of love that the mind can comprehend. Mystical love is a gift of grace. Just as you must prepare to receive God, you need to prepare—to be open and accepting—to receive mystical love.

See the Earth becoming larger again. See your heart filling with love of the Earth and all within it. Imagine your heart becoming as big as the planet. Gradually surround the planet and all humanity with your mystical heart. Close your heart within your soul and send your soul on a walkabout, one nation at a time. As your soul visits each nation, allow your heart to radiate mystical love. Breathe and pray that love into that country and into the faces of the people you meet. Feel your connection to humanity. Now return to your Castle and feel your oneness with the heart of the sacred and the whole of humanity.

Let this become a part of your soul's mystical practice.

THE FOURTH ROOM:
Channeling Mystical Love

Mystical love is a powerful healing agent and you can channel it. This is an act of mystical service that you perform in private or with soul companions. Keep it between you and God. Don't tell someone you're going to channel love and grace to them or that you have done so. Always maintain silence about this practice—period.

Channeling mystical love for healing is part of a contemporary mystic's practice. Prayer engages the flow of grace by centering your attention and settling the fragments of energy spinning in your psychic field. In contemplative prayer, you are able to ignore sounds and thoughts that could distract you. Withdraw into the silence of your Castle. Focus on a prayer, such as: I open myself as a channel for grace and light in this world. In this world of so many, God knows my name. Every thought matters and every prayer is heard in some way that is incomprehensible to our minds. Just when I think that so much doesn't make sense, I see a miracle. I am reminded again that everything and everyone matters. In the silence of my Castle, I withdraw from the distractions of my world and rest quietly for a moment in the company of the divine, the stillness in my soul. When I reach this stillness, I know that all is well and that I have once again allowed myself to be distracted by illusions. Illusions pass. God is constant. It is the constant I must rely on. I open my soul willingly and with love as a vessel of mystical love in this world.

Open your soul and accept the role of channel for mystical love in the world. Now, visualize people who you know who need love and healing. Then visualize people who you do not know who need it. Imagine mystical light flowing through you so fast that you have to step aside, inwardly, to let it pass. Where there is hatred, sow love. Where there is pain, sow love. Where there is chaos, sow love. Pray but do not become attached to the consequences of your prayer. You are only a channel.

This is part of the soul's mystical practice.

THE FIFTH ROOM:
Channeling Healing Grace

Channeling healing grace is much the same as channeling mystical love. They both come from the same source, the divine, but we name that light according to our needs. Pray whenever you are engaging in any exchange of grace with or for another person. You are praying as much for their sake as for yours. Channeling healing grace is very powerful, and, as a channel, you can do more for this world than you imagine. But perhaps it is better that we cannot ever fully comprehend the power of grace.

Prayer is the conduit of healing grace in this world. Open your soul with a contemplative prayer, a prayer that helps you to come into a state of being, of centeredness. Acknowledge that you are working from the consciousness of the Fourth Mansion, the realm of the supernatural. With that thought in your blood and bones, enter into this prayer of contemplation: With God's blessing, I open myself to be a channel of healing grace for others. Within my Castle walls, I am surrounded with tranquility and quietude and I remind myself that the mystery of healing is in God's hands. The sweetness of grace flows through a loving and open heart, which is all I have to offer. God utilizes that love which I willingly release. The wonder of love is its boundless capacity to heal, to bring forgiveness, to soothe the angry soul, to repair broken relationships, to make things right in all ways. I must trust in the power of love in my life and rely on its goodness, even when I see no immediate proof of its power. Love is God in action in this world. I am a conduit of love and of grace and I open my soul to channel that healing force to those in need.

If you slip into a mental state, forgetting that you are in the Fourth Mansion, remind yourself that you are in your soul, in your Castle, holding open your soul for healing grace to travel through. Refer to the prayer: I return to the center of my Castle, to the center of my inner soul, where the only voice I hear is the voice of God alone. You will stray into the mental domain again and again, so be patient with yourself. Visualize the people who are in need of healing and let the grace rush through you. Close with a prayer of gratitude.

THE SIXTH ROOM:
Better to Love Much than to Think Much

In the first three mansions we were accustomed to our love having an object: a person, pet, thing, place, or pastime. Love without an object or a goal—love for the sake of loving—is foreign to our way of thinking. There, love is personal. When we view the world as impersonal, sharing love seems foolish because we think it makes us vulnerable to emotional, business, and financial predators. Now that you are in the Fourth Mansion, however, your concern is the love that arises in cosmic consciousness. Here, you practice praying mystical love into the world. Here, you also embrace your mind and blend its gifts with the capacity of your heart. This union of the mystical heart and the intellect defines the illuminated soul.

In this practice, you consciously rely on your soul to redirect a person or a situation through grace and love. Your role is not to determine what the outcome will be or how it will change; your task is to facilitate a change through channeling divine light.

Center yourself with a prayer. You are in your Fourth Mansion. You have crossed into the realm of the supernatural. Imagine that this room is where you go to think, but your practice here is to cease thinking and worrying about the issue at hand. Quiet your mind and connect it to your heart. Channel love to the situation or person who brought you here. Channel love to yourself, as well. Let love flow through you and into the stress areas of your life. End with a prayer of gratitude.

THE SEVENTH ROOM:
Messages from the Divine

You are more accustomed to talking to God than to listening and hearing him. You are more accustomed to putting your five senses on alert for responses than you are to receiving simple messages. Therefore, you are likely to anticipate receiving guidance or instructions.

One woman reported, "I had this feeling as if I were suddenly wrapped in a blanket of stars while I was praying one evening. All of a sudden I felt lifted out of my body and had this cosmic sensation of hovering way above the Earth, wrapped in this illuminated blanket of stars. I felt suspended in eternity, completely bathed in a sense of divine love, as if God knew exactly who I was, where I lived, and even how much I owed on my water bill. I felt ridiculously, outrageously intimate with God. I wanted to stay up there and float forever, but just as suddenly as I was taken into that celestial wonderland, I was returned to Earth and into this dense, painfully overweight, middle-aged body of mine. Immediately, I began wondering, What am I supposed to do with this experience? I kept talking about it to my friends, trying to figure out what I was supposed to *do* with it. Then I started to wonder why none of my problems had been resolved as a result of that experience. I mean, there I was hovering above the Earth, but, like, so what? I was still overweight and still in a lot of pain—so what good did that do me? Finally—*finally*—I realized that I received a most profound, mystical message from God, who let me know that I was being watched over. I was intimately known to this divine being who drew me off the Earth one evening to let me know my prayers were heard—that *was* the answer to my prayers, but I didn't see it at the time because that wasn't the answer I wanted. That answer wasn't good enough for me. I didn't want a mystical experience; I wanted a practical solution. I wanted God to suddenly make my body thin so that I would not have to work at losing weight. In fact, what I really wanted was to be able to continue to eat anything I wanted and wake up thin. I wanted a custom-designed miracle, which is why it took me quite a while to realize I actually had received a miracle. I was not yet able to receive mystical gifts of grace. I still wanted my goodies from God to come in earthly packages. Luckily for me, I caught up with myself and finally saw the gift."

Prepare to receive God by emptying yourself of expectations. See God only as God is. Live within this room for a day at a time by taking this practice out with you into your world: At various times during the day, become aware of your setting and view it as if you had just entered a sacred place. See yourself within your Castle, viewing everything and everyone as if they were a part of a grand cosmic plan vital to your well-being, and you to theirs. You are exactly where you are supposed to be, as are they. Appreciate every detail and let that appreciation turn into this prayer: Is there anything you need of me in this moment, in this place? Then be still for a moment, wait. Take a deep breath and resume what you were doing, but maintain your connection to your Castle. At this point on your journey, you can remain as mystically active out in the world as within your Castle.

THE EIGHTH ROOM:
Allow Your Heart to Shatter

We love whom we want to love until we are called to love those whom we cannot easily or comfortably fit into our hearts. Having your heart shattered by the force of the sacred and enveloped by the cosmic heart of the divine makes you a servant of divine love. You are guided, directed, led by the force of that love to venture where you would not otherwise. The walls around your heart that once protected you from strangers and stragglers, vagrants and thieves, and outcasts and aliens are dismantled. You feel an overwhelming compassion without boundaries. Perhaps, for instance, you answer calls to help victims of a hurricane. Where once you could walk away thinking, Someone should help those poor people, now that someone is you.

You can't initiate a mystical shattering. Teresa had many divine visitations and once reported that an angel pierced her heart with a spear, causing an indescribable pain of supernatural proportions. Being directed to love in such a way is a mystery—a wonder of God that directs our lives once we become cosmic servants.

In this room, contemplate what it means to be called to love in a place you would rather not go. Whom can you not love? How would you recognize if your heart opened and you were directed to embrace someone whom you had previously banned from your heart? Do you have to make an effort to fuel an old anger or bitterness? Your heart may begin to crack open. Do you discuss old hurts and traumas again and again, out of habit? You may be consciously preventing your heart from opening. Being judgmental of others and holding on to negative thoughts blocks the emergence of mystical love. You cannot be bitter or unforgiving and be a conduit for love and grace. Heal your heart. Allow it to give up old wounds.

Practice forgiveness, but also take this practice to the mystical plane, as you are in the Fourth Mansion. Forgiveness is an act of spiritual alchemy through which you detach your consciousness from the entire paradigm of human justice. You remove yourself from the center of righteousness and self-righteousness, where you usually find your personal justification for any behavior, no matter how grievous. Only the soul is capable of the mystical act of forgiveness, in which you surrender to the power of God, withdrawing any personal need or desire to remain attached.

Discovering this capacity to respond with transcendent compassion to one's aggressors is exactly the quality of love that John of the Cross discovered during his imprisonment, which led him to write *The Dark Night of the Soul.* A much greater and profoundly cosmic love lies within us, but we must break through the forceful power of our injured egos to discover this love. Forgiveness is truly a mystery, for it challenges every bit of common sense and rational thought operating within us, and yet that is precisely the way of the mystic—to transcend reason and act within the power of divine mystery.

Begin with a prayer such as: I desire to forgive more than I am capable of forgiving, but not to forgive is even more difficult. Help me break through the walls of my ego and let me experience even a drop of the love that transforms resentments into compassion."

THE NINTH ROOM:
Receiving the Power of Grace

Be still and receive grace. There is no other aim in this room. Be silent. Contemplate what it means to receive God, and let your soul drift into that image. Withdraw from your senses, withdraw from the mind. Move into divine light.

THE PRAYER OF RECOLLECTION:
SOUL FLIGHT

Teresa's Prayer of Recollection is a mystical treasure. "Supernatural recollection," in her words, "is not about sitting in the dark or closing your eyes or being subject to any external thing. . . . It seems that without any intervention a temple is being built through this supernatural recollection where the soul can go to pray. The senses and other external things begin to lose their hold, and the soul starts to recover what she has lost. . . . Sometimes the soul enters within herself and sometimes she rises above herself. . . . Let's say that the senses and the faculties, which are the inhabitants of the Interior Castle, have gone outside. Let's say they have been hanging around for days and years with strangers who despise all that is beautiful about the Castle. When they realize their error, they come back. But before they can reenter the Castle, they have to break the bad habits they have been accumulating. They are not traitors. They willingly linger in the vicinity of the Castle until they can be allowed in again. (*The Interior Castle,* Starr)

During the Prayer of Recollection, the soul recovers what it lost—its timeless nature, its cosmic perspective, its greater heart and consciousness. You don't lose your senses, you detach from them so that your soul and being are lighter—enlightened—undistracted by earthly attachments or feelings. You are congruent, comfortable in the Fourth Mansion, living in both the earthly and spiritual worlds.

By the Fourth Mansion, Teresa was adept at this detachment, which she called "mystical flight," the experience of having the soul separate from the body and rise above it, to wander deeper into her Castle. Virtually every spiritual tradition records journeys of the soul or consciousness beyond the personal into other, higher, supernatural spheres for revelations.

Teresa also uses the metaphor of a temple to describe an even more inaccessible place within the soul—inaccessible through the senses, that is. A temple is suggestive of a place in the soul that is a holy sanctuary, deeper into the Castle than you can reach through the lower three mansions—a place past the senses, closer to God.

At this stage of the soul's journey, Teresa changes the imagery she wants us to use to grasp the divine. We are no longer to strive to imagine God as dwelling within us. God *is* within us, but you cannot feign or force the voice of God with your imagination. There is no logic or reason to the mystical path, no formula that brings God to your door. You go toward God as you get further into your soul—into your Castle—and detached from the chaos of the world, although you are still of the world and care about the world and the people you love. Detachment means that nothing in your exterior world has authority over you. You withdraw your soul from your history, from chapters of your life that are over and done with. Let your past fade into the past, where it belongs. You do not keep company with the dead—including people, places, and past memories—that do not serve your well-being. You draw your spirit back—recollect it—into present time and out of the wastelands, cemeteries, and swamps that can make you emotionally and physically ill.

The Prayer of Recollection lets you enter a mystical state of consciousness in which you transcend your physical sensations, including pain. It occurs spontaneously, but you can take steps to prepare to receive it—and God, who brings it.

Open to your soul. Be still. Be silent. Open your heart. Feel it grow large and encompass all the world. Prepare yourself to feel abundant grace. Feel your soul detach from your body and hover above it, still encompassing everything. You are above and beyond your senses. Your mind is still and quiet. Pray that you will be filled with love and grace. Then return to your body.

A Moment of Contemplation

By the Fourth Mansion, all inner work is gentle and serene. To do anything else, to cause pain or anxiety for yourself, is harmful and unnecessary. With that lovely advice, you can now take leave of the Fourth Mansion, mindful that it is mystical consciousness that continues to live within you. Mystical consciousness is not a part-time occupation for the soul. To channel mystical love or healing grace is a calling. Since you have responded to that call, you have become a cosmic servant, a mystic without a monastery, active in the transformation of this world. Your soul is now your greatest companion and God your greatest resource, as they were for the mystics who lived centuries ago.

Nothing is easy about living in mystical consciousness, but it is even more difficult to live outside it.

Let us leave the Fourth Mansion with the inspiring words of Teresa, who sounds here like a loving mother preparing her chil-

dren for the world: "In dealing with the Prayer of Recollection
. . . an expansion of the soul takes place, as if the water rising up
from the fountain doesn't just overflow and move on. Instead,
the more water that comes up the larger the basin grows to receive it. That's what this kind of prayer does to the soul. And God
works many other wonders in her, shaping and preparing her to
contain abundant grace.

"This sweet inner expansion frees the soul from constraints
in her service to God. She is no longer oppressed by fear of the
underworld. Although she desires more than ever not to offend
God, she is anything but groveling now. She is fully confident
that she will find her delight in him. While she used to be afraid
of austerities, concerned that they would compromise her deli-
cate health, now she knows that in God she can do everything.
Her desire for self-sacrifice is much greater than before. She no
longer worries about trials. Her faith is revitalized. She understands that any hardships she suffers are for God and that His
Majesty will give her the grace to bear them patiently." (*The Interior Castle,* Starr)

Mystical grace may be forthcoming, but you must continue
to practice. Practice the mystical gifts of the Fourth Mansion.
Channel mystical love and healing grace. Live in preparation for
receiving God. Return to the rooms in this mansion continually,
as these are the training rooms for your soul. As Teresa wrote,
"All good lies in perseverance."

THE FIFTH MANSION

Dissolving into Holiness: From Silkworm to Butterfly

Oh, friends! How could I ever describe the riches, the treasures and delights to be found inside the fifth dwelling? There is no way of knowing how to talk about such things . . .

—Teresa of Ávila
The Interior Castle, Starr

I N THE HINDU TRADITION, the greatest mystical poet of South India, Manikkavacagar, went to live in a temple after a lifetime of serving Shiva through poetry. There, he was rewarded by a blinding illumination of the divine light, into which he is said to have merged— and then vanished.

Ignatius of Loyola had a profound conversion experience in which his senses, his will, and all the ambitions that he had held for himself as a young man dissolved into spiritual pursuits. Before his conversion, he was a soldier with dreams of accomplishing fame and glory through war and had to be saved twice by interventions of the Blessed Mother. But he was gravely injured in battle and almost died. During his long recovery, Ignatius passed the time by reading and also in erotic fantasies of a noblewoman whose company he desired but could not attain. Although he'd asked for romances and dramatic stories, all that was available in the house where he was confined were books on the life of Christ and the saints. He discovered that his erotic fantasies left him completely dissatisfied while his spiritual thoughts brought him peace. The readings awakened his brilliance for what would become his trademark for spiritual discernment, and he was told in prayer that he was to serve God and bring back an ancient order and practice of devotion. In this pursuit in his *Spiritual Exercises,* Ignatius dissolved fully into the union of his soul with the divine.

In a workshop, when I first brought up the Fifth Mansion and its challenge of dissolving into holiness, one student gave me a look and said, "I can't imagine what that means, but I'm completely seduced by the notion of dissolving into divine light. When I visualize what it could be, I feel as if I am releasing burdens and old rubbish and floating in divine fluffy clouds. Sometimes I envy those saints because I think, What is it that you experienced? Who and what is that God that so captured you? I mean, they were in love beyond love." This man's face had just touched the power of this mystical experience.

Dissolving into holiness means to merge without boundaries into divine consciousness. Teresa describes this transformation from body to soul as turning from a silkworm into a butterfly. This can happen within the context of your contemporary life as the soul becomes on fire and dissolves much of the ego's familiar landscape. This final release of the ego's hold on you is like a silkworm breaking out of its confining cocoon and lifting into flight as a beautiful butterfly.

This mystical experience is enabled and encompassed by a state of consciousness that Teresa calls the Prayer of Union, which she compares to the sacrament of marriage. In this mansion, you assume a conscious relationship with timelessness. You no longer doubt your mystical experiences and dialogue with the divine. You now know the interior of your soul and your way around the Castle. You know your way to God. The Castle is no longer an exercise of the mind and imagination—it is part of you.

And your personal spiritual sojourn has now changed into an archetypal one. You are following a path that others have traveled.

Of the exquisite mystical state that Teresa calls the Prayer of Union, she writes:

> Don't think that this union is some kind of dreamy state like the one I was talking about earlier. The reason I would even use the term "dream" is that the soul seems to fall asleep. But she [the soul] is neither sleeping nor awake. It's the faculties that are asleep in this state—deeply asleep—to things of the world and to the self. In fact, during the short time the Prayer of Union lasts, the soul transcends both sense and reason. She couldn't think a single thought even if she wanted to. Any prescribed technique for suspending consciousness is rendered utterly unnecessary.
>
> . . . She [the soul] doesn't know what she wants. She has died completely to this world so that she can fully live in God. This is a delicious death. It is as if the soul were being plucked out of all of the activities of life on earth. . . . If she is still breathing, she is entirely unaware of it. . . . Even if the soul does not totally lose consciousness, she can't move a hand or a foot. She resembles a person who has fallen into such a deep faint that it seems like he's dead."
>
> —*The Interior Castle*, Starr

As we dissolve the bonds of the physical world here within the consciousness of the Fifth Mansion, we become timeless, cosmic beings.

LIVING IN A HIGHER STATE

Given your day-to-day life in the physical world, it is appropriate to wonder, Why would I want to experience such a state of consciousness? How would piercing the cosmic veil possibly serve my life path? The deeper you go into the Castle, it seems the more impractical your journey becomes. But consider this: Mystical experiences may not be glorious in their practicality, but how practical are negative states of consciousness, such as anger, depression, addiction, or resentment, which render you dysfunctional or even hurtful to people on your personal and professional radar screen? Given the power of these negative states of mind and how exceedingly impractical harming yourself and others is, I would offer that a mystical state of consciousness that leads you to become more compassionate, aware, and, ultimately, involved in service to the world is quite practical.

Even here, within the Fifth Mansion, the nature of mysticism remains mysterious. You, the pilgrim, may sometimes feel like an outsider trying to get in . . . but into what? Are you seeking an out-of-body experience? A momentary flight-out-of-form into blinding light that hints of immortality? Is all your inner work only to achieve random mystical experiences—gifts of grace from a loving but often whimsical God?

On a trip to South America, a few of my fellow travelers went off one evening to meet with a shaman to do a mushroom ritual. Eager to experience an altered state, they believed that participating in this sacred ritual would help them into a mystical state of consciousness that would produce visions that would resolve their career crises. Of course that did not happen. One person actually wanted a different shaman for the next evening, determined to get what he wanted and expected from the experience. Among the many problems with this approach is the fact that this ritual's entire paradigm of the sacred has no authentic sacred meaning for most nonnative visitors. While people can read up on another culture's rituals, such an intellectual crash course does not facilitate reverence or belief in the traditions and spirit that activate the rituals' power. The most for which outsiders can hope—in general—is a few good hallucinations.

What they get is some bad headaches. You can't force your way into mystical consciousness—period.

Teresa warns her readers not to force their way into the Castle or into mystical states of awareness. "Only the Lord of the Castle can let you in," she writes. Thomas à Kempis also reminds us, "It belongs to God to give comfort when He wills to whom He wills and as much as He wills—all according to His good pleasure and not more." And *The Cloud of Unknowing* affirms, "God gives the gift of contemplation freely and without recourse to methods; . . . methods alone can never induce it." In other words, only through grace will you get into this consciousness. If you are not called, do not enter.

How would a forced entry happen? Perhaps in medieval days contemplatives would have tried to force God's hand by prolonged fasting or extreme lengths of meditation and prayer, which could bring on hallucinations or mental breakdowns. As Teresa pointed out, this is not true prayer or a humble approach to God; it is a practice of personal vanity and expectations. Thankfully, I can say I have rarely encountered such extremes.

Mystical experiences are generally episodic. We usually cannot conceive of maintaining it as a way of life. Yet, mystics undergo a significant shift in their relationships with power and reality that also changes their everyday mind-set. For most people, power is an external force that they perceive as coming toward them or attacking them, so they always feel defensive. But with mystical consciousness, your power is inside you. Instead of power coming *toward* you, power now flows *through* you. You can make better, more conscious choices because you see beyond the personal ego.

For example, mystical consciousness allows you to view the trauma of a job loss or divorce as a new beginning. You can see that you have been forced to grow out of a symbolic cocoon and made to change into something new. Certain life changes are, in facts, altars of transformation. Mystical consciousness can give you the grace to illuminate your every moment, not just the difficult ones.

Individuals who have access to mystical consciousness are not necessarily quiet illuminates: Bach, Beethoven, Francis Bacon, Thomas Jefferson, Einstein, Thomas Merton, Michelangelo, Leonardo da Vinci, Rumi, Emily Dickinson, Helen Keller, Mother Teresa, Nicholas Roerich, and many others were great channels of light whose contributions transformed the world. They were mystics within their own fields. Mind you, their mysticism did not make them perfect, but they were divinely inspired. Like Teresa of Ávila, they were larger than life, their experiences as exaggerated and exceptional as their genius—which was not intellect alone, but the soul working in harmony with the intellect that has faith and vision.

Although inspiring, their life journeys—what they had to endure—are also intimidating. Emily Dickinson lived in isolation, wearing only white and never leaving her home in Amherst, Massachusetts, until her death. Her intuitive abilities had become so hypersensitive that she could hardly bear to be near another person without feeling great pain. Mother Teresa lived among the poor and, long before her fame, went without many meals herself in order to feed orphans and lepers for whom she was called to care. Teresa had absolutely no fear of illness, physical suffering, or her own death, whereas most people are terrified of all three. She was a fully liberated transcendent soul. For that reason, many people keep their soul's mystical genius contained in order to try to live a safer, more ordinary life, believing that these great individuals paid too high a price for the mastery of their talent. Yet, Helen Keller, who struggled with blindness and deafness as a child, came to say that she would not have wanted her life to be any other way; she opened up the world for hearing- and sight-impaired people. Living an exaggerated life is characteristic of an illuminated genius.

And Now You

We all undergo some exaggerated life experiences in archetypal circumstances. For example, everyone suffers the loss of a loved one; some people even lose everyone and everything they love. We all experience some sort of betrayal, but some people are betrayed in breathtakingly cruel ways. Most of us go through periods of boredom and depression, but some seem never to break out of these cycles. Individuals in states of extreme exaggerations of the human experience may seem as if they are frozen in one season of the year, unable to cycle from winter to spring, summer to autumn. But these situations are meant to force you to make a choice between living as a victim—powerless—and growing in a new way with a new awareness, ripe for personal transformation. It is a cosmic standoff: It forces you to face and use your inner power. You decide: Is your life a spiritual sojourn or just a day-to-day existence to suffer until the end?

A cosmic standoff might unfold for an alcoholic, for example, who lives a life in which every day begins and ends the same way, always focused on getting the next drink. Nothing else matters; the entire world exists only to satisfy that craving. The soul cannot find its way into this person's intuitive circuits, either through the conscience or through the dream state, which is saturated with alcohol. Then he bottoms out. Will he continue to be subject to the excuses and stories his ego tells him—that he's not an alcoholic and can quit anytime he likes—or will he animate the power of his soul and begin his withdrawal from the authority of the ego and surrender it to God? This is his moment of transformation, his opportunity to leave the cocoon.

When John of the Cross was stuck in a small, stifling prison for nine months, he was visited with divine consolations that inspired some of his most beautiful poetry, the *Spiritual Canticle* and, of course, *The Dark Night of the Soul.* John called on heaven to help him in this cosmic standoff, when he was sunk in despair and isolation and also tortured with weekly public lashings. Besides giving him divine comfort, John was also helped in what some considered a miraculous escape.

Perhaps you have a gift or talent that longs to be unleashed and developed. You can feel it running through your bones and your psyche: It speaks to you in dreams and in your imagination. This is the way the unexpressed you makes itself known within the cocoon. Eventually, however, the unrealized you becomes impatient; all butterflies must eventually break free. You have to decide whether you will destroy the butterfly within the cocoon or allow it to fly. The divine calls you to express your talents as much as you are called to express your soul—your talents are animated *by* the grace of your soul.

So again I would ask you, as I did at the beginning of this section, Why would you want to experience mystical states of illumination? Indeed, why would you *not* want to? Some part of your life is always going to be exaggerated or difficult. Releasing your soul to a higher consciousness will likely necessitate further changes in your life. They are likely to be beneficial, although they may also be challenging, but they may well unleash the greatness of your life. Why would you not embrace the opportunity to experience illumination? Why live an ordinary life when you know in your soul that you can have an extraordinary one?

DISSOLVING INTO YOUR SOUL

In the consciousness of the Fifth Mansion, the soul is an ever-more-present companion, taking charge when it must of your external and internal life. Your soul is already expanding into your life and dissolving nonessential parts of it little by little. The notable shift that occurs within the Fifth Mansion is that you gain the strength to allow yourself to change. You progress from relying on your physical senses to relying on the interior wisdom of your soul.

You have recollected your life force, and your soul is now focused on expanding its receptivity to the divine, and on becoming a greater reservoir of cosmic love. Instead of continually reviewing its attachments to the physical world, your soul is now being called into transcendence—to release itself into an abiding surrender to the divine. You accept the requirements for the interior life, the regular practice of prayer, reflection, and contemplation, and, as in a successful marriage, you recognize that union with God takes constant work and attention. But mystical truth can give you tranquility, inner peace. This interior peace results from your purposeful transcending of conflicts, contradictions, and personal challenges. You will always cycle in and out of tranquility and restlessness and will always have to work to balance the ego and the soul. But, as a mystic, you learn that you have the power to use light for transformation, no matter how great the obstacle.

In the Fifth, Sixth, and particularly the Seventh Mansions, we leave behind the concept that there is purpose to the design of the cosmos or to mystical experiences. We become observers of patterns of communications and exchanges of grace between the soul and God. The Fifth Mansion was where Teresa's soul dissolved the boundaries of time and space and separated itself from its earthbound consciousness. This cosmic shift in sensory perceptions is a natural consequence of progressing toward illumination, which is a by-product of grace. Teresa herself interpreted these profound mystical experiences as passionately intimate, but she remained impersonal in her instructions, charting a course that all could follow.

As an example of a Fifth Mansion moment of transcendence, imagine that your soul shut down your senses and allowed you to perceive your life through a wide-angle cosmic lens. Instantly you are aware that you are "above and below" simultaneously; you can feel the ground beneath your feet while being at eye level with the stars. You feel at one with every life form. Your cell tissue is part of everything and everything lives within you, from the smallest spinning particle of energy, to a breathing tree in the forest, to the collective consciousness of all nations. Your consciousness expands to embrace the galaxies. In the microseconds of this mystical experience, you realize that your soul has dissolved the boundaries in your mind and your senses, a container so small that it now feels painful to squeeze your soul back into your body. But as soon as you are back, your first thought is, When can I leave this body again?

You don't necessarily receive personal direction during this experience, yet your field of reality is transformed. You are graced with an awareness of the interlinked vitality of life, the "interbeing" and interrelationship of the universe. The universal truth "as above, so below"—as it is in heaven, so it is on Earth—is active in your biological tissue and in your veins. You don't just know it intellectually, you can *feel* the pollution and decline of nature; your breathing becomes tight as images of the rain forests—the lungs of the Earth—scream to you as they slowly die. You are no longer separate from the whole of life. You have become a part of the living mystery—a conscious mystical activist.

Such an experience gives you an intimate connection to the universe. Does your soul have the stamina to manage a conscious connection to the entire fabric of life? Your life, your health, and your consciousness are one with the world's soul and psyche, which are afflicted by an epidemic of depression, anxiety, chronic fatigue, bipolar and other mood and attention disorders, heart disease, and any number of psychosomatic sufferings. You are also connected to the love that binds the collective soul of humanity. The suffering of humankind is so obvious, but the impact of love and of prayer is always apparent. You have such power and the potential to change so much through the grace that runs through you. You can see that power, taste it, connect with it within a mystical experience that ties you to the people and souls of other lands. Little by little, you shed the illusions that you are of a certain faith, skin, and nation, and replace them with the truth that you are part of the one collective soul of all species on the planet.

We have entered the era of the soul and the psyche. We know we are psychic beings. We know we have more than five senses. We know we are sensitive to the energy fields around us and those of negative people. At this point, we can acknowledge that we have an active psychic field around our physical bodies; the ability to perceive over long distances, outside the boundaries of time and space; the ability to receive information from souls who have passed over; the ability to receive information from angels and guides; the ability to receive energetic data regarding incoming health problems that can prevent those problems from becoming physical; the ability to channel grace through our systems into the physical world for healing physical disease, emotional disease, or, on a larger scale, political disease. In short, we are now a species that must acknowledge the full participation of our souls in every aspect of life.

You cannot experience cosmic sight and return to ordinary life. You cannot be lifted out of your body into timelessness and then reenter your physical form without changing your perceptions of reality.

Let's go back into the Castle.

Entry Prayer

I cross the bridge into the silent bliss of my Castle. I close the drawbridge and forbid all outside influences from entry into this holy place that is my soul. Here in my Castle, I am alone with God. Under God's light and companionship I discover the depth and beauty of my soul. I embrace the power of prayer. I open myself to divine guidance. I surrender myself to become as a channel for grace, healing, and service as God directs my life.

Rooms to Practice Dissolving into the Soul

You'll use these rooms in the Fifth Mansion many times, some for the rest of your life. Each new day will remind you that something old is passing away, dissolving out of your life. You will continually shed your history, because the soul's nature is to be light, liberated from unnecessary weight. Imagine an emergency in which you are given ten minutes to take only the essentials from your house because all the rest is about to be destroyed in a flood. What would you save? You would save your treasures, not your wounds. And you would survive and build a new life.

Dissolving into your soul is a powerful spiritual practice. Imagine, for instance, a situation in your everyday life that would make you tense. Would you not find it soothing to be able to dissolve that tension before it penetrated your cell tissue and destroyed an entire day of your life? Why would you not want to utilize a similar power to become one with your soul?

The most challenging feature of your work in the Fifth Mansion is the call to look upward, not to your past or into your shadow. Even though you visit rooms in which you are directed to do exercises that require you to visit your past, the underlying goal here is to transcend this history. In this work with your soul, you dissolve these old bonds in order to become one with your soul. This companionship is the backbone of your mystical life.

As you progress with the exercises in the following rooms, always begin with a prayer. Many of these exercises are rigorous and will take you deep into your interior. You need to maintain your daily prayer life, too, to build your strength and help you especially in exercises in which you will consciously shift your connections to time and space. You will use the gifts of your mind as well as of your soul, but, as always, pray as you perform these visualizations.

THE FIRST ROOM:
Dissolving the Past

Living in the past is like living in a cemetery. Memories and unfinished business control your emotional well-being, mind, and
soul. You hold on to the past because it is familiar, but that is dis-
orienting to the soul, which is in present time. If your thoughts
and emotions are in the past when you pray for guidance in the
present, you are living in too many time zones. This makes it
hard for you to hear guidance or make decisions about what to
do in your present life. You're actually listening for guidance so
that you can go where you cannot go any longer—no amount of
prayer can help you there. Clinging to the past is like praying for
God to raise the dead. If your past is distracting you from your
present life, you need to dissolve your connections to it.

Soul Work: Focus your inner awareness on dissolving misper-
ceptions about your past. You are not dissolving your memories
or images of people or places, but any illusions you hold about
them. Release them. Visualize them melting like ice on a hot
sidewalk on a summer day. Deanimate them by consciously withdrawing your energy and spirit from them. Surround your memories with grace, blessing every experience. Your goal in this
room is to replace all illusions from your past with light and
grace. You may need to do this exercise several times to recall
your soul from its different psychic time zone.

THE SECOND ROOM:
Dissolving Space

The soul is not bound by physical parameters, so it can receive guidance unobstructed by time and space. Mystical con-

sciousness communicates in the archetypal languages of intuition, symbols, dreams, and experiences. Mystics and people who have had near-death experiences know the sensation in which physical coordinates of time and space dissolve. When Teresa moved into the realm of expanding consciousness, she, too, felt as if the boundaries of time and space had been left behind on Earth.

What does God want from you in this moment? Within the interior of your soul, God is present.

Soul Work: Ask both your soul and your ego for their interpretation of meaning and purpose. Each hears God differently. How does each map the route differently? For instance, the ego will usually follow a route that reinforces your insecurities and fears. List the paths that you take. Be very honest. Reflect on them. Mark where your soul is likely to collide with your ego. How can you resolve the differences?

THE THIRD ROOM:
Surrendering Your Senses into Healing

Ultimately the divine determines whether we recover from an illness. A genuine healing is a mystical experience, not a rational one and requires a soul animated by faith. Without it, a complete healing is not likely to occur. Yet, even with faith, you must surrender into the process of healing; that is, you must place your complete faith in the treatment by which your healing will be accomplished. An ill person wants to recover as quickly as possible, of course, but often you cannot see at what level the process of healing is unfolding. By surrendering your senses, you investigate your understanding of how you expect healing to work between you and God.

Soul Work: Reflect on how you see your healing processes at work. What arises each time life presents you with something that requires healing? Where do you feed doubt into your healing? How do you torment yourself with impatience? With this practice of self-reflection, you can test when you choose to perceive through mystical consciousness rather than ordinary thought. Think of some things in your life that need healing. Include on this list at least one negative attitude that doesn't serve you, or one addiction, or someone you need to forgive, as well as any pain or illness. There is no such thing as a shortage of things to heal.

Choose one thing on which to focus a healing practice that includes prayers and whatever else is required. For the next fourteen days, return to this room to reflect upon the influence your healing practice is having on you as a person. (Among the points to note in your evaluation is whether you *can* maintain a fourteen-day healing practice.) You are looking for results in *the* healing challenge itself, but you are also looking to see how your life as a whole is being affected by your healing practice. Appreciating that a healing practice influences your entire life engages the mystical nature of healing. A medical approach targets only the illness.

THE FOURTH ROOM:
Dissolving Illness

Teresa noted in the Fifth Mansion that the body is secondary to the soul, a temporary vessel that will disintegrate once it has served its usefulness. Nonetheless, she counseled us to take care of the body so that it can serve the soul. Today, however, we live in a culture that adores the body and ignores the soul. We love the energy of connection, the social spirit of spiritual practices today. We love to talk about them and be social butterflies flitting from practice to practice. But the social butterfly spirit is quite different from the empowered soul that inhabits the Castle. Only the soul can channel grace "hot" enough to burn disease out of cell tissue, for instance. Only the soul has the force to burn the negative time lock that is lodged in diseased cell tissue and replace it with timeless grace.

Soul Work: This room is for healing. You will need to practice, practice, practice the art of healing in this room. You will need to build up the strength of your soul to master the consciousness required for this art. Even then, you can proceed only so far. Remember that healing is a calling unto itself.

Center yourself with a prayer. Ask your soul to channel "hot grace" into your cell tissues that are unhealthy or tired. Repeat the words *hot grace* or pray, "I am a channel of grace and I give permission for the healing fire of grace to take over my body and burn through my [fill in your request]." Practice holding that image and sense the flow of grace through your body.

You can heal at a distance through the channeling of hot grace. Once you receive permission to work with an individual, enter into the consciousness of this room and again, center yourself through prayer. Visualize the individual as surrounded by light and then say the prayer, "I am a channel for grace and I willingly open my soul as a conduit of healing for (name the individual). Then hold them in the light of grace for three to five minutes. And then close this practice with a prayer such as, "I thank the divine for the healing grace given abundantly to (name the individual). Amen."

As with all practices that involve prayer and soul work, devotion to the practice builds your own stamina for the task. Remain detached as to the outcome. Trust that with every prayer for a healing, a healing occurs.

THE FIFTH ROOM:
Dissolving Conflict and Power Struggles

You will always have conflicts, power struggles, and bad days in Earth School, as well as joy and wonder. You may prefer to avoid conflict, only to find that you begin to implode because you have stuffed inside all the tension and resentment that you should have worked out externally. Much conflict, however, can be dissolved, and therefore resolved, by relying on the soul's ability to detach and ascend into a cosmic perspective. You may still need to confront someone in the everyday world to discuss and resolve a conflict, but you approach the conflict already seeing through it, seeing from a higher viewpoint. In this room, you recognize the power conflicts, as you did in the lower mansions, but now consciously transcend them. In the earlier mansions, you looked to old power plays and observed the untrained soul within you. Now you must develop insight to recognize them as ego illusions. They are classic temptations, the kind that Jesus had to resist in the desert. Now your task is to learn to dissolve conflicts immediately, before they can incarnate into a reptile.

Soul Work: This is the perfect room to come to if you have actually had a power struggle with someone and are presently off balance as a result. Disconnecting from a power play does not mean you walk away from a situation. This is not like physically storming out of a room. Dissolving a soul connection in a power struggle is an act of mystical alchemy, and it can occur in the middle of a business lunch. It is between your soul and God, and all the while your business and the lunch can go on and not skip a beat.

Imagine a power conflict in action. Withdraw your spirit from this power conflict. To transcend it, you recognize the power play, imagine yourself returning to the Castle, close the drawbridge so that you feel protected, and consciously dissolve any threads connecting you to that situation. Take this practice into every situation in your life. Learn to live in the consciousness of your Castle.

THE SIXTH ROOM:
Dissolving Fear and Blame

You will always have to confront fears. But you can dissolve the hold that fear has over you just as you can dissolve all other illusions.

Soul Work: Bring your fears into this room, one at a time. Imagine yourself in conversation with your soul, requesting that you become more fully aware of the impact that your fears have on the greater environment of your life.

Reflect on why you have the fears that you do. Pray to be given a transcendent or mystical understanding of them. Releasing your fears may not be a matter of learning more about them or understanding the root cause—you may need to ask for the healing grace to have them lifted from your shoulders.

Assume your prayer has been answered and leave this room with the understanding that your fears no longer hold the same authority over you. You may need to return to this room again whenever you discover that you hold fears within you. Always remember that, once a prayer is said, that prayer is answered.

THE SEVENTH ROOM:
Dissolving into God

Enter into this room as if you were entering a sacred chamber. Imagine a celestial hot tub and picture yourself stepping naked into that hot tub under the night sky. The sky is brilliant, full of stars. The air is satiny, warm, fragrant with jasmine and roses. You are alone, completely content, and comfortable. Allow your body to rest comfortably as you go inward, leaving it and all your senses behind. You lift up outside your body and into cosmic flight. Your senses are numb, you are floating, alone with God. Dissolve into that cosmic night sky. Release your soul.

When you return, say a prayer of gratitude and closure if you are leaving the Castle.

CHARACTERISTICS OF A MYSTICAL EXPERIENCE

Equally important to the companionship of your soul is your growing familiarity with the cosmic realm and your interconnectedness with it. Little by little, as you ascend through the mansions, the soul expands, learning to trust the visions of its place within the cosmic grand design. In the Fourth Mansion, the soul ascended into the cosmic heart of the sacred, divine love. Here in the Fifth Mansion, your senses recede further and your soul gains the strength to maintain cosmic perceptions that often cannot be reinforced by other human beings.

Mystical experiences are both personal and impersonal, with universal characteristics as well as unique intimacies shared between the individual and God. In the Fifth Mansion, however, mystical experiences are likely to be more archetypal. Teresa writes:

> In a state of union, the soul sees nothing and hears nothing and comprehends nothing. Union lasts such

a short time, and it seems even shorter than it really is. God presses himself so fully against the inside of the soul that when she returns to herself the soul has no doubt whatsoever that God was in her and she was in God. This truth remains with her forever. Even though years may go by without God granting this blessing again, the soul can never forget. She never doubts: God was in her; she was in God. This knowingness is all that matters.

How, you might ask, could the soul see this truth and understand it if she is incapable of seeing or understanding anything? Well, it is not in the moment of union that the soul is cognizant of this truth, but she sees it clearly afterwards. It isn't some vision that convinces her. It is an unshakable certainty, and God himself has put it there.

—*The Interior Castle,* Starr

Teresa adds, "We need to stop looking for reasons to explain how all these blessings happen. Our minds cannot grasp these things, anyway. Isn't it enough to know that he who causes all this is omnipotent? It is God who does it. No matter how much energy we expend, we have nothing to do with making this happen. We need to give up our desire to comprehend divine blessings." (*The Interior Castle,* Starr)

In *Paradiso,* Dante agreed, "Even Heaven's most enlightened soul,/that Seraph with his eye most set on God,/could not provide the why . . ."

One needs only the briefest encounter with God in the walls of your soul to be convinced for the rest of your life that you have been visited by the divine.

Before you embark on this next set of rooms, reinvoke a state of grace with prayer, then reenter the Castle.

Rooms with a Mystical View

THE FIRST ROOM:
God in the Walls of Your Soul

Imagine the interior of this room as if the walls themselves were animated with God. Let images of this room speak to you; let them become vaporous, floating off the walls and surrounding you with light. Allow them to separate you from the sensations of your external world, as if you are surrounded by a benevolent cloud that blocks all your senses.

Soul Work: Be present to God. Listen. What is being revealed to you? Be still and listen. Listen and receive. Breathe God into the walls of your lungs as if they are the walls of your soul. Incarnate the sacred into your cell tissue. And wait, listen for what is to be revealed to you. This room is not about asking. Listen and receive and feel God in the walls of your soul.

THE SECOND ROOM:
Mystical Depression

In *The Interior Castle,* Teresa recognized mystical depression and wrote about symptoms that can include anxiety, mood swings, chronic fatigue, and feelings that you have become completely disconnected—not detached, but disconnected—from your life. You may feel as if God has abandoned you.

If you become depressed or anxious by the difficulties of living a conscious life, stop all inner practices. Teresa—and even Zen teachers—advise working in the garden or at other tasks that ground you and take your mind off yourself. The spiritual path is about the pursuit of God, not the pursuit of yourself. If the object of your inner journey becomes yourself, then you will break down and suffer depression, anxiety attacks, and discontent because you are imploding from attention to your fears as opposed to your release from them.

St. John of the Cross coined the now commonly used phrase *the dark night of the soul* for his spiritual crisis. Writing his book of the same name while in prison, he described the passages of the soul from the darkness of its awakening to its confusion about its identity to its reception into the lightness of the divine.

In this room, you examine your psychological and emotional experiences with God. This is a complex exercise; perform it deliberately and thoughtfully. You may also want to enlist your soul companion or spiritual director to help you through it. Spiritual directors are trained professionals, often with theological and psychological backgrounds, who guide and counsel people devoted to their spiritual path.

Soul Work: Enter into a dialogue with your soul; examine the nature of your psyche and emotions. Do you frequently feel depressed? What are the triggers of depression? Describe your depressions in detail. Have you ever considered a depression to be a spiritual crisis? Does depression strike you rapidly, without warning? Speak with your soul about the causes of your depression, asking for insight into the spiritual significance of your dark nights. How should you handle them? Should you feel overwhelmed at any time, always reach out for appropriate support.

THE THIRD ROOM:
Choosing Mystical Consciousness

Mystical consciousness can melt the illusions that surround the ordinary problems of your life. Looking through a mystical lens does not make your problems go away, but it helps you to see them symbolically and to choose better solutions to them. With mystical consciousness, your soul becomes your co-worker, a working companion, an intimate resource on which you rely to help you understand the spiritual and symbolic meaning in life. Without a way to find meaning and purpose in what we do and in our experiences, no matter how small, we are lost.

Soul Work: What part of your life—any situation or relationship—distracts you from your soul? Look for the symbolic meaning that this situation has for you. What does it teach you about your power struggles? About forgiveness? What insights can your soul give you to transform this situation or relationship? What other questions about your life should you now consider from the perspective of a mystic? You can gain insight into any situation through mystical consciousness.

THE FOURTH ROOM:
Your Search for Purpose and Meaning

When did you first ask, "What is the purpose of my life?" What motivated you to ask that question? How did you expect the answer to come? How did you expect your life would change?

Soul Work: Be very honest in your dialogue with your soul as you pursue the question of meaning and purpose. Note that the emphasis on these questions returns you to the beginning of your search, not to the present moment. Who were you then and who are you now? How have you changed and matured

since you began your spiritual journey, and what have you discovered about your purpose in life? What would you need to
hear in order to recognize that you were just told your meaning
and purpose in life? What are you waiting to hear? If you cannot
hear from your soul, are you blocking what you don't want to
hear?

INTO FLIGHT: THE SILKWORM BECOMES THE BUTTERFLY

The silkworm, wrote Teresa, is like the soul. "She comes alive
with the heat of the Holy Spirit and begins to accept the help
God is offering." (*The Interior Castle*, Starr)

The soul builds a cocoon where it will die, says Teresa, only
to be liberated into flight once fully mature. She could not have
chosen a more perfect metaphor, for the caterpillar has no
choice but to spin a cocoon and become a butterfly. It is its destiny. The same is true for the soul. This is the perfect metaphor
to describe the ending of one cycle of consciousness and the beginning of another.

The time within the cocoon is difficult, however, for the soul
does not know how long it must remain in the darkness. The silkworm is in a highly vulnerable state, unable to protect itself, relying on camouflage to conceal it from predators. The soul is
between worlds, in between identities.

What cocoons have you had to endure? The experience of
dying to a certain kind of life and being born into another is archetypal, like the Phoenix descending into the ashes, only to be
reborn and rise once again.

You may struggle all the way into the cocoon, but you cannot
sidestep a cocoon experience if it is time for one in your life. You
can choose, however, how to experience the cocoon. You may be
able to draw comfort from recognizing that you are preparing
for emergence into the light, rather than fear that you are alone

in a dark, lonely place. To be able to illuminate your most painful moments—or days or months—with the mystical truth that you are living a transformation in progress brings God into the walls of your soul.

THE FIFTH ROOM:
Into the Cocoon

The cocoon experience is the archetype of death and rebirth, an ending and a beginning. You have been in a cocoon before and will return to one again. That is the wheel of life. What matters is what takes place within the cocoon.

Soul Work: Imagine that you are wrapped in a cocoon with your soul, waiting for a new life to begin. You cannot see the new life forming around you, but you know that the old life is dying. As you take time to rest from the old life, you recognize that you are growing wings.

What parts of your life do you need to let die? Are there habits you need to release or attitudes that simply do not serve you any longer? If you are in a cocoon, then you are dying to something. What is it? Work with this consciousness no matter how painful it is for you. Trust in the insights you receive and the mystical act of rebirth.

THE SIXTH ROOM:
Mystical Flight

Mystical flight inevitably follows your cocoon experience. You will emerge a butterfly. Hold that image. The ego dies in the cocoon so that the soul can take flight.

*S*oul *Work:* What must you leave behind in the cocoon and shake off as you emerge? You cannot have secrets from your soul. Ask your soul whether you are willing to be released into mystical flight. Is there any ego fragment left that you need to slip off? As you emerge from the cocoon, what do you see? Rest outside the cocoon. Dry your new wings. Can you fly in the new light around you?

MYSTICAL MARRIAGE

By the time Teresa wrote *The Interior Castle,* her relationship to Jesus had become mystically sensual. Often Teresa would enter into states of such transcendent bliss with Jesus that she experienced what can only be described as "mystical orgasms"; indeed, she became famous for these experiences in particular and for levitating during pinnacle moments of illumination and ecstasy.

> The comparison is a crude one, but the sacrament of marriage is as close as I can come to evoking the bonding that unfolds between the soul and God. The difference is that human marriage contains all things while in this spiritual wedding nothing remains that is anything other than spiritual. Pleasures of the body have little to do with this union; the spiritual delights the Beloved shares with the soul are a thousand leagues removed from the pleasures married people must experience. *It is all about love melting into love.* Its expression is absolutely pure, exceedingly delicate, and gentle. There is no way to describe it, but the Beloved knows how to make it deeply felt . . . he

arranges for them to meet alone together, as they say, and joins himself with her.

—*The Interior Castle*, Starr

A Moment of Contemplation

Your union with God is a union of a human soul and a cosmic force. As above, so below. By entering your Castle, you no longer leave the world, but empower yourself within the world. You are learning to love heaven and Earth, God and self, to be one with the soul of humanity. The exploration of your Castle is indeed long, but what a worthy journey it is.

Exit Prayer

I am a channel of grace. As I leave my Castle, grace surrounds me and grace protects me. I enter my life under the blessing of God and I remain open to receive guidance from my soul.

THE SIXTH MANSION

Essential Wisdoms and the Final Fire

> Remember: in this state of prayer nothing can be seen—
> not in the ordinary seeing, anyway—not even in the imagi-
> nation.
>
> —Teresa of Ávila
> *The Interior Castle*, Starr

I WAS TWENTY-FOUR YEARS OLD when I first saw a holy man from India and heard him lecture. Not yet having attended graduate school in theology, I had not truly opened up to the messages of spiritual teachers from all world traditions. The holy man was dressed all in white and had a long beard. I still recall his radiant smile. Everyone in the room was awestruck by him, bowing to him, which at the time made me so uncomfortable that I left the room and listened to the lecture from the hall. Distracted, I heard only bits and pieces until almost the end, when I stepped just inside the doorway and heard someone ask, "What is the greatest gift we can give the world?" The holy man smiled and giggled, and replied, "A fully healthy you."

I thought, What a ridiculous answer.

Of course, today I would think, What a wise, wise response. If we could each be fully healthy, what a world this would be. This illuminated soul passed on to me a true gift of wisdom that has guided me ever since to try to help others find their real power.

The Sixth Mansion is a masterpiece of mystical literature, an archive of instruction and wisdom. "If one is not oneself a sage or a saint," Aldous Huxley wrote, "the best thing one can do . . . is to study the works of those who were, and who, because they had modified their merely human mode of being, were capable of a more than merely human kind and amount of knowledge."

Teresa ascends fully into her role as an illuminated mystic, writing extensively about the signatures of mystical experiences. In this mansion, which could stand on its own as a treatise of the soul's experiences with God, Teresa is authoritative. In the lower mansions, she often asked, "But what do I know?" Here, she discerns authentic from inauthentic mystical experiences with details that would have been unappreciated in an earlier mansion. Every line of instruction in the Sixth Mansion is as applicable to us today as it was to the nuns she guided four hundred years ago. It is apparent that she intended this to be a no-nonsense instructional classroom for those students who managed to make it this far in their inner pilgrimage. Instructions end at the Sixth Mansion. The Seventh Mansion is the experience of being "consumed" by God, taken into divine consciousness.

Teresa shares her personal life with God throughout *The Interior Castle,* but her revelations in the Sixth Mansion sometimes read as if she is copying pages from her diary, particularly when she writes about some of her most intimate encounters with her beloved. Among these exquisite passages is the one describing her most well-known mystical apparition (depicted in Bernini's sculpture, *The Ecstasy of St. Teresa*) in which an angel pierces her heart with an arrow, sending her into an altered state of cosmic pain and ecstasy. To show that no soul is free of the challenges of ordinary life, regardless of how intimate its relationship with God, Teresa also includes among her mystical experiences recollections of her personal sufferings. For instance, she felt harshly judged by her community for the grace she obviously received from heaven. She was thought by some to be a spiritual exhibitionist and had even been accused of consorting with the devil. After a point, even her spiritual directors—before John of the Cross—did not support her interpretation of her mystical experiences.

Nonetheless, Teresa maintains her commitment to remain humble. Had she written about one mystical experience after another, she would have created an impression of herself as flawless, so I suspect that she quite deliberately included her failings. And yet, even her characteristic self-deprecation is noticeably reduced in this mansion, as if she is saying, "I haven't got time to keep that up and transfer all my wisdom."

Although this mansion is but one away from the Seventh Mansion, where divine marriage is discussed, the mystical sojourner is still like an initiate: so close to God and yet so far. Revealing so many secrets of the soul draws evil as well as light, for light always attracts the dark. Final tests and obstacles arise in this mansion, as if you are going into the desert for forty days—a final walk of fire, a last cleansing. Simultaneously, the interior life and insights are heightened further, as if God is stretching your consciousness to its full capacity. You must contain your humanness and divinity, shadow and light, all consciously. Your soul may be flooded with realizations from the collective unconsciousness or divine illumination, which can cause agony and ecstasy. Your challenge is to find the stamina to maintain your human and heavenly connections with prayer.

As with much of Teresa's writings, woven in among her profound mystical instructions are praises and prayers written to the divine as her beloved Jesus. This imagery of a passionate relationship to Jesus as a partner in a mystical union can be difficult to comprehend until you consider that Jesus is the equivalent of the Buddha, Krishna, the Great Spirit, the Goddess, or the Beloved in Rumi's poetry. Teresa is describing a transcendence of the physical, five-sensory world and all its illusions. She reached enlightenment, nirvana. She was released from the wheel of samsara, or however one wishes to frame the cosmic pilgrimage of this great soul who, in the sixteenth century incarnated as St. Teresa of Ávila.

FIVE ESSENTIAL WISDOMS ABOUT PRAISE AND CRITICISM

Teresa probably never thought that her writings would fall into the hands of non-Catholics and help them find their souls and God. That would have been incomprehensible at the time, even though Spain had been home to Jews and Muslims for seven hundred years before their expulsion in 1492, and even though the Protestant Reformation was in full swing after Martin Luther's 1577 revolt. Her Catholic spirit comes through every word, but you read it in archetypal ways. You do not take the imagery literally. At one workshop, while teaching this material, a student told me that she was offended by the bad rap that reptiles were getting from Teresa's characterization of them. This is nonsense. Though her language is archaic, underlying it is a deep understanding of human nature, the soul, compassion, and cosmic consciousness. You can use this road map in the Sixth Mansion every moment of your life.

Teresa understood the pain of betrayal, having been the subject of her fellow nuns' gossip and criticism. But, she points out, praise is equally painful. Both praise and criticism test the ego and the soul; illusions of earthly power can seduce anyone who is unable to remain humble. A rise in power and status always brings challenges, and everyone around you—professional colleagues, friends, or family—will have opinions of your conduct. Few people will praise you, especially if they perceive that your empowerment diminishes theirs. You will be a target of criticism—on that you can count. Thus, it is wise to know how to maneuver through ups and downs, through cycles of power and disempowerment. Teresa gives five specific rules for dealing with your need for praise and vulnerability to criticism. Each is as valuable to someone on a spiritual path as it would be to anyone in the outside world, because the underlying issues concern the management of power, vanity, ego, and the control we give to others over our lives. Here are her rules to hold to in your inner and external life:

- Do not be judgmental. Everyone, including you, is quick to make both positive and negative judgments of others and of the trials God sends us. You never know the truth of what God has in mind. To judge anything at all is an error.
- Never envy the experiences of others, spiritually or otherwise, because envy reveals a lack of humility. By your actions and attitude, you are demanding to be given what is not rightly yours. To envy the mystical experiences or the spiritual life or calling of others hurts the soul. Envy is a reptile.
- Everything good about you comes from God—your talent, your skills, and all your abilities; thus, you should not take credit. To fuel your ego shows a lack of wisdom. Control your ego, be humble about your gifts so that you do not misuse them; when you keep yourself focused and clear that God is truly the source of your gifts, your struggle with being pulled apart by either praise or criticism will cease.
- Remain humble. Do not look for praise. When someone praises you for your gifts, do not let the energy of that praise penetrate your ego or your mind. It will fuel your insecurities rather than support your soul. You will begin to think, What if I lose this talent? or, What if I fail? You will begin to torment yourself with thoughts of how others are judging your actions. You will create goals for yourself instead of listening to inner instructions and guidance for how you are supposed to use your gifts. Soon your gifts will fall under the control of others, as you will fall prey to their judgments of you and lose sight of your trust in God.
- Develop a special appreciation of those who criticize you;

do not resent them. They are your allies. Look on them as sacred adversaries in action in your life. They are more helpful than those who praise you because they support your humbleness. They have a true spiritual role in your life. To resent those who criticize you is to forget that you have also criticized others. Remember to use your soul's ability to illuminate your shadows so that you see clearly through seemingly negative events. Always, beyond the darkness, God's greater plan is in motion. That is the truth you need to trust. It is a truth reached through prayer and the security of humility.

Entry Prayer

I cross the bridge into the silent bliss of my Castle. I close the drawbridge and forbid all outside influences from entry into this holy place that is my soul. Here in my Castle, I am alone with God. Under God's light and companionship I discover the depth and beauty of my soul. I embrace the power of prayer. I open myself to divine guidance. I surrender myself to become as a channel for grace, healing, and service as God directs my life.

Rooms of Gifts

THE FIRST ROOM:
The Source and Meaning of Gifts

Your entire life is a gift from God, not just your talents and abilities. Yet, do you really believe that? Do you live in that truth or are those just words that you speak because they are the right thing to say? Could you ever declare a suffering or an illness or a handicap a gift from God and mean it?

What gifts have you been given in this lifetime? What gifts do you have beyond your obvious talents? A gift does not have to be glamorous. You may overlook many of your gifts because they require too much effort to develop or they cause you difficulty.

Soul Work: In this room, reflect upon the many gifts of your soul, most of which you have never noticed. You know the obvious ones; you have yet to discover the many jewels in your soul. Consider this the resource room of your soul, the place where you come to discover untapped potential, talent, and vision. The more you learn about your soul, the more you will discover yet a new gift, yet another jewel. Each time you enter this room, ask your soul to reveal at least three new gifts that are waiting to emerge. Do not look for the obvious, which your rational mind is inclined to do. You must approach this exercise as a mystic, as someone who recognizes the value of the subtle abilities of the soul and the power of a positive attitude. Let your soul reveal its potential to you in this room. This exercise will change your life each time you do it.

THE SECOND ROOM:
Do You Need Praise?

In this room, consider how you react to praise. We face criticism every day and are also overlooked or invisible. We like praise because it proves that we are visible, that we matter. People say that they give gifts with no strings attached, but they generally have an underlying agenda. To be able to give freely of your gifts, you must transcend both the need for praise and the fear of being criticized.

Soul Work: Ask your soul for guidance: Are you still seeking praise? You have done a lot of work to free yourself from the control that others' opinions have over you. Where and under what circumstances are you still wounded over lack of praise or recognition? How can you reengage your humility to protect you in these situations? Remember that praise and criticism are the opposite ends of the same power. To be detached from both is to be truly free.

THE THIRD ROOM:
Cycles of Power

You are never fully empowered and you are never fully disempowered. Power is a cycle like all other forces in nature, but you always have the power of prayer. Be mindful of your cycles of power. When you feel yourself slipping into a time of disempowerment, do not be afraid. It is only a cycle of nature. You can see past and transcend it.

Soul Work: Enter into a dialogue with your soul about your relationship to empowerment and disempowerment. When do these cycles come and go? Study them so that you can learn to remain centered through both extremes. Neither is permanent. Your task is to acknowledge the fear and then to respond as if you were a mystic, reminding yourself that divine power *is* permanent.

THE FOURTH ROOM:
Invisibility

To walk invisibly in the world tests your soul. Invisibility means that you are able to receive guidance and act on it in silence, following through with detachment and faith. You are released from the ego's need to judge the significance of your actions and see their consequences. You are able to trust that all that you do has value or you would not have been guided on your course.

Soul Work: Test yourself in your world. Opportunities to serve in invisible ways exist in every moment, from offering a prayer of support to a kind word about another person in private. There is no end to how you can be of service and remain an invisible source of grace in this world.

THE FIFTH ROOM:
What Is Not Rightly Yours

If you are envious, you are in danger of being deceived and you will prostitute your soul to anyone who you think can offer you a shortcut to what you want, whether that is wealth, happiness, success, fame, power, love, or a path to God. But ultimately you learn—and it is always very painful—that there is no such thing as a shortcut where the soul's journey is concerned. Envy is a reptile, a dangerous force that can lead to destructive choices. Teresa would call it evil. And the worst suffering of all is that envy blinds you to the wonders in your own life.

Soul Work: Do you love your own life? That question introduces the task in this room, which is to take your life apart, piece by piece, examining each fragment for its beauty, purpose, and value, in order to decide whether you love your life. Perhaps you love part of your life, but not all of it. Or perhaps you love your life, but not all of the people in your life. To love your life with conditions indicates that you are bargaining with the divine, and that you harbor anger and disappointment at the package your life came in. The inability to love your life makes you crave someone else's; from that craving comes envy. From a mystical perspective, every part of your life is as it should be and all parts are moving pieces—a truth to dwell on and work with.

This exercise can be on-going as you continue to acquire more relationships and more belongings and more of everything. As a way of organizing your thinking process, try starting with the letter A and going to Z, listing all your items in alphabetical order. However you make your list, as it grows, evaluate the item as something you love or not. If you don't love it, why not? Can you have a change of heart? If it is not important, don't bother. If it is, work on it. This is a rigorous practice for discovering how seriously you take the business of loving your own life.

THE SIXTH ROOM:
What Are Your Hidden Desires?

When you want something, the imagination finds it easy to take over and provide fantasies, telling you whatever you want to hear. You become vulnerable to seduction. The imagination has no capacity to reason or to see clearly through the shadow of desire.

Soul Work: Examine the hidden desires and emotions that stir negative images and bring only restlessness to your mind and soul. If these desires were rightly yours, you would not feel consumed with negative feelings. Instead, you would be guided toward their fulfillment. These despairing emotions are your soul telling you that you are focusing your attention where it should not be. What choices are you making that come from wanting what is not yours? What actions do such desires lead you to make? What do you tell yourself to try to convince yourself that these desires are good for you and will serve your life path? And why do you not listen to the restlessness coming from your soul? Why do you deny that this restlessness is guidance?

THE SEVENTH ROOM:
Releasing the Gifts of Your Soul

It is fair to wonder why you must do all the rigorous work of self-reflection and constant inner maintenance. What is the purpose, after all? Your soul is a vessel of sacred graces: compassion, harmony, wisdom, love, endurance, humor, patience, healing, and vision. The fierce work of inner cleansing and the building of stamina lead you to discover these qualities in yourself, not as theory but as fact. These become the true substance of who you are in the world; these are the essence, the building blocks of your highest potential.

*S*oul *Work:* Choose one quality of the soul listed above at a time. Reflect on that quality at length in your journal, applying the meaning and significance of its power in your life. How would that divine force change the quality of your life? How would it change your life's direction? Then take that power into the world with you. Imagine yourself connected to that grace, as if it is flowing through you constantly, influencing your thoughts and actions. Reflect at a later time upon the difference that grace has made in your life.

THE EIGHTH ROOM:
Reverse Envy

If you envy others, convincing yourself that you know what you need in this world, none of your decisions and choices will bring you happiness. From envy comes poor judgment. Envy is poison in your eyes and in your heart.

Soul Work: In this room, dialogue with your soul about people you envy or have envied. One at a time, look for their difficulties, fears, or hardships. Meditate on what they have suffered and imagine yourself in their place, suffering their losses, their illnesses, their pain. Does anyone truly know the sufferings in your soul? How foolish does this envy seem now?

THE NINTH ROOM:
Which Choices Have Brought You Happiness?

How much of your happiness was really the result of something you chose? Or was your happiness the result of an odd mixture of experiences that seemed to come out of the blue? Some seemed to be disasters at the time, and others were the best things that ever happened to you.

Soul Work: In this dialogue with your soul, examine your choices compared with God's choices for you. Which have worked out better? Which choices have required that you accept the circumstances *before* everything worked out for the best?

ON SUFFERING

Not a path exists in the physical world that is without pain, fear, suffering, grief, loss, and trauma. Yet, quite clearly, we cause much of our own problems. You may suffer a bit as a result of your choice to become conscious, but the decision to expand your self-knowledge and knowledge of God does not mean the *beginning* of suffering—it means a different type of suffering. When you violate your conscience and consciousness—when you know better but choose to think or act otherwise—you will indeed suffer. And the greatest suffering comes from self-betrayal—that is, when you have heard your intuitive guidance but repressed, denied, or deliberately acted against it. Indeed, this causes pain because you made the *choice to become more conscious* yet betrayed your soul when it spoke to you.

To Teresa, pain and suffering are caused by not trusting God on your spiritual journey and not listening to your inner voice. To disconnect from that voice is to wander into the dark woods alone. You need to pray in order to find your way back to the path.

Another source of pain can come from personal betrayal and inadequate spiritual direction. When Teresa listened to unhelpful counsel, she felt more isolated. Some, envious of her inner life, broke her confidences, exploiting their private conversations to create scandals and sensationalism. Be very careful before you share any sorts of insights, even nonspiritual ones. Imagine that you have shared a deeply personal secret with someone, trusting that this individual would keep your confidence. Within a day you learn that it took all of one hour before your secret was betrayed. You feel pain at such a betrayal and pain at having to cope with the consequences of the secret being exposed. You can blame this individual, who of course is at fault, but at the same time you must also question your wisdom in choosing to share your confidences. Whom did you choose and why? Were you looking for emotional validation and attention? Were you looking to feel special in that moment?

A secret is actually a unit of power. You must exercise great discernment anytime you are considering releasing that type of power, be it spiritual, personal, or financial, into the hands of another person. You must question your motives, illuminate your desire and aim, and ask yourself, "Why am I doing what I am doing in this moment?"

Use discernment especially when sharing spiritual or mystical experiences. These gifts of grace are meant to be held within your soul. They are to fill you and feed you during contemplation, a kind of divine fuel, a spiritual manna, as Dante called it. This grace animates cosmic insights that can comfort or inspire you, "aha" moments that channel grace into your system, providing a perspective you could not see ordinarily. Keep your grace within your Castle. Practice silence. Apply grace where it is clearly needed. Share your insights only with carefully chosen soul companions.

Rooms of Secrets

THE FIRST ROOM:
Secrets You Have Not Kept and Why

To be a keeper of secrets is a sacred trust and requires a strong soul. If your soul lacks the stamina to maintain a secret, you should say to the person who wants to confide in you, "Do not tell me your secret because I am not strong enough to keep it." Then, discuss this with your soul.

Soul Work: Why are you not yet strong enough to keep a secret? Why would you share someone's secret? What if God gave you a secret to hold, perhaps a revelation to keep only in your soul? Could the secret someone gave you actually be a divine trust? What do you need to do to prepare to receive secrets?

THE SECOND ROOM:
Are You the Goal or Is God?

You can lose your focus on the spiritual path, making yourself the goal instead of mystical illumination. This happens, understandably, because you are in your body and in your life and your body can become weak and your life can become overwhelming. But your body and your life are in service to your soul—that is the vision you must strive to animate. When you lose your focus and are taken in by an earthly concern that causes you suffering, enter into a dialogue with your soul in which you ask to see the symbolic meaning of your suffering.

Soul Work: Let your soul reveal the deeper meaning of the suffering you are temporarily enduring. Detach from the grip it now has on your life. Rise above the suffering; see it from high above. Ask your soul to illuminate your interior, to transform your suffering into insight and purpose. Pray for this profound act of transformation.

THE THIRD ROOM:
How Do You Embrace Grace?

Grace is divine fire, cosmic power, that runs through your being, calming your body, inspiring your thoughts, healing your physical pain, preventing you from an accident, guiding your inner journey. Grace is the indescribable breath of God entering into your being while you pray. Grace is the energy you call upon to help another person in need of comfort, healing, or inspiration. To embrace grace, become aware of its presence in your life, mindful of the reality of this divine substance.

*S*oul *Work:* Ask your soul how you can know grace as an essential force in your life. Pray and be still so that you become aware of what your charism—your special grace—feels like when it enters your system. Practice consciously embracing grace with your soul. Come back to this room. As you practice, your capacity to contain grace for others expands.

BE MINDFUL OF EVIL

Evil was a genuine adversary for Teresa and had many manifestations. She was not physically chasing demons down the halls of her convent, but she saw evil as ever present, a force against which you must be on your guard. Doubts and fears qualify as the workings of evil; for example, doubting your inner experiences of God is evil. The force of evil finds a weakness in your psyche and takes advantage of it at every possible opportunity. If you have a fear of being rejected, for example, evil would animate that fear every time you felt insecure. You would interpret everything you heard in every conversation through your fear of rejection, drowning out all other reasonable interpretations. This noise in your head would then lead you to make poor choices in your relationships and other areas of life.

Prayer and faith are your protection. I once asked a very blessed mystic for advice about some matter that would require that I meet with a person whom I considered harmful. His counsel to me was to prepare for that meeting by spending a couple of hours in prayer. He said, "You must always prepare to meet evil by building a field of grace with prayer. Evil cannot penetrate grace." I understood then that the individual I was meeting was not evil; a psychic field of evil had gathered around him and was taking advantage of his fears; as a result he was making decisions that harmed many people. But I built a field of grace that allowed me to be near him and not lose my center.

Evil is a very real force, just as goodness is a real presence in the world. Never be so proud as to believe that because we live in a modern world with electrical lights and plumbing and computers, darkness and the devil have vanished.

CHARACTERISTICS OF MYSTICAL EXPERIENCES

The divine comes upon or speaks to the soul unexpectedly. In the Sixth Mansion, you open yourself to mystical encounters or visitations but you do not expect them. Teresa never expected any of her experiences with God, and this teaching of no expectations is among her most important contributions. Even though these raptures can seem miraculous, Teresa cautions us not to expect miracles. Stay mindful of your limitations; stay humble. You are a vessel, a conduit for grace, not a generator.

One characteristic of the mystical experience is the pain that is not a pain, a sensual, mystical fire that ignites within the soul. The fire takes you over, but, just before the point where you feel that you are about to burst into flames, it goes out, leaving you wanting more of God. The experience ends as instantly as it began, lasting only seconds, not minutes. Another, similar experience is to feel as if you suddenly burst into flames and a powerful fragrance has engulfed you and spread through your senses. Unlike the pain that is not a pain, this mystical experience activates a divine fire of love.

The divine may also speak to the soul through *intellectual* visions. These transmissions are in absolutely clear words that are spoken "even though He speaks them in secret." During an intellectual vision, you are disconnected from the world, and though the soul is able to remember the revelation in every detail, you cannot communicate it verbally. This is a deeper, more personal experience than in earlier mansions when the divine appeared in signs or symbols that you had to interpret. These visions are not fleeting or volitional. During a true vision, a powerful stirring occurs and then suddenly everything goes quiet. Without any effort on the soul's part, wisdom overcomes unconsciousness and certainty replaces all doubt. Teresa also describes visual revelations, or imaginative visions, which she says are useful because they match up more with our animal nature; our senses are engaged.

In intellectual visions, the soul suddenly feels the presence of God beside her, not with the five senses but through the intellect. According to Teresa, deception is not possible in an intellectual vision. The effects it creates inside the soul are so beneficial that the spirit of evil could never be responsible for them. Goodness flows from the vision. This experience could not be the result of a mental imbalance, either, because the results are too glorious. The soul is awash with a profound serenity and left with a special knowledge of God. God alerts you that he is always beside you. The constancy of divine companionship gives rise to a most tender love for God, awakening a more profound purity of consciousness because the presence at your side makes your soul more sensitive to everything.

The still, small voice is a common way through which God speaks to us. Yet, many times I have suspected that the voice people tell me they heard was simply their imagination, because the details and demands were fairly earthbound. Every now and again, though, I meet someone who radiates a certain grace that indicates a rich inner life. Now, as ever, if you ask for inner guidance, *you are going to receive inner guidance. And it will come through your interior channels.* A letter will not drop out of the sky into your lap; the phone will not ring with God on the other end; you will not be transported into the next phase of your life without effort.

The Bible and other sacred literature are filled with stories of spiritual voices, from Moses and the burning bush to Mary receiving the message that she was about to become the mother of Jesus. People have told me countless wonderful stories of a voice that told them to sell their homes, or quit their jobs, or that they would marry the man or woman they were with. Two women told me that they heard a voice tell them that, regardless of what the medical tests said, they would indeed get pregnant. And they did.

People often ask me, "I am praying for guidance, but I don't hear anything. What am I doing wrong?" I have even had people say they must be using the wrong prayers, as if prayers were magical spells. Many people are simply not prepared to handle the consequences of receiving guidance, so they don't hear their guidance. Most people receive responses to their prayers through intuition rather than a direct communication from God, which can be overwhelming. You need a ferocious degree of stamina in order to deal with both the experience of guidance and the message. You need to trust in the authenticity of your experiences and unconditionally trust in God.

Teresa, one of God's great conspirators, heard the voice of God in many expressions. The five characteristics of a genuine spiritual voice are as valid today as they were a half millennium ago:

1. It is so clear that the soul remembers every word as well as the tone. The messages carry divine power and authority.

2. It is unexpected. Frequently, these messages come when we are preoccupied with other thoughts, and they so thoroughly eclipse the usual mind-body conversation that they jolt us into paying attention. They often reveal a future that the soul never believed could or would happen. Imagination cannot make that up if it's never occurred to the mind. Because this communica-

tion interferes with the rational mind's preoccupations, it is a strong indication that the communication is not self-generated.

The message also converts into powerful action for good. Imagine a time when you were sad or upset by something. If a person who truly does not care about you says, "Oh, things will be okay. Don't worry about it," you would feel no comfort at all. But if someone you love and trust says, "Be not troubled," you would feel that she was sent by God to deliver that message to you.

Many people have shared stories with me of how a dear person happened to show up at the right time, delivering just the right message, a coincidence that they viewed as divinely choreographed. Teresa would hear, "It is I, fear not," during some of her more troubled moments and would know that all would be well.

3. It is the truth. In a false spiritual voice, the imagination tells you what you want to hear. A spiritual voice that comes from God leaves the soul in great quietude. A calm beyond calmness lingers in the soul, sometimes for days. One woman told me that when she was rushing to work, desperately worried that she and her partners were going to lose their fledgling business, she saw a church on her way. She closed her eyes and said a prayer of surrender: "I give the entire situation over to God. I release everything." Later, during a meeting at the office, when fear gripped the entire team, she "suddenly . . . felt completely enveloped by the most awesome power of transcendent quiet. I could hear everyone, but I knew I had been taken out of the toxic field of stress and placed into this indescribable divine calm. The uselessness of fear became so apparent. I always return to the sense of this quiet in my memory, even if I can't attain that state of complete tranquility. Still, the memory that I had such a mystical state is itself bliss."

Another man shared his experience: "I was doing all the things that a person does to get ready for Christmas, and the commercialism of Christmas had begun to annoy me. I had to wrap presents and finish other shopping for the kids and my wife and I could tell she was getting uptight because of the holidays, so I just withdrew to my study and pulled out a book by Thomas Merton. I opened it randomly, glancing at various lines until I read, 'This day will not come again.' Immediately, I looked up and saw my children and my wife, the Christmas tree, the lights, the house, the presents, and pictured them grown-up and gone and my wife and me alone in this big house. Suddenly I was overcome with the gratitude of being reminded once again of the preciousness of each moment, and I entered into a deep prayer of thank you, thank you, thank you. And then, as if a soft, comforting, warm breeze had found its way into my office, I was overcome by a depth of quietness, a sacred quietness, that I have never experienced before in my life. God visited me in that moment."

4. Your comprehension is instantaneous, as if you are transferred from a state of not knowing to one of complete knowing at the speed of light. The message does not fade from your memory, ever, whereas we forget, sometimes in minutes, other things we hear. Authentic words are burned into your memory and soul.

I had the pleasure of knowing a man who was a member of the Brothers of the Sacred Heart. He told me that he had gone to the chapel to pray about his vocation because he was deeply troubled and didn't know how to tell his spiritual director about his doubts or even when to bring them up. He was kneeling in front of a statue of Jesus with his head down, deep in prayer, and when he was finished, he got up to leave, only to see his spiritual director seated at the back of the chapel. The director rose to greet him, saying, "I myself was in prayer when the holy spirit told me to come to you because you were troubled. Shall we talk now?" My friend broke into tears at the very thought that God would work so perfectly through the prayers and revelations of those in our lives. An understanding of the well-being of another person or of the depth of his pain can be given to you as a way of consoling him—a true gift from the spirit.

5. The truth that is conveyed transcends all words. In this case, you communicate that truth through personal transformation or through shifts in your charism or spiritual power. These changes are often more noticeable to others than they are to you. Many mystical experiences are experiences of truth that cannot be conveyed in words but are absorbed into and conveyed through the power of the mystic's soul. One of my dearest friends had a near-death experience during a serious illness that left him in a coma for weeks. His recovery was dubious for months. During his long recovery, he had to rely on his soul for all the stamina he could muster, and as a result of his inner spiritual work, he discovered that he had unlocked the ability to heal. He had experienced his immortality and returned to his physical body, and the truth of that vision of light not only transformed his health but flowed through his hands as a healer.

On the other hand, if a spiritual voice is a product of your imagination, the first four characteristics do not apply. You will have to work to remember the details of the communication, and frequently the message will become unclear. The message will not be calming but agitating. Most people will be inclined to reveal such a message all too soon.

The Different Spiritual Voices

In spite of Teresa's many spiritual communications, including visitations from angels, saints, and the divine, she was overwhelmed with feelings of isolation at times. She was remarkably strong to experience such a vast cosmic life with only herself to rely on for its validation.

She described five characteristics of spiritual voices:

1. Spiritual voices have one of three sources: God, evil, or our imagination. There are no others.
2. Some spiritual voices come from outside the soul and oth-

ers from the depths of the soul. Spontaneous experiences of either or both are possible.

3. Some of these experiences filter down from the highest part of the soul; others are so external that it can seem as if a physical voice has spoken audible words.

4. Sometimes a spiritual voice is simply a figment of imagination or an artifact of a mental imbalance. Should you come across people whom you suspect are involved with a false spiritual voice, listen to them with compassion, but do not encourage them to pursue their spiritual practice or to spend time alone. Hearing false spiritual voices is one indication that you lack the stamina to continue internal work for now. You may require a more external life. If you are hearing these other voices, you are susceptible to psychic attacks, depression, and spiritual illnesses, as well as to attracting the energy of evil. When your imagination is stronger than your soul, then the imagination can hurt you, and you can be swayed by fear, greed, envy, or pride.

5. Divine messages are of pure intent. They will never contain a shred of criticism or negativity about another human being, as that is not the dialogue of God. Finally, dismiss any message that does not completely and fully support revealed truth.

Rooms with Divine Communications

THE FIRST ROOM:
An Authentic Voice

To listen for an authentic voice requires that you spend time in contemplation, silence, and prayer. And you must work through the inauthentic voices chattering in your head, making noise and creating distractions. Everyone has said at one time or another that he was following inner guidance when it was really his own will behind his actions.

Become aware of your soul's voice. This will make self-deception more difficult. The soul is a relentless representative of God. After you hear it once, you can never turn off that connection. Establishing that clear connection to your soul is done in several ways, one of which is acknowledging what is *not* the voice of your soul.

Soul Work: What are the inauthentic voices telling you? What do you listen to in your head all day long?

THE SECOND ROOM:
Divine Intervention

God comes into your life in many ways and, without doubt, incidences of divine intervention are among the most sacred and mysterious. These are acts of mystical intimacy. These interventions can manifest in infinite varieties—subtly, as when you hear a slight, swift voice in your head that says, "Don't say that," or, "Say this." Or, visibly, as when you actually see a figure who talks to you. Appreciate all of them.

Soul Work: In this room, work with your soul to recall how God has communicated with you through acts of divine intervention. Seeing God in the details of your life helps you recognize the constant occurrence of acts of divine intervention and helps you develop mystical vision—a deliberate practice of seeing God in the unplanned experiences of your life. Appreciate these each day and keep a record of them in your spiritual journal.

THE THIRD ROOM:
Being a Mystic Without a Monastery

Living in the world as a mystic without a monastery is your new challenge. But it will not be as difficult as you might think. Mysticism and mystical consciousness is a way of seeing the whole of your life with divine vision and of seeing the presence of God in the details of everything you do and in everyone you are with. Meaning and purpose exist even in the smallest of tasks, and above all, you have the knowledge that you are a constant channel for grace in this world and you can silently, invisibly illuminate every situation you are in.

Soul Work: Enter your world as a mystic. Think of yourself as a channel for grace, and practice engaging in life through detachment and by not allowing the ordinary reptiles of negative thinking to penetrate your Castle. Live in fearless bliss and allow the divine to awaken your soul's greatest potential.

THE FOURTH ROOM:
Evaluating Your Stamina

Soul stamina requires a devoted practice to prayer, self-reflection, and living a life enhanced with inspiration. It is not enough to do this practice once a week, as life runs in cycles of stress and joy, hardships and wonders. Every part of life must be absorbed and appreciated for the wisdom it brings. And above all, you must always remain attuned to the voice of your soul.

THE EXPERIENCE OF HOLY RAPTURE

Rapture is the experience of spontaneously being lifted into an altered state of consciousness, taken away from your body and senses, and becoming absorbed into the presence of God. No one was more surprised than Teresa. Of her experiences of levitation in particular, she writes, "Does the soul have any power to resist this transport? None whatsoever. In fact, resistance only makes matters worse. . . . The interior part of the soul has even less power to stop wherever she happens to feel like stopping." (*The Interior Castle*, Starr)

People today do have the experiences that Teresa describes—receiving the grace of quietude and perceiving soul guidance. *The Cloud of Unknowing* notes, "Some people experience . . . rare moments of ecstasy called ravishing, while others experience [God] . . . amid their ordinary daily routine." Experiences of holy rapture are rare, which is not to say that they cannot happen. As Teresa so often points out, it is not for any human being to say what experiences God will visit upon anyone.

The Kinds of Rapture

In one type of holy rapture, the soul isn't even in prayer but is struck by a word it remembers that "makes the spark of a soul's yearning for God burst into flame so that the soul burns entirely and then, like the Phoenix, is reborn. All errors are forgiven. It is a purification." During this rapture, the faculties and senses of the body go dead, but the soul is more alert than in any other state. "During this state, the Beloved likes to show her some secret things, heavenly mysteries and imaginative visions, . . . They are so firmly pressed into her memory that she could never forget them." But they cannot be conveyed with words. "Still, when the soul regains possession of her senses, there are many things they can say about these visions. But, you will ask me, if there are no images and the faculties cannot comprehend anything, how can the visions be retained? I don't understand this, either. What I do know is that there are truths about the greatness of God that are so firmly planted in the garden of the soul that even if she didn't have faith dictating who he is and compelling her to believe that he is God, the soul would adore God from that moment forward." (*The Interior Castle,* Starr)

Sometimes, God carries off the soul and takes your breath away. Your senses may still function, but you cannot speak or move. This is not a seizure or a spell, for there is no pain or black-out or fatigue. After a very short time of absorption, the body seems to come back into itself. After this brief mystical encounter, you are profoundly moved to act only out of love. This force of will and love endures for many days afterward.

In another type of sudden rapture, it really does seem that the spirit is whisked away from the body. Clearly you are not dead, but you cannot say whether you were in your body at certain moments. The sheer speed of this movement is terrifying at first and you feel as if you have been in an entirely different zone from the one in which the rest of humanity lives. In this experience, you and your soul must be brave and trust in God. This is surrender. You are shown a light so rarefied that if you were to spend the rest of your life trying to imagine that light and everything revealed to you there, it would be impossible to catalog them.

As a result of holy raptures, you become more deeply conscious of the greatness of God, you gain humility through self-knowledge, and you lose your appetite for worldly things.

Soul Prayer: To be lifted off the ground in a holy rapture, swept into a divine embrace of light and grace, punctured to the depth of my soul by the force of your existence—could I endure that?

Or do I need doubt to keep me from it? Do I need to keep my faith just in my mind and not allow it to melt into experience? If I surrendered to the experience of you—and ceased talking about you, thinking about you, and thinking about me—and ascended into the experience of you, what would life in this physical world feel like to me again? I would have melted through my body and been taken into the embrace of divine consciousness, only to be put back into my stiff body. Would I have to deliberately welcome back my fears just to feel normal again? Would I do that? Could I actually adjust to having a cosmic soul?

Am I afraid to look upon your face? What would a vision of you change for me? Would that prove you existed for me? Should I fear it? What if you gave me an uncomfortable task? What if I were given a vision that had nothing to do with me or for me, yet my life would be changed as a result?

AUTHENTIC CONTEMPLATION

Some of Teresa's nuns remarked that they could remain in their states of contemplative ecstasy forever, perhaps trying to impress her with their sentiments. Her response was, "This is impossible." For Teresa, mystical experiences are spontaneous; they have a timeless feel but last only moments; and, although they last only moments, they have a far longer-lasting influence.

As a result, God remains in the soul. God in the walls of your soul has a profound effect on you. For instance, you might usually find it difficult to meditate. Meditation is all about seeking God and is usually a state of mind. But once you've found God, the soul doesn't see any reason to wear herself out searching for God through the intellect, for she has already found a direct route.

There's an old Zen story of a traveler who encounters a wandering monk with a great burden of sticks on his back. The traveler asks the monk if he knows the way to enlightenment. The monk nods that he does, so the traveler asks him, "What happens when you get enlightened?" The monk immediately drops his burden. "And what happens after the enlightenment?" the traveler asks. In answer, the monk picks up his bundle and continues on his way.

As Jack Kornfield writes in *After the Ecstasy, the Laundry*, "We all know that after the honeymoon comes the marriage. After the election comes the hard task of governance. In spiritual life, it is the same: After the ecstasy comes the laundry." Even after mystical union, your life is next. You meditate or pray not to avoid your life or your loved ones, but to face them, to be better with them, to do better for them.

There is no place left to go but directly into the Seventh Mansion, directly into the embrace of the divine.

Exit Prayer

I am a channel of grace. As I leave my Castle, grace surrounds me and grace protects me. I enter my life under the blessing of God and I remain open to receive guidance from my soul.

THE SEVENTH MANSION
Divine Marriage, Healing, and Reentering the World

Once you have been shown how to enjoy this Castle you will find rest in everything, even in the things that challenge you the most. You will hold in your heart the hope of returning to the castle, and no one can take that from you.

—Teresa of Ávila
The Interior Castle, Starr

A WOMAN WROTE ME a letter describing an experience that is a type of mystical union. While she was journaling one afternoon, she began to think about the things that mattered to her in life. She found herself locked into an exercise of appreciation that she could not get out of. "It was as if I was given a list of everything and everyone in my life. I felt as if I was being asked how much each person and each thing mattered to me." One by one, she responded, "Yes, this person is important to me, but I am aware that my inner life exists well beyond the boundaries of my relationship to that person, and to that place, and to that thing." Upon completing that exercise, she wrote, "I just sat there, feeling as if I had shed my skin. I felt weightless and then suddenly I was weightless. A light pierced my soul and melted my body and then melted the world around me. I was instantly one with God. This magnificent sensation lasted a second or maybe a minute. I don't know. But when it was over, I was transformed. I felt whole, complete. I felt one with heaven and Earth, as if I contained both without separation, and that feeling has never left me."

In the Seventh Mansion, your soul sheds its earthly skin and becomes completely absorbed by the presence of God. The essence of mystical marriage, for Teresa, was two streams of light coming into a room from two windows, forming one bright river in which the boundaries distinguishing the two vanish. It was also like rain falling into a pool of water, leaving no trace of the individual raindrops in the water. Still, for all her exquisite attempts to lift us into her mystical world, we can only observe her experience and try to follow. For the nature of mystical experience is an intimacy between only the mystic and the divine. Ultimately, as you might discover through your mystical experience, you cannot communicate in words the sensation of the divine entering the walls of your soul any more than you could sell acreage in paradise.

Having mystical experiences or feelings of union, however, does not mean the end of difficulties in life for the soul-journer. No magic number of mystical experiences of quietude or rapture—even if they include the most extraordinary divine revelations—will curtail your need to return to your daily life. You will still have to face the cycle of birth and death, love and betrayal, vengeance and forgiveness, youth and aging, disease and healing. To imagine that being graced with an encounter with God will somehow allow you to manipulate or avoid these challenges would be to forget your basic commitment to humility. The difference between mystics and the individual who stands outside the Castle is that mystics transcend the reasons why suffering is present in their lives. A mystic doesn't find clever or magical ways of avoiding life's chaos. He deals with them with compassion, grace, faith, and trust in God and in his soul connection. He strives to be a servant of God in his thoughts and actions.

As a mystic you should not take your own experience, as the author of *The Cloud of Unknowing* writes, "as the criteria for others. . . ." Do not think, speak, or judge other people on the basis of your experience. "It may be that in God's wisdom those who have in the beginning struggled long and hard at prayer and only tasted its fruits occasionally may later on experience them . . . in great abundance. So it was with Moses. At first he was permitted to gaze upon the Ark [of the Covenant] only now and again and not without having toiled long on the mountain, but later when it was housed in the valley, he gazed on it as often as he liked."

A mystic attempts to work with God and not to offend God by his life—in thoughts or actions. This may seem an outdated, medieval attitude, that God could be offended by an individual's actions. While Hamlet's uncle worried, "O, my offence is rank it smells to heaven," we may only casually sigh, "God forgive me for saying this," or, "God have mercy on us for this war," and immediately move on to the next thought. Teresa was genuinely pained by the thought of human acts that offended God, not because she was judgmental or sentimental but because in divine revelations she had seen and felt the consequences of humanity's misdeeds. She saw that evil was not the will of God but the result of human fear, greed, and vengeance. She saw very clearly that humanity had been given options—that the brutal suffering and destruction caused by war were completely unnecessary.

We have all been stuck in difficult situations at times and have complained, "No matter what I do, nothing seems to change." Teresa also mused that, no matter how much one does, nothing seems to make any real difference in the greater scheme of things. Yet, she emphasized that, nonetheless, we must continue doing and having faith that, somehow, our actions do matter.

At this point on your journey into your soul, you cannot ever really leave the Castle. You cannot withdraw from God. You cannot experience the grace of quietude and then deny it. In fact, once you chose to enter the Castle, you made a one-way decision that is as eternal in its consequences as the eternal nature of the soul itself. You are on a continual journey of spiritual maturity; you are coming of age spiritually through prayer, contemplation, and the arduous task of self-inquiry. You do this in order to comprehend the power of creation that is contained within your soul and to become a channel of truth and grace. All these attributes you then devote to the service of humanity in ways great and small, silent and public, through prayer, action, love, and compassion. You take the warehouse of platitudes you have mouthed over the years—such as, "Life is a spiritual journey," and, "I was born for a purpose"—and finally live your life in accordance with those truths.

Talking about these spiritual teachings, and reading about them, is not a substitute for living them on a daily basis in the arena of your life. You must be willing to incarnate your theology and illuminate the world around you with the power of your soul, a power that ironically may not even require your voice at times. Such power comes through even in silence. Your sole/soul requirement is to commit to being devoted to your inner authority—to the divine. That devotion will give you the will to follow through on all that you are guided to do, say, and become in this life.

The archetypal teachings of Jesus can help guide us to work with and not against our souls and God: his cosmic consciousness, his call to love one another as we love ourselves, to forgive one another as often as necessary, to be of service to one another, and to alleviate suffering. This consciousness burned within Teresa after her vision that her heart was pierced by a divine arrow. She was consumed with the heart of the sacred, immersed in cosmic love, but there she could also feel the pain of humanity that did not know such love. For her, that was a great suffering—a mystical grief—which she attempted to remedy in her writings and teachings.

A mystic necessarily returns to the world and lives a conscious life. You don't remain hidden in prayer and contemplation. You go out into the world to be of use to God by helping others. This is the soul's greatest fulfillment on Earth. The greater the light in the soul, the more difficult one's life is, but not because God sends pain and difficulty. Rather, as we will examine in the next section, truth, revelation, and mystical consciousness are their own particular burden in a world saturated with fear and illusions.

THE MYSTICAL TRINITY REVEALED

The holy trinity is one of the foundational doctrines of Christianity, a mysterious, complex belief that the nature of God comprises the father, the son, and the holy spirit. The sign of the cross—the blessing ritual—honors this belief. The symbolic meaning is the metaphysical, alchemical power of the merger of three cosmic forces into one power, represented in the all-encompassing compassion and consciousness of Jesus. The merger of substance (matter) with power (the soul) and knowing (enlightened consciousness) is the sacred alchemy of Christ Consciousness, the mystical meaning of the trinity, in which all powers are united.

Teresa had a vision in which the divine mystery and power of the holy trinity was revealed to her. It was such a profound vision that she put it into a special category of revelations that she called secret inspirations.

In the Seventh Mansion, Teresa reveals:

The soul enters the innermost chamber through a transcendental vision of the three divine Persons, which imparts to her a particular representation of truth. At first, an incredible clarity descends on the soul like a luminous cloud, setting her spirit on fire and illuminating each of the three aspects of God individually. At the same time, through a wondrous kind of knowledge, she apprehends the truth that all three divine Persons are one substance and one power and one knowing and one God alone.

The soul realizes then that what the rest of us know by faith, you might say, she understands by sight. But this is not seeing with the eyes of the body or even the eyes of the soul. It isn't a visual revelation. Here, all three Persons communicate to the soul. They speak to her, explaining things.

—*The Interior Castle,* Starr

God reveals to Teresa that the divine has no sexual identity or gender. It is a consciousness of light. For a sixteenth-century Catholic nun, this was heresy. God also revealed that the nature of the divine has three expressions: knowledge, power, and substance. All physical teachings are but symbols for a much greater truth. This dismantles the patriarchal view of God completely. It also shows the divine to be a universal, unifying force—both cosmic and intimate—that transcends Christian views and can underlie any religion.

It would be liberating, extraordinary, and profound to have the biological image of the holy trinity converted through spiritual alchemy into a universal, elemental—golden—truth. To be given such a transcendent vision forces your soul wide open and you risk losing any connection to earthly authority. For how could you possibly listen to the arguments of theologians discussing the biological interpretation of the trinity after the truth itself had illuminated your soul? How could you possibly maintain the same relationship with secular or church authorities once you had such an insight? After such experiences, you must put up a front, live behind a mask, and tolerate with a soft heart the gap that exists between what you know to be truth and what others still need to believe.

Thus, Teresa's great awareness was extremely painful. It wasn't fear of the Inquisition—which was in full force at the time—that gave her pain. She had been lifted to the top of the mountain where she could see the beautiful skies and breathe air uncontaminated by Earth's illusions—but she couldn't communicate her vision because most people simply would not have understood. Teresa mystically sensed the collective soul of humanity including the collective fear that comes from not understanding or following the truth. She could see the tragic consequences of human foolishness against a cosmic background and what could be, were they to choose a positive path. Many other mystics have written about the same challenge. Said one extraordinary monk to me, "To experience the divine directly and be among those who doubt the presence and power of God is unendurable." Another contemporary mystic commented, "To experience divine love, to truly experience the floodgates of love opening and flowing into all of life, and then to return to ordinary life where people are so bound by dark emotions and so afraid to love—this is a true suffering for me because I cannot seem to find the way, the path, or the words to free people from their prison. They cling to their fears far more than they trust the power of love."

Another wrote to me, "I find that the most painful part of my journey is repressing my heart to fit into my body again. I have experienced cosmic love, a love of all humanity. That love was given to me. I could not have attained that on my own. I could never really feel love for all of humanity by myself. Then the great love was taken away but not the memory of it, not the impact of it. A stream was left flowing in my heart, like an invitation to follow it back to the ocean of love. Yet it is a bittersweet stream from which to drink because humanity is in such pain and to love anything that suffers too much is to take on that suffering. My only recourse is to pray while I love. I have no other choice, now."

A Moment of Contemplation

Even in the Seventh Mansion, where Teresa merges with God, she encourages us to remain introspective and humble at all times. This is so that, when you are given—or graced with— higher truths, you will be ready to utilize them. You must be willing and prepared to use truth, not just to speak about it. Truth is a tool, a force through which you move life forward. When you go from not knowing that thoughts and attitudes influence your reality to knowing it, you are being given the grace of truth. You must change your life and live according to that truth. You cannot do otherwise. An instinctual gut reaction is guidance, truth from God. You may want to dismiss that guidance because it is too overwhelming and you do not want to become aware of that particular truth, but you cannot deny that you are aware of your guidance. You can no longer deny that you hear the voice of God.

THE MYSTICAL ROOTS OF HEALING

A genuine healing of the body, the heart, and the soul is fundamentally a mystical experience. Besides searching for the meaning and purpose of our lives, we strive to solve the mysteries of our psychic imbalances and physical illnesses. Yet, these days, the need to find the root cause, or reason, for why we break down has become so obsessive that it is a pathology unto itself.

During the years that I gave medical intuitive readings, the people I was trying to help frequently turned their readings into "crime solving" sessions—they were looking for the person or situation that caused the stress or unhappiness that led to their illness or depression or other condition. Many seemed to think that finding this criminal stressor would automatically result in a healing. Their approach also often felt to me like a witch hunt more than a search for healing, except that they were hiding their demons behind terms like *emotional trauma* and *stress,* as if validating their wounds and blaming someone for doing something to them would free them at last.

Crime solving and witch hunts do not heal, as many people eventually discover. Crime solving is soothing for a time to the rational mind, which loves the feeding frenzy of facts and details, especially those that build a case for righteous anger. And hunting witches may give people grounds for burning witches. Only very rarely does a genuine act of forgiveness result. And forgiveness is what heals, not discovering causes, not assigning blame. A genuine healing does not occur in the domain of reason and rational thought. The mind is not an instrument capable of healing the body, much less the heart or the soul. For most people, the mind is full of hissing reptiles that can hardly be silenced—fears, illusions, misgivings, endless anxieties, and misinterpretations of what people have said or done to them. Yet people think this chaotic instrument called the mind has the stamina and focus to dissolve cancer in the cell tissue and stabilize all the systems of the body. Hardly.

Healing is not a rational experience that can be brought about by simply visualizing healthy cells running through your body and replacing malignant ones while the rest of you lives a life so filled with fear that you are unable to make the essential choices you need to in order to release your soul to take over. Unless you are willing to let your soul fully take charge without any conditions, you will never completely heal.

Genuine healing is not physical. It is greater than your rational mind. Indeed, you have to transcend the boundaries and the reptiles of your rational mind to open yourself to the grace that can dissolve illness. During the mystical experience of a healing, your soul becomes more empowered than your body, mind, and heart. It frees itself from the ground rules governing your physical body and your physical life. Your soul becomes more empowered than your body when you truly, deeply, unconditionally surrender the whole of your life to the divine—including your need to know what will happen next and whether you are going to be safe and healthy. You need literally or symbolically to get on your knees in a position of humility and break down or break through the control that reason holds over you. Finally, you do the most unreasonable act imaginable—you trust an invisible force much greater than yourself to reorder the whole of your life. Let God clean house for you. The prayer, "Lord, get me out of my own way," helps many people who want so much to be able to surrender in trust, but cannot do it. Then you say, "I let go and let God."

The divine alters the mystic's relationship to time and space. As Teresa noted many times, she could not recall if she was in the experience of quietude for seconds or minutes. Time always ceases to exist during a mystical experience as you disengage from five-sensory reality. Getting better is always just a matter of time, but healing is another matter entirely. Healing in the mystical sense means that you are not just better, you fully transcend the experience, the history, the setting, and the physical illness that was disrupting your body. A new beginning is given to you—a new life.

And yet, such a healing does not necessarily imply that your physical body has recovered, as the focus of healing within a mystical consciousness is the soul's well-being. One woman, for instance, was burdened with chronic pain because of a birth defect. One day, while praying for someone else, she felt grace course through her body, taking away, melting all the pain. Her body remained handicapped, but the pain was gone. As far as she was concerned, she was fully healed.

Such a healing can occur instantly. Or it could take a week, a month, or a year. Healing is a mystery. But you cannot expect a healing merely because you said certain prayers or made a pilgrimage to a sacred site. Expecting anything specific from God, as Teresa would say, is a source of personal suffering. When you wait in faith, all will be provided. And yes, it is difficult . . . and yes, it is splendid.

A Moment of Contemplation

Teresa did not write directly about healing and thus none of her mansions is devoted to specific instructions about personal healings. Nor did she experience any personal physical healings, even though she suffered throughout her life from pain and various chronic illnesses. But Teresa's soul was healed of countless ailments, and the soul's ills were the only ones that mattered to her. Physical ailments were generally considered necessary spiritual irritants. Suffering created a language of intimacy between medieval mystics and Jesus, a means through which they could break through fear and the rational mind. Union with the divine was their only goal. Teresa would have been appalled at the very suggestion that she ask the divine to make her physical body healthier so that she could enjoy the fruits of the everyday world. Such a way of thinking was completely foreign to her. To ask God to heal your body instead of to meet with your soul would be like asking Shakespeare to teach you how to write graffiti when he is prepared to teach you to become a poet. Teresa's main task was to lead others into the Castle, away from the world of form and flesh, to meet their eternal souls and God. The body was a necessary but temporary vessel for the soul, a form to be cared for but not revered or pampered. The soul was what needed to be cleansed and taken to higher and higher states of grace.

Healing is a lifestyle for us today, an industry, and we search for ways to heal emotions, relationships, minds, and, in some cases, even our past lives. Many people engage in an endless cycle of crime-solving therapeutic activities, unearthing who did what to whom and when and what should be done or said to heal that wound, and who is still angry, and who is working on forgiveness. Four hundred years ago, people died fast and young. They had few medicines, frequent epidemics, and untreatable injuries. Death was everywhere, not hidden in hospitals and convalescent homes. Healing was not a pursuit because few people ever healed from anything.

On the other hand, it was accepted wisdom in many spiritual traditions that suffering was a gift from God. Finding solace by giving an illness or other difficulties divine meaning and purpose was clearly a choice to utilize the power of one's consciousness to transcend a disease for which there was no other treatment. The suffering of Jesus, whom they considered a divine human being, therefore became an archetype. People projected their own suffering onto him, feeling united with him on a human, intimate, and divine level. This union of divine suffering with human suffering was a medieval match made in heaven. Suffering became more tolerable and meaningful when viewed as a test given directly from God, and one that opened mystical passageways. You could endure the unendurable nourished by that belief. Meaning and purpose work like morphine; prayer helps transcend physical pain.

Nonetheless, intimacy with God does not bring suffering. Your journey of awakening into consciousness will bring some pain with it, but it will be the cleansing pain of self-knowledge and greater awareness, not a punitive pain from a vindictive God. When you engage the power of your soul, you see the purpose and meaning in your life, not just your suffering. But the journey also bring endless joy. All roads ultimately lead to the Castle.

Entry Prayer

I cross the bridge into the silent bliss of my Castle. I close the drawbridge and forbid all outside influences from entry into this holy place that is my soul. Here in my Castle, I am alone with God. Under God's light and companionship I discover the

depth and beauty of my soul. I embrace the power of prayer. I
open myself to divine guidance. I surrender myself to become as
a channel for grace, healing, and service as God directs my life.

Healing Rooms

You are in the Seventh Mansion. You are in a field of grace that
dissolves fear and doubt. You are in the atmosphere of the divine.
You can pray yourself into the light of the Seventh Mansion. You
cannot imagine yourself into this altitude of consciousness but
you can pray or meditate to enter it. The following is a suggested
prayer:

Though I cannot image the unimaginable, I surrender my
soul to receive the grace of this mansion. I am within the embrace of the Seventh Mansion. I am present with the divine as I
repeat, "I am still because I know God is with me."

THE FIRST ROOM:
Your Humble Request

Enter this room with the intention of stating and releasing your
healing requests. You must already realize that all is known, but
here acknowledge that which you need to heal. Pay attention to
how you phrase your request, not because it matters to heaven
but because it matters to you. You do not want to make a self-
serving request or to ask heaven to do all the healing work. Many
people do not want to change their lifestyles, give up their addictions, or change their diets in order to take care of their bodies.
They do not want to become forgiving, to face emotional
wounds, to stop complaining, to make tough life choices, to become generous and honest. They simply want to heal and get on
with the business of being the way they were.

Examine your requests and expectations of God by asking
yourself the following questions:

- What are you really willing to change?
- When?
- Can you change with a willing, cheerful heart or will you have to let others know how difficult changing your life is?
- Will you expect God to heal you immediately? How soon?
- What kind of attitude will you have if you don't see results right away?
- Are you willing to change, not look back, and have no expectations?

THE SECOND ROOM:
Dissolving Doubts

Enter this room whenever you are filled with fear and doubt, whether or not you are ill. Even Teresa continued to have earthly struggles after her mystical experiences, but she dealt with them by remaining within the field of grace that is the Castle. Being in the Castle helps you dissolve doubts and fears.

In this room, remind yourself:

- I reside within the Castle that is my soul. Here within my soul, all of my doubts and fears are dissolved and have no authority over me. My life is in God's hands.
- All doubts are self-created. Something activated this doubt, but it's not even important to know what that was. Be in the Castle, close the drawbridge, and lock out the reptile of doubt.
- Enter into prayer, and breathe deeply. Keep silent for a bit. See yourself in a field of grace.
- You live in mystery. Your life is a mystical experience. Trust that the outcome of each prayer is a miracle.

THE THIRD ROOM:
The Grace of Miracles

Miracles are instantaneous change—prayers answered at the speed of light. They could happen all the time if people were comfortable with having their prayers answered that fast. Mostly, people prefer to receive their answers in keeping with earthly time. The rules of life change for someone who is the recipient of a miracle—make no mistake about that.

Nonetheless, miracles do not result from faith or endless prayers alone but from unconditional trust in God's will. Miracles indicate that you are involved in an intimate relationship with God, that you accept the unconditional terms of the miracle. You are never again allowed to make lesser choices of consciousness.

As you enter into your prayers, do so in a spirit of humility. If you are going about your prayers only "when you have time," then consider that against the size of your request.

- Do not request specifics either for yourself or for others.
- Maintain your prayer life. God is not Santa Claus. Healing is not about good behavior and being rewarded. It's about knowing that your prayers are answered immediately in some way, and your job is to say thank you and accept how the answer unfolds in your life.

Here is a healing prayer for you:

I am in need of healing and I release the way of my healing path into your care. I know that I am graced by a miracle because all who ask for your intervention are received. I am grateful for my healing. I believe in the grace of miracles. I know all can be healed and that all of life is your creation and in your care. My job is to trust and to follow the guidance of my self within the text of each day. In this way, I serve a lifestyle of miracles. Where healing is needed, let that grace flow abundantly and let me serve that and let me be served by that. As the mystic Julian of Norwich wrote, "All will be and all will be well and all manner of things will be well."

THE TRANQUIL SOUL

Although a soul on Earth can never rest, it can attain a permanent tranquility. You know your soul has arrived—that God is fully present within the walls of your soul—in a number of ways: You feel the presence of God. You have a deep awareness that the longest search in life has finally come to an end. Fears and reptiles that once possessed you have been ejected and you know with absolute certainty that they will never return—they have been exorcised from your Castle forever. Your soul ceases to yearn for spiritual gratification, knowing that it is secure in the Castle and its connection with the divine. You are satisfied in your spiritual practice and confident in the messages you receive from God. The interior pressure from the spiritual quest comes to an end in this mansion.

In the Seventh Mansion, you no longer fear death and illness. Your sense of eternity and connection with your soul is so authentic that you know there is no death. Detachment has become a natural practice rather than an effort. You have earthly goods that you want, but not because you need them or need to feel empowered by them. Your detachment does not mean that you make a commitment to a life of poverty, but that you have made a conscious commitment to manage your relationship to the material world—including abundance—in such a way that you do not negotiate your soul in order to acquire earthly goods, fame, power, status, or control. No acquisition on Earth is worth a fragment of your soul, but, if you are insecure about your ability to survive, you will not believe that. Detachment is the soul's power to be free of earthly illusions.

Other indicators that God is in the walls of your soul include a need for time alone, for contemplation as well as the need to help other souls. Such "holy impulses," as Teresa calls them, come from within, like a soft touch that continually reminds you of the presence of God. Your link to the divine cannot be broken now; it is a sealed, eternal bond.

A RETURN TO THE WORLD

Like a perfected piece of divine art, mystics without monasteries must return to the world for others to appreciate. As I've said, the world is the contemporary mystic's monastery. Teresa's instructions in the Seventh Mansion tell us how to return to the world in order to be of service to others. I had anticipated that she would encourage her readers to maintain a more reclusive practice, but she wants only to serve the divine through others and to have others act in service. Service is a vital part of her message in this mansion: Take your soul out into the world and allow God to work through you as a channel for grace, a vessel of power and transformation.

Here are your instructions:

• Pray every day. You find illumination through prayer, and now you must pray for others, for the sick, and for those who do not pray for themselves. In one of the mansions, you may have seen or experienced the power of prayer and the impact that prayer has on the world. Prayer is power. Use it to be of service to the world.

• Be virtuous. Be kind of heart and compassionate.

• Don't shrink, as Teresa would say. Be bold and stand for your principles.

• Take care of your physical body. It is a gift from God. Teresa paid little attention to the body in the previous mansions, but now, as the soul is ready to emerge into the world in order to be of service, she acknowledges that the body is an important vehicle for the soul.

You Are a Container for God in This World

Whenever societies have cycled through crises, mystics have arisen to address them. Like hidden angels of the divine, they emerge in every walk of life. Today, mystics without monasteries are wives and mothers, husbands and fathers, teachers and lawyers, bankers and doctors, soldiers and policemen, therapists and writers, social workers and salespeople. They are everywhere.

Mystics salvage the good of one culture and carry those treasures into the birth of the next. Mystics are not silent containers of God, make no mistake. Many are the loudest noisemakers. They wrestle with the great questions of life and death. They remind a people and a society of its principles and its vision. They inspire others through their example of living in accordance with their souls' direction, through their intensity and clearsightedness. Mystics recognize the signs that a society's soul is starving and has gone unconscious.

Mystics have the courage to see through common fears. They see beyond calls for destruction and violence as means for solving problems. They see the contradictions in others' statements—for instance, that war creates peace.

The one great difference between Teresa's time and ours is that God's new mystics are everywhere. And the new mystic should rightly be called a mystical activist.

Yet, the journey itself has not changed. There is no shortcut to God. Centuries may have passed since Teresa wrote her masterpiece, but her genius, wisdom, and guidance are as valuable today as in the sixteenth century.

It takes great courage to cross your drawbridge and enter

your Castle. It is not easy to enter each room and begin a dialogue with your soul. It can be as painful as it is awesome and empowering. It is long and arduous. You have to be prepared to meet your shadow and to embrace your soul. Your life will change. But then, your life will change anyway. You are being called.

The divine will find you in your Castle. God will find you. And you must ask yourself, "Why does God want me? Why have I been called?" You are being called inward so that you will also be able to move out into the world.

Perhaps you have been called because you have that certain mystic's profile: strong, stubborn, independent, a silent (or loud) warrior type with a hot temper and a relentless will that's searching for something to serve. Perhaps your soul, a restless creature of eternity, is finally forcing you into the quest for your highest potential, after your many delays.

Something compels you to want to know more of the nature of God. This desire, this need, is what it feels like to be called. You don't necessarily want to withdraw from the chaotic influences of this world until the only voice you hear is that of the divine. In the middle of your earthly chaos, you discover a passion to follow that may even bring more chaos for the moment, but underneath it you will find a new order, a divine order.

TAKING LEAVE

The first time I actually heard Teresa—really heard her voice—was when I started teaching *The Interior Castle* in the workshop and she said, "Daughter, follow me." The only other time—and the last time—I heard her was at the end of our work together on this book.

As I wrote *Entering the Castle*, I observed regular silence and an intense prayer practice. As I worked, I would wait for Teresa's arrival and guidance and I would know when she had come because of the subtle change in the silence of my office. In an instant, it would become sacred silence. As I studied Teresa's writings and prayed, she would communicate to me through the transmission of subtle thoughts that I knew were not mine—just a thought that would animate my thinking, such as, God seduces in the First Mansion. Aha, thought I. Okay, then, this chapter is about the seduction of God. And off I went, reading, researching, dwelling in that idea, thinking and pondering what that meant and how to put it into a spiritual practice.

In the middle of writing about the Seventh Mansion, I knew that Teresa and I were coming to the end of our time together, and I wondered, Teresa, what did you look like? This had not really occurred to me before, since so many great artists have given us their inspired paintings and sculptures of her. But two hours later, Federal Express arrived with a package for me. An artist named Pat Benincasa had sent me a poster and a postcard of her work, a beautiful diptych called the *Difficult Saints*. On the right, she depicted St. Catherine of Siena and on the left St. Teresa of Ávila. I treasure this portrait.

Finally, when I had finished the work in the Seventh Mansion, I sat back and dissolved into tears. I asked, "Is this it? Is this goodbye?" I sensed that Teresa wanted her favorite prayer to close the book, and then I heard, "Farewell, daughter," and felt her gentle energy depart my office.

After she left, I walked around my house and felt as if I had lost the most authentic soul companion I would ever know.

I am so grateful to have Teresa's writings, especially *The Interior Castle*. I am so grateful for the guidance she gave me, so grateful to have been a recipient of these teachings about the Castle. I'm grateful for the depth of knowledge I now have about my soul and my life. I hope that *Entering the Castle* will help you and many others find your way into your soul, your purpose, and also that it helps you take your unique quality of grace out into the world as a mystic without a monastery.

It's funny, but until I began teaching about the medieval mystics and about mysticism, I had never been a big fan of Teresa or her work. In grad school I'd thought it too complicated; I didn't really like Teresa; she was difficult. After following Teresa's call into the Castle and finishing the writing of this book, I went to Scotland to teach a workshop on the Castle. One of the students came up to introduce herself; it was Colette, the woman who had sent me the bookmark with Teresa's inspiring quote at the beginning of my journey, and who had told me that she was praying for me. I had received two other cards from her while writing the book, and here, at the lecture, she revealed that she had been told to pray for me through her inner guidance. She didn't know why and she admitted that she didn't like me much at the time. But she had her orders, so she held me in prayer. Colette looked me in the eyes and asked, "So, is it over? This thing you're doing?"

I said, "Yes, it's over."

"Good," she replied. "Then I can stop praying for you." She turned to go, then stopped, looked back, and said, "I thought I would come see you. When I first saw you at a distance, I thought you looked so intense and so stressed. Then I heard a voice that told me that I was instructed to pray for you and not to judge you. I have to admit, you're not so bad."

I'm holding you in prayer as you start and pursue your work in the Castle and as you make your way in the world. Remember that to read a prayer is the same as to say a prayer. Either way, the grace will come through. To enter the Castle, you pray the Castle. You are asking to see your soul and God. And the grace will come through.

ESSENTIAL GUIDANCE FOR MYSTICS OUTSIDE THE CASTLE WALLS

- **Maintain your work in the Castle.** Do not stay away from the interior work of your Castle for too long. Revisit the rooms that need the most attention, where you can finish only one exploration at a time. Add a room as you need to when a crisis arises in your life and then go into that room to resolve that crisis. This book is meant to be your companion for a lifetime—or for as long as you need before you feel God in the walls of your soul.

- **Practice illumination.** Do not treat your spiritual life as a hobby. Maintain the practices in the Castle, among them illumination. The mystic's life is not about showing up for a twenty-minute, close-your-eyes-and-listen-to-soft-music meditation. Mystical activism is proactive; it requires dedication and a soul with stamina.

- **Develop and share the gifts of your soul.** Do not keep your talents hidden from others. Do not be shy about your capacity to see a problem clearly and understand its symbolic message. Be available to bring illumination into another person's life, but be humble about it. Allow your inner guidance to alert you to act; if you do not receive that instruction, then remain silent and serve that individual through prayer. Always stay humble.

- **Keep alert.** Evil exists. And the greater the evil, the more difficult it can be to grasp, to see. Take refuge in your Castle, close the drawbridge, and enter into prayer. Insecurity and fear rule, but not within your soul.

- **Fly under the radar.** Never position yourself as an authority or presume that you are better than another. Never put yourself in a position to be criticized for your spiritual practices. Stay humble at all times.

- **Avoid power plays.** Your job is not to win arguments or prove anything to anyone. Power plays drain your soul and serve only the ego, and only temporarily.

- **Stop blaming others.** No other human being is responsible for your choices, even though that individual's choices may have affected your life, just as your choices have affected others' lives. Focus only on understanding the motivations behind your choices.

- **Don't use the word *deserve*.** To decide who deserves what in this world positions you as judge and jury over others. When have you ever had all the facts? Never. That is a cosmic position only. Believing you deserve something means that you think you are entitled. I am entitled to heal; I am entitled to guidance; I am entitled to an easy life. Entitlement is a self-inflicted form of suffering. Many times people use the word *deserve* as an excuse to buy or indulge in something special. As a result, their purchases land them in debt and sweet desserts make them gain weight. If you want something special, just get it. Leave out the game of "deserve." As Teresa wrote, never approach God with an expectation, either. You do not deserve to be healed because you prayed; you do not deserve to have your prayers answered because you are a good person. To believe in entitlement and divine obligation is to ask for self-inflicted suffering.

- **Let your first response in any situation be, "What can I do?"** You may not be able to build a house or repair a levee (although, to be frank, you don't know that). Sometimes you are called into action and sometimes that action is what you can do silently. You can change anything and everything with prayer and faith. You are never to assume a helpless posture. Inspire others with that truth *when appropriate*. You are not a preacher. You wait for your instructions to come through your soul to make you an invisible act of power.

- **Channel grace on a daily basis.** Understanding that you are a channel for grace is a core part of your identity as a mystic. Countless ways exist to channel grace; certainly daily prayer is a must. Make this a part of your daily practice—a priority, not a convenience. The length of time is not an issue, but daily devotion is required. Devote, for example, ten minutes a day to opening a channel on the cosmic grid.

- **Form a circle of grace with soul companions; such friends are essential to your well-being.** Soul companions support one another's spiritual journeys. The intent of a circle of grace is to empower every person in that circle. In a circle of grace you can channel grace for healing and for sharing higher guidance. You encourage one another's creative abilities, courageous decision making, and spiritual life. A book club can be part of a circle of grace, as you can also discuss the rich literature of the soul and spirituality. As you gather together, open the circle with prayer. If a member has a decision to make or an illness to heal, have him or her pose the dilemma or question. Open yourselves to the clearest guidance that you can bring to bear upon the questions. Pray for grace, and channel it to the person or situation.

- **Live congruently.** Make sure that your mind and your heart are in agreement with your soul in your actions, decisions, and thoughts. Mind, heart, and soul are your interior trinity. Keeping the integrity of your soul is extremely challenging, requiring serious introspection and inner work. This is a perfect theme for a group of soul companions.

- **Be devoted to truth.** Mystics are keepers of truth. No matter who you are or what you do professionally, a nonnegotiable devotion to truth is an essential life practice. A part of a mystic's task has always been to find new truths, to further intellectual pursuits, and to dismantle outdated, superstitious systems of thought. Nourish your mind and heart with reading material.

- **Stay active in the world.** Mystics are servants. Do not run and hide from this world. Violence, pollution, and war are challenges that require a response from you that serves the good of humanity. You cannot run and hide and expect others to make this world safe for you.

- **You are a source for healing.** Healing has many expressions. Prayer and the channeling of grace are the instruments of healing. You might find yourself in situations in which your help is needed; for instance, someone may want to confide in you who would normally not open up to anyone. In these moments, silently ask for a blessing and visualize grace flowing through you and into the person who is speaking to you. That is all you need to do. In rooms where there is tension, visualize grace flowing through you into the room, blessing and healing the atmosphere. Stay silent always about these actions.

- **Remain active in your Castle.** Use the visualization of the

Castle. See yourself as safe within your Castle walls, surrounded by love and the blessings of other people. Animate the love in your life; do not always feed the idea that you must just protect yourself. Use your Castle as a source of positive replenishment. Make it a stronger and stronger psychic source of love and a field of creative and tranquil grace. See God in everything. Appreciate the presence of the divine in the details of your life every day.

Let your Castle become the sacred ground beneath your feet. Live the power of your soul. Listen to and follow the voice of your soul. You are not alone. No higher purpose in this life exists than to be called into a mystical relationship with the divine.

> Let nothing disturb you.
> Let nothing frighten you.
> All things pass away.
> God never changes
> Patience obtains all things.
> He who has God lacks for nothing.
> God alone suffices.
> —Teresa of Ávila

BIBLIOGRAPHY

Armstrong, Karen. *Visions of God.* New York: Bantam, 1994.

Babinsky, E. L., trans. *Marguerite Porete: The Mirror of Simple Souls.* Mahwah, NJ: Paulist Press, 1993.

Bangley, Bernard, ed. *Authentic Devotion: A Modern Interpretation of the Devout Life by Francis de Sales.* Colorado Springs, CO: ShawBooks, 2002.

Bangley, Bernard. *Nearer to the Heart of God: Daily Readings from the Christian Mystics.* Orleans, MA: Paraclete Press, 2005.

Barks, Coleman, trans. *Essential Rumi.* New York: HarperSanFrancisco, 1995.

———. *Like This: Rumi; Versions by Coleman Barks.* Athens, GA: Maypop Books, 1990.

Barks, Coleman. *The Soul of Rumi.* New York: HarperSanFrancisco, 2002.

Bartholomew, S. *Hymn to the Universe.* Translation. New York: Harper & Row, 1965.

Bauerschmidt, Frederick. *Why the Mystics Matter Now.* Notre Dame, IN: Sorin Books, 2003.

Bishop, Jane, and Mother Columba Hart. *Hildegard of Bingen,* Scivias. Mahwah, NJ: Paulist Press, 1990.

Blakeney, R. B. *Meister Eckhart, a Modern Translation.* New York: Harper & Row, 1941.

Bowie, F., and O. Davies. *Hildegard of Bingen, an Anthology.* London: Society for Promoting Christian Knowledge, 1990.

Butcher, Carmel Acevedo. *Incandescence: 365 Readings with Women Mystics.* Orleans, MA: Paraclete Press, 2005.

Mother C. Hart. *Hadewijch: The Complete Works.* New York: Paulist Press, 1980.

Cohen, J. M., trans. *The Life of Saint Teresa by Herself.* London: Penguin, 1957.

Colledge, E., and J. Walsh. *Julian of Norwich, Showings.* New York: Paulist Press, 1978.

Cunneen, Sally, trans. Thomas à Kempis. *The Imitation of Christ.* New York: Vintage, 1984.

Davies, O. *Meister Eckhart, Selected Writings.* London: Penguin, 1994.

De Caussade, Father. *Abandonment to Divine Providence.* Kila, MT: Kessinger, 2004.

Dejaegher, Paul, ed. *An Anthology of Christian Mysticism.* Springfield, IL: Templegate, 1977.

De Mello, Anthony. *Awakening, Conversations with the Masters.* New York: Image Books, 1992.

———. *The Way to Love.* New York: Image Books, 1991.

Dods, M., trans. *The City of God.* New York: Modern Library, 1950.

Dreyer, Elizabeth A. *Passionate Spirituality: Hildegard of Bingen and Hadewijch of Brabant.* Mahwah, NJ: Paulist Press, 2005.

Dulles, Avery. *The Spiritual Exercises of St. Ignatius.* New York: Vintage, 2000.

Egan, H. D. *What Are They Saying about Mysticism?* New York: Paulist Press, 1982.

Elizabeth of the Trinity. *Reminiscences of Sister Elizabeth of the Trinity, Servant of God, Discalced Carmelite of Dijon, a Benedictine of Stanbrook Abbey.* Westminster, MD: Newman Press, 1952.

Erdman, D.V., ed. *The Complete Poetry and Prose of William Blake.* Berkeley and Los Angeles: University of California Press: rev. ed. 1982.

Ernst, C. W., and M. A. Sells. Preface, *Early Islamic Mysticism, Sufi, Qur'an Mi'rag, Poetic and Theological Writings,* 1. Mahwah, NJ: Paulist Press, 1996.

Evans, G. R., trans. *Bernard of Clairvaux, Selected Works.* Mahwah, NJ: Paulist Press, 1987.

Fanning, Steve. *Mystics of a Christian Tradition.* New York: Routledge, 2001.

Finley, James. *Christian Meditation.* New York: HarperCollins, 2004.

Flanagan, Sabina, trans. *Secrets of God: Writings of Hildegard of Bingen.* Boston: Shambhala, 1996.

Flinders, Carol L. *Enduring Grace: Living Portraits of Seven Women Mystics.* New York: HarperCollins, 1993.

Fowler, James. *Stages of Faith: The Psychology of Human Development.* New York: HarperSanFrancisco, n.e. edition, 1995.

Fox, M., ed. *Hildegard of Bingen's Book of Divine Works.* Santa Fe: Bear & Co., 1987.

Fox, Matthew. *Creation Spirituality.* New York: HarperCollins, 1991.

French, R. M., trans. *The Way of a Pilgrim: and The Pilgrim Continues His Way.* New York: Harper, 1954.

Ganss, G. E., ed., P. R. Divarkar, E. J. Malatesta, and M. E. Palmer, trans. *Ignatius of Loyola: Spiritual Exercises and Selected Works.* Mahwah, NJ: Paulist Press, 1991.

Griffiths, Bede, and Thomas Matus. *Bede Griffiths: Essential Writings.* Maryknoll, NY: Orbis Books, 2004.

——, and Peter Spink. *The Universal Christ: Daily Readings with Bede Griffiths.* London: Darton, Longman & Todd, 1990.

Hague, R., trans. *The Heart of Matter.* New York: Harcourt Brace Jovanovich, 1979.

Hamilton, Edith. *Mythology.* New York: Vintage, 1942.

Happold, F. C. *Mysticism, A Study and an Anthology.* Harmondsworth, New York, Ringwood, Markham and Auckland; Penguin: (1963, rev. ed. 1970)

Harvey, Andrew. *Essential Mystics.* New York: HarperCollins, 1996.

——. *Teachings of the Christian Mystics.* Boston: Shambhala, 1998.

——. *Teachings of the Hindu Mystics.* Boston: Shambhala, 2001.

Henry-Couannier, M., and V. Morrow, trans. *Saint Francis de Sales and His Friends,* Staten Island, NY: Alba House, 1964.

Hughes, S., trans. *Catherine of Genoa: Purgation and Purgatory, The Spiritual Dialogue.* New York: Paulist Press, 1979.

James, W. *Varieties of Religious Experience.* New York: Penguin, repr. 1982.

Jantzen, G. M. *Julian of Norwich, Mystic and Theologian.* Mahwah, NJ: Paulist Press, 1988.

Johnston, William. *Arise, My Love: Mysticism for a New Era.* Maryknoll, NY: Orbis Books, 2000.

——. *Mystical Theology: The Science of Love.* Maryknoll, NY: Orbis Books, 1995.

——. *Still Point: Reflections on Zen and Christian Mysticism.* New York: HarperCollins, 2000.

————. *The Cloud of Unknowing and The Book of Privy Counseling.* New York: Doubleday, 1973.

Kavanaugh, K., and O. Rodriguez, trans. *The Collected Works of St. John of the Cross.* Washington, DC: ICS Publications, rev. ed. 1991.

————. *Teresa of Ávila, The Interior Castle,* New York: Paulist Press, 1979.

Keating, Thomas. *Intimacy with God.* New York: Crossroad Classic: 1996.

————. *Manifesting God.* New York: Lantern Books, 2005.

————. *Open Mind, Open Heart.* Harrisburg, PA: Continuum International Publishing Group, reissue ed. June 1994.

Kempis, Thomas à. *The Imitation of Christ.* New York: Vintage.

Kornfield, Jack. *After the Ecstasy, the Laundry.* New York: Bantam, 2001.

————. *Buddha's Little Instruction Book.* New York: Bantam, 1994.

Ladinsky, Daniel. *Love Poems from God.* London: Penguin, 2002.

Lawrence of the Resurrection, Brother, O.C.D., C. De Meester, ed., S. Sciurba, O.C.D., trans. *Writings and Conversations on the Practice of the Presence of God.* Washington, DC: ICS Publications, 1994.

Luibheid, C., trans. *Conferences—John Cassian.* New York: Paulist Press, 1985.

Sister M. Faustina Kowalska. *Divine Mercy in My Soul, The Diary of the Servant of God.* Stockbridge, MA: Marian Press, 1987.

Mackey, H. B., trans. *St. Francis de Sales, Treatise on the Love of God.* Westport, CT: Greenwood Press, repr. 1971.

Magill, Frank Northen, and Ian P. McGreal. *Christian Spirituality— Essential Guide to the Most Influential Writings of the Christian Tradition.* New York: HarperCollins, 1988.

Maloney, G. A., trans. *Hymns of Divine Love by St. Symeon, the New Theologian.* Denville, NJ: Dimension Books, 1975.

Mandelbaum, Allen, trans. *The Divine Comedy of Dante Alighieri: Paradiso.* New York: Bantam, 1986.

Marion, Jim. *Putting on the Mind of Christ: The Inner Work of Christian Spirituality.* Charlottesville, VA: Hampton Roads, 2000.

McGinn, Bernard. *The Mystical Thought of Meister Eckhart: The Man from Whom God Hid Nothing.* New York: Herder & Herder, 2003.

Merton, Thomas. *The Ascent to Truth.* New York: Harcourt Brace, 1951.

————. *Conjectures of a Guilty Bystander.* Garden City, NY: Image, 1968.

————. *Contemplation in a World of Action.* Notre Dame, IN: University Press of Notre Dame, rev. ed. 1998.

————. *Mystics and Zen Masters.* New York: Farrar, Straus and Giroux, reissue ed. 1986.

———. *New Seeds of Contemplation.* New York: New Directions, 1961 rep. 1972.

———. *Run to the Mountain: The Story of a Vocation, The Journals of Thomas Merton 1, 1939–1941.* New York: HarperCollins, 1996.

———. *Seeds of Contemplation.* Norfolk, CT: New Directions, 1949.

———. *The Seven Storey Mountain.* New York: Harcourt Brace Jovanovich, repr. 1978.

Montaldo, Jonathan, ed. *A Year with Thomas Merton: Daily Meditations from His Journals.* New York: HarperSanFrancisco, 2004.

Nash, A. E., trans. *I Have Found God, Complete Works, II, Letters from Carmel.* Washington, DC: ICS Publications, 1995.

Noffke, S., trans. *Catherine of Siena, the Dialogue.* New York: Paulist Press, 1980.

———. *The Letters of St. Catherine of Siena.* Binghamton, NY: State University of New York at Binghamton, 1988.

Nouwen, Henri. *The Inner Voice of Love.* New York: Image Books, 1998.

——— and Wendy Greer. *The Only Necessary Thing: Living a Prayerful Life.* New York: Crossroad Classic, 1999.

Pagels, E. *The Gnostic Gospels.* New York: Vintage, 1981.

Peers, E. Allison, trans. *The Interior Castle by St. Teresa of Ávila.* New York: Doubleday, 1989.

———. *The Way of Perfection by Teresa of Ávila.* New York: Doubleday, 1991.

Rohr, Richard. *Everything Belongs: The Gift of Contemplative Prayer.* New York: Crossroad General Interest, rev. ed 2003.

Ryan, J. K., Trans. *Introduction to the Devout Life—Francis de Sales.* New York: Image Books, 1972.

Shannon, W. H., ed. *The Hidden Ground of Love, the Letters of Thomas Merton on Religious Experience and Social Concerns.* New York: Farrar, Straus and Giroux, 1985.

Skinner, J., trans. *The Book of Margery Kempe, a New Translation.* New York: Image Books, 1998.

Spearing, A. C. *Revelations of Divine Love: Julian of Norwich.* London: Penguin, 1999.

Starr, Mirabai, trans. *The Interior Castle—Teresa of Ávila.* New York: Riverhead Books, 2003.

Suzuki, Daisetz Teitaro. *Mysticism—Christian and Buddhist—The Eastern and Western Way.* New York: Routledge Classics, 2002.

Teasdale, Wayne. *The Mystic Heart.* Novato, CA: New World Library, 1999, 2001.

————. *The Mystic Hours: A Daybook of Inspirational Wisdom and Devotion.* Novato, CA: New World Library, 2004.

St. Therese of Lisieux. *Story of a Soul, The Autobiography of St. Therese of Lisieux.* Peabody, M.A.: I C S Publications, Institute of Carmelite St., 3rd ed., 1999.

Teilhard de Chardin, Pierre. *The Divine Milieu.* New York: Harper & Row, 1960.

Tetlow, Joseph. *Ignatius of Loyola: Spiritual Exercises.* New York: Crossroad Classic, 1992.

Tobin, F., trans. *Mechthild of Magdeburg, The Flowing Light of the Godhead.* Mahwah, NJ: Paulist Press, 1998.

Ullman, Robert, and Judyth Reichenberg Ullman. *Mystics, Masters, Saints and Sages.* Berkeley, CA: Conari Press, 2001.

Underhill, Evelyn. *Mysticism.* London: Methuen, 12th ed. 1930. New York: E. P. Dutton, 1930; Meridian, 1974.

————. *The Mystic Way, A Psychological Study in Christian Origins.* New York: Dutton, repr. 1998.

————. *Practical Mysticism.* Cincinnati, OH: Ariel Press, 1988.

Wolters, C., trans. *The Cloud of Unknowing and Other Works.* New York: Penguin Classics, reissue 2002.

ACKNOWLEDGMENTS

I am indebted to many people for their constant gifts of love and support in order to give birth to this book. As always, my gratitude, love, and appreciation for my editor, Leslie Meredith, is immeasurable, not only because of her brilliance as an editor but because once again she allowed me to shift gears in the middle of a book project, toss out the first book I was writing, and begin this one a handful of months before the deadline. Words can never convey the gratitude that I carry in my soul for the faith she has in me. And to the entire team of Free Press/Simon & Schuster, my sincere thanks for your support in the production of *Entering the Castle*, most especially Andrew Paulson, editorial assistant, who carefully ensured that all the chapters made the electronic journey successfully into my computer. To my agent, Ned Leavitt, my thanks for constant support and care. And to the formidable Ken Wilber, whom I admire without parameters, my most sincere thank you for writing the foreword to my book. I am so honored to have you with me in this book.

I am blessed with a loving family and a circle of friends who wrap their lives around the demands of my creative life and my high-strung personality, which gets even more high-strung during the writing of a book. I consider the following individuals my earth angels. Not only has each one enthusiastically supported the birthing of this book, for which I am eternally grateful, but they are my good and forever friends. They make my life rich. They are, in the words of St. Teresa of Ávila, the companions of my soul. To Tom Lavin, PhD, a gifted Jungian analyst and an even more blessed visionary, I will always believe I was guided to meet you. And so to Mary Neville, Jim Curtan, Georgia Bailey, Tom Williams, Meryl Martin, Charles and Sue Wells, Jill Angelo, Chandra Sammons, Steve and Sarah Fanning, Linda Monahan, Peter and Eleanor Buxton, Ellen and John Gunter, Julie and Patrick Flaherty, Judi Butner, Francis Pollard, Peter Shaw, Priscilla Haddad, Lynn Bell, James Garrison, Andrew Harvey, Peter Occhiogrosso, Michael Gluck, and my dearest, Donald Meshirer, all my love, gratitude, and devotion is returned.

My family is the shining blessing of my life. We are abundant in love for one another and I draw upon that surplus constantly, especially during intense periods of creativity. As always, they were ever at the ready, beginning with my mother, the adored head goddess of the family. My sister-in-law, Amy, is also my assistant, and it gives me great pleasure to acknowledge that functioning without the assistance of either Mother Goddess or Amy and my brother, Ed, would be impossible. My cousin, Colleen Daley, is yet another treasure who banged at my door with her massage table and I-Health equipment, determined to keep my stress levels low. I'm not sure she succeeded, but oh, how I love her for trying. My nieces—Angela, Allison, Rachel, and Sarah—and nephews, Joe and Eddie—remain my joys and phone companions, always checking in to see if auntie is okay. And to my wonderful cousins Pam, Andy, Marilyn, and Mitch, let me say that I am so glad we are family. Who could not love such a life?

Also a part of my family is David Smith, business partner turned soul companion, best friend, confidant, and life blessing. David is the reason why I am free to create and to teach, and he endures my mood swings like a trooper. David is the "thread to heaven" through which this material came to Earth. I'm not surprised heaven would choose him—he's the archetype of the good man. During the summer of 2005, he came to my house to share his thoughts about the changing patterns he was observing in the field of human consciousness and how those changes were influencing the subjects that people were interested in studying. Ever the optimist and always one to project a field of protection, David was eager to assure me that "CMED would be all right," even if we did have to go through a transition period. Following that conversation, I said a prayer: Where to from here? Within weeks, *Entering the Castle* exploded into the world. Within one month of the first lecture, invitations to bring "the Castle" to Europe were coming into the office, and within a few weeks of that, plans were under way to do workshops in castles . . . and finally, in Ávila, Spain. And so, to my dear friend David, I extend my deepest thanks for your ceaseless integrity, courage, and faith in our work and for listening to your own guidance. I would not have prayed, Where to from here? had you not come over on that summer afternoon, asking me, "Where to from here?"

To Cindy Funnfsinn, who is a jewel on the CMED team, and Chuck Hodges, my thanks for your excellent high standard of professionalism in running the tech-support end of CMED. My workshops on Entering the Castle rely on your skill. These workshops were born slowly but grew rapidly as word spread of the power of the journey into the Castle. Nancy Levin, the event manager from Hay House, saw the potential of *Entering the Castle,* and as a result, Hay House sponsored the first workshop tour, which helped introduce this material to the public. I am indebted to Nancy and to Hay House for their sponsorship and their faith in my work. Their support continues, as they are the production company for the audio set of *Entering the Castle.* Thank you, Hay House.

And finally, to Colette Newman, whom I did not meet until

this book was written. A card from her arrived at my home on the day I decided to write this book. For more than a few moments, I had questioned my judgment, wondering if I was doing the right thing. Then I opened my mail to find a bookmark sent by an unknown woman informing me that she was keeping me in her prayers. I flipped over the bookmark and read the printed message: "Let nothing disturb you. God alone suffices."—St. Teresa of Ávila. Colette held me in prayer as I wrote this book, and I had no idea why this stranger was praying for me. To you, Colette, my endless admiration and gratitude. How I admire your ability to be a true, "invisible act of power and mystic" on this Earth.

Caroline Myss
Oak Park, Illinois
August 2006

INDEX

Keller, Helen, 271
kindness, unexpected, 1–2, 13
Kingdom of Heaven, within us, xx
Kornfield, Jack, *After the Ecstasy, the Laundry,* 321

"Let nothing disturb you" (Teresa), 346
letting go, 61, 212–13, 220–21, 331
life, difficulties of, 239–40
light:
　consciousness of, 327
　darkness and, 183–85
　divine, 167, 168
　pierced by, 78–79, 88
　recognizing, 182–83
loneliness, 194–95
love:
　cosmic, 245, 262
　divine, expression of, 159–60
　God as, 90, 151
　mystical, 243–44, 255–56
　objects of, 260
　for sake of loving, 258
Luther, Martin, 296

Madonna, 58
Manikkavacagar, 266
mansions, *see specific mansions*
mantras, 51
Mary, Saint, 311
meaning, search for, 288–89
Mechthilde of Magdeburg, 152–53
meditation, 15, 44, 51, 69, 103
Melville, Herman, 38, 68
mind:
　distractions of, 238–39
　emptying, 185
　intellectual capacity of, 225
　power of, 221
　separate from soul, 49, 211–12
mindfulness, 42
miracles, 336
mirror mind, xvii
Mitchell, Edgar, 36

Moses:
　and Ark of the Covenant, 324
　and burning bush, 41, 311
　at Sinai, 54
mudras, 51
Muhammad:
　hiding from the angel, 14
　on revelations, 40
　surrender of, 160, 213
Myss, Caroline:
　grand mal seizure of, 3
　spiritual beliefs of, 1, 4–5
mysterium, pure, xix
mystical depression, 286–87
mystical experiences, characteristics of, 284–85, 309–14
mystical fire, 309
mystical flight, 263, 290–91
mystical grief, 326
mystical illumination, 192
mystical insight, universality of, 41
mystical love, in Fourth Mansion, 243–44, 255–56
mystical marriage, 291–92, 294, 323
mystical renaissance, second, 19
mystical trinity, 326–29
mystical union, 322–26
mystical water, 254
mysticism:
　central ideas of, xiv
　mysterious nature of, 269
　scientific nature of, xxii, 00
　soul engaged in, 14
　spiritually radical nature of, 36
　truths of, 27, 274
mystics:
　changes in, 167
　in contemporary culture, 25, 28–29, 34–37, 39, 40, 45–47, 52
　"Holy Anorexics," 18
　life purpose of, 36
　medieval, 18–19, 39–42
　profile of, 340

ABOUT THE AUTHOR

Caroline M. Myss is the author of the best-selling *Invisible Acts of Power, Anatomy of the Spirit, Why People Don't Heal and How They Can,* and *Sacred Contracts,* and is a pioneer and international lecturer in the fields of energy medicine and human consciousness. Since 1982 she has worked as a medical intuitive: one who sees illness in a patient's body by intuitive means. She specializes in helping people understand the emotional, psychological, and physical reasons why their bodies develop illness. She has also worked with Dr. Norman Shealy, MD, PhD, founder of the American Holistic Medical Association, in teaching intuitive diagnosis. Together they wrote *The Creation of Health: Merging Traditional Medicine with Intuitive Diagnosis.* In 2003 she founded the CMED Institute, an educational program that specializes in intensive classes on archetypes and Sacred Contracts. She lectures internationally and around the United States regularly. She lives in Oak Park, Illinois.

The author and publisher of this volume thank the copyright holders of the following works for permission to reproduce selected passages:

From *The Interior Castle* by St. Teresa of Ávila, translated by Mirabai Starr, copyright © 2003 by Mirabai Starr. Used by permission of Riverhead books, an imprint of Penguin Group (USA), Inc.

From *The Interior Castle* by St. Teresa of Ávila, translated by E. Allison Peers, copyright © 1972 by E. Allison Peers. Used by permission of Sheed & Ward, an imprint of Rowman & Littlefield Publishers, Inc., Lanham, MD 20706 USA.

Excerpt from *Tagore: The Mystic Poets* © 2004 by SkyLight Paths Publishing (Woodstock, VT: SkyLight Paths Publishing). Permission granted by Sky-Light Paths Publishing, PO Box 237, Woodstock, VT, 05091. www.skylight paths.com.

"Fringe" (p. 255) from *The Soul of Rumi: A New Collection of Ecstatic Poems*, translated by Coleman Barks, copyright © 2001 by Coleman Barks. Reprinted by permission of HarperCollins Publishers.

Excerpts from *Mechthild of Magdeburg: The Flowing Light of the Godhead*, from the Classics of Western Spirituality, translated by Frank Tobin, Copyright © 1998 by Frank Tobin, Paulist Press, Inc., New York / Mahwah, N.J. Used with permission. www.paulistpress.com.